The Detroit Wolverines

ALSO BY BRIAN MARTIN
AND FROM MCFARLAND

Pud Galvin: Baseball's First 300-Game Winner (2016)

*The Tecumsehs of the International Association:
Canada's First Major League Baseball Champions* (2015)

*Baseball's Creation Myth: Adam Ford,
Abner Graves and the Cooperstown Story* (2013)

The Detroit Wolverines

The Rise and Wreck of a National League Champion, 1881–1888

BRIAN MARTIN

McFarland & Company, Inc., Publishers
Jefferson, North Carolina

LIBRARY OF CONGRESS CATALOGUING-IN-PUBLICATION DATA

Names: Martin, Brian, 1950– author.
Title: The Detroit Wolverines : the rise and wreck of a National League champion, 1881–1888 / Brian Martin.
Description: Jefferson, North Carolina : McFarland & Company, Inc., Publishers, 2018 | Includes bibliographical references and index.
Identifiers: LCCN 2017047178 | ISBN 9781476665078 (softcover : acid free paper) ∞
Subjects: LCSH: Detroit Wolverines (Baseball team)—History. | Baseball—Michigan—Detroit—History—19th century.
Classification: LCC GV875.D65 M37 2018 | DDC 796.357/ 640977434—dc23
LC record available at https://lccn.loc.gov/2017047178

BRITISH LIBRARY CATALOGUING DATA ARE AVAILABLE

ISBN (print) 978-1-4766-6507-8
ISBN (ebook) 978-1-4766-2786-1

© 2018 Brian Martin. All rights reserved

No part of this book may be reproduced or transmitted in any form or by any means, electronic or mechanical, including photocopying or recording, or by any information storage and retrieval system, without permission in writing from the publisher.

Front cover: The 1887 National League champion Detroit Wolverines (National Baseball Hall of Fame Library, Cooperstown, New York)

Printed in the United States of America

McFarland & Company, Inc., Publishers
Box 611, Jefferson, North Carolina 28640
www.mcfarlandpub.com

To the baseball fans of Detroit,
past and present

Table of Contents

Acknowledgments ix
Preface 1

1. Late to the Game 5
2. The Hollinger Nine 20
3. Getting Back in the Game 36
4. A Fine Debut 50
5. A Wild Ride 67
6. Thompson and the Tail-enders 82
7. Retooling 99
8. A Big Deal 116
9. Going for It 132
10. Getting There 150
11. Collapse 170

Epilogue 185
Appendix: Detroit Baseball Rosters, 1879, 1881 to 1888 191
Chapter Notes 197
Bibliography 208
Index 211

Acknowledgments

This book would not have been possible without the help of many people who went above and beyond their duties as guardians of records and other information to assist the author. My sincere apologies to anyone who may have been missed in the following list. While I did not deal with them directly, Michigan baseball historians Peter Morris and Richard Bak provided invaluable assistance in the early days of my research because of their fine books, *Baseball Fever: Early Baseball in Michigan* and *A Place for Summer: A Narrative History of Tiger Stadium*. I think this book about the Wolverines fits nicely between their works and complements them.

I can't say enough about the Detroit Public Library, a wonderful institution that like other public services has struggled mightily with funding cutbacks through Detroit's financial woes. Staff members were always cheerful and happy to help this researcher, who is a proud non-resident member. In particular, Mark Bowden, at the library's Burton Historical Collection, was outstanding. He was invariably helpful, prompt and supportive in the search for files, microfilms and images. So, too, were Dawn Eurich and Romie Minor, who took a keen interest in my work. At the Detroit Historical Society, where I became a research member, Nathan Kelber, the manager of digital collections, was of great assistance by sharing rare images of the Wolverines and their park. He, too, took a lively interest in this project.

At the University of Michigan's Bentley Historical Library in Ann Arbor, thanks are extended to lead reference archivist Malgosia Myc and reference assistant Diana Bachman. They provided some wonderful images of Frederick Stearns, including when he played baseball for the university.

Paul Egan, a reporter for the *Detroit Free Press*, a good guy and brother of a former journalistic colleague of mine, could always be counted upon for advice on matters pertaining to Detroit or Michigan and to some of the characters about whom I learned. Isabelle Donnelly, of the Grosse Pointe Historical Society in Grosse Pointe, graciously helped me learn more about prominent early lakefront residents James McMillan and John S. Newberry. In Port Huron, Michigan, Ben Plonk, supervisor of parks and forestry in that city, pinpointed the final resting place of former Wolverines manager Bill Watkins.

At the National Baseball Hall of Fame and Museum in Cooperstown, John Horne was again at his helpful best. The coordinator of rights and reproductions for the Hall shared a variety of images of the Wolverines and various players. Thank you, yet again, John, your professionalism is unmatched.

Finally, there is Don Murray to thank. My longtime friend, colleague, sailing buddy and all-around fine fellow is a terrific first-line editor whose suggestions and attention to detail helped me immensely. A real fan of baseball and proper English usage, he was tireless in finding errors, trimming copy and suggesting improvements.

Preface

There was a time when Detroit was known as the Paris of the West. It featured elegant homes for its blue-blooded entrepreneurs and manufacturers, along broad, leafy thoroughfares, with fine public buildings and noteworthy architecture. It had become one of America's great cities.

The City of the Straits (from the French *de étroit*, of the narrow [strait]) had graduated from a remote fur-trading post established by the French to become the country's fourth-largest metropolis, with ready access by rail and water to eastern markets for its manufactured goods and the raw materials harvested in its vast hinterland like timber, iron and copper.

There was a time when the economy of Detroit was vibrant and diversified, when it was the pharmaceutical and stove capital of the world, a leading center for the production of paint, soap, chemicals, steam engines, rail cars, bridges and iron works. Many of the nation's new millionaires amassed their fortunes in the city while Henry Ford was still on the family farm in nearby Dearborn.

There was also a time when Detroit was not sure about professional baseball and whether it deserved support. The city trailed other American cities which had already embraced the game. The first real test came in 1879 when local entrepreneurs and business leaders opened Recreation Park, a privately owned facility for harness racing and other sports. Its shareholders believed that a professional baseball team would help draw patrons and make it a success. They hired a manager and players for a team to attract patrons to the new facility, but the independent club soon failed, unable to find good, suitable competition or develop a base of supporters. That did not deter some leading businessmen who felt Detroit belonged among the ranks of America's baseball cities. In 1881, a group led by newly elected mayor William G. Thompson established the Wolverines club and gained admission to the National League for its sixth season. Success, however, was elusive. After several lackluster seasons and the departure of an embittered Thompson, the Detroit club reorganized and found on-field glory when businessman Frederick K. Stearns spent lavishly to acquire some of the top talent of the day. Stearns hired the great hitter Sam Thompson and Buffalo's "Big Four" sluggers of Dan Brouthers, Hardy Richardson, Jack Rowe and Deacon White. A prominent pharmaceutical manufacturer, Stearns knew baseball. He had played baseball for the University of Michigan and was determined to produce a winning team for his city. He proved to be wily—and effective.

The Wolverines captured the National League pennant in 1887 and the 15-game "world's series" over defending champion St. Louis. The following year, attendance at Detroit games, which was never particularly strong, plummeted. Directors claimed they took a bath financially and wanted out. They sold the players to the highest bidders and the franchise itself to Cleveland, which wanted into the League. Part of the problem besetting the Detroit club was Stearns' free-spending style. With poor local support, the Wolverines needed strong attendance in all League cities to cover the high salaries of their well-paid stars. Stearns was resented by other clubs upon whom he relied financially to help pay top salaries in order to beat them. The League retaliated by limiting the share of the gate for visiting clubs, a move protested by Stearns, who threatened to bolt. After a year, the League recanted, but by then the fate of the Wolverines was sealed. Detroit retrenched in baseball, fielding its professional team in lesser leagues. A Detroit club to become known as the Tigers joined the Western League in 1894. That circuit morphed into the American League, with Detroit as a charter member. The Tigers have enjoyed a solid following and identity as an American League pillar ever since. Some of their stars became household names, such as Ty Cobb, Sam Crawford, Charlie Gehringer, Hank Greenberg, Al Kaline, and George Kell.

Today, Detroit is America's poorest city, with a population of about 700,000, down from a peak of 1.8 million in 1950, although its greater metropolitan area exceeds four million inhabitants. Partly because of a shrunken tax base due to abandoned properties, the city declared bankruptcy in 2013, from which it emerged a year later. Unemployment remains stubbornly high among a poorly educated workforce. Poverty is pervasive. The Wayne County morgue is filled to overflowing because relatives of the dead held there can't afford to claim them, acclaimed writer Charlie LeDuff discovered. Abandoned homes and other buildings have been bulldozed in a multi-million-dollar program to eliminate crack houses and places of prostitution. Thousands more remain standing, awaiting their fate. All are mute testament to better times in the Motor City. Also blighting the cityscape are the skeletal remains of an industrial powerhouse that was once the envy of the nation. Some of them, such as the massive former Packard automobile plant, the former American Motors headquarters, or the once-grand Michigan Central railroad depot, are ghostly reminders of a Detroit that once was. There is growing evidence, however, that the city has begun to recover from its economic nightmare. It will take time.

Throughout its rise, fall, and recalibration, Detroit has had baseball. For eight years, a long time ago, that team was the Wolverines. Many Detroiters may be unaware that their city was once a member of the National League and captured its pennant.

The Detroit Wolverines tells the story of the early days of baseball in the City of the Straits. It's a story with many ups and downs, the raging and ebbing of baseball fever, a tale that should resonate with Detroiters and with a wider audience that has witnessed the struggles of Tiger Town.

There was a time when Detroit flourished, but baseball struggled.

This is the story of that time.

1

Late to the Game

It can be said that the roots of professional baseball in Detroit lie in Cleveland. At least in part. Compared to other cities, such as its Ohio neighbor some 175 miles to the southeast, Detroit was relatively late to catch the baseball fever which swept America and its citizens slow to accept the professional game. Amateur baseball had many followers, but pay-for-play was a distasteful concept among many observers, seen as somehow tainting the game.

The first recorded game in the City of the Straits was played in August of 1857 by members of the newly established Franklin Base Ball Club, consisting mainly of local printers and employees of the *Detroit Free Press* and *Detroit Advertiser*.[1] They took their name from Benjamin Franklin, the famous newspaper writer, printer and publisher, and one of America's founding fathers. Participation by the newspapermen was likely among the reasons the game attracted public mention. Two games of "base" were played on a vacant lot along Beaubien Street, a mere pop fly east of today's Comerica Park. In the first game, a team led by Henry Starkey, a clerk in recorder's court, and Jonas H. Titus, a printer, won, 75–40. In the second contest, the side of printers George Atkins and Michael Dempsey prevailed, 40–12. The first game went to 22 innings, while the second lasted for 32. At the time of that game, there was little interest in baseball. Cricket was the most popular team sport in Detroit, and clubs found ready competition in Michigan and just across the border in the British colony then called Canada West, soon to be renamed Ontario.

A surge of interest in baseball followed the Civil War with several amateur clubs springing up in Detroit, primarily the Detroit Base Ball Club and the Early Risers, but also the Creightons, Alerts, Eurekas, and Athletics. Then came the Cass Club and the Aetnas, who developed a strong rivalry. To get an edge, some clubs began paying non-locals to play for them, a move that most observers sharply criticized as contrary to the interests of the game itself. The gentleman's game was gradually being replaced by one in which winning was paramount. But going so far as to engage imported players to achieve victory was generally frowned upon in Detroit. And clubs began to feel the heat. In 1868, Jonathan Van Norman, president of the Detroit club, confessed that his organization was wrong to hire outsiders.

> We lost sight of the best interests and legitimate objects of baseball when we began to have an itching for foreign aid.... What we haven't the brain and muscle to accomplish ourselves, by education and practice, we had better leave unaccomplished. So soon as our club becomes obsessed with hankering after professionals, that moment there is the danger of its becoming prostituted from its beneficial and noble aims, and thus can no longer either claim or expect countenance from the public.[2]

Despite public assurances that its future lay with local amateurs, the Detroit club quietly continued to pay some players. Helpfully, the *Detroit Advertiser and Tribune* insisted the team relied strictly on hometown lads, rather than professionals. The 1869 season was the last for the Detroit Base Ball Club, however, as, for reasons that are not clear, interest in its games waned in the city. At the same time, the game picked up in Jackson and Kalamazoo and at the University of Michigan in Ann Arbor.

The move to professionalism in baseball was inevitable. In 1869, the Cincinnati Red Stockings became the first openly professional team and toured the country for more than a year before losing their first game. Cincinnati demonstrated how successful a professional organization could be, both competitively and financially. Eyes were opened. Baseball was no longer just a social event, played by wealthy gentlemen. It was becoming a commercial venture, and players and businessmen alike were taking an interest in its possibilities. Encouraged by the success of Cincinnati, the National Association of Professional Base Ball Players was established in 1871, organized and run by players hoping to earn a livelihood from the suddenly successful game. Its charter members were Cleveland, Chicago, Philadelphia, Boston, New York, Washington, Fort Wayne, Troy (New York), and tiny Rockford, Illinois, population 11,000. Cleveland had a population of about 93,000 at the time, slightly more than Detroit's 80,000. The latter city, however, was not ready for professional baseball and watched developments from the sidelines. For years, there had been an ebb and flow to baseball interest in Detroit, and its latest ebb was underway. Peter Morris put the situation this way in his *Baseball Fever: Early Baseball in Michigan*: "Michigan was accustomed to brief periods of baseball excitement that were followed by long periods of apathy, and to seasons that began with great interest and soon fizzled."[3] During the early 1870s, without aspirations to a bigger stage, the Cass, Aetna, Kalamazoo and Jackson teams were content to vie for the state championship. Elsewhere, professional baseball had already gained a secure foothold in many American cities which took to the ball field for national bragging rights.

In Cleveland, baseball was played in its public square as early as 1857, the same year the Franklins first appeared in Detroit.[4] The pastime quickly spread, but interest fell off during the Civil War years. In 1865, the Forest City Base Ball Club was established, taking its name from the unofficial title of leafy Cleveland. Regular games were played against the local Railway Union Club and also the Detroit Base Ball Club. Other contests were arranged with nines from Toledo and Buffalo. The Forest City club fared poorly against the top touring clubs from New York and Philadelphia, however, and sought outside help. In 1868, the club hired its first professional, Jim "Deacon" White, a pitcher from Corning, New York. To supplement his baseball income, the lanky newcomer, whose nickname was derived from his sterling character and clean living, found a job in a local railroad car shop. White's twisting delivery puzzled opposing batters but also seriously challenged his catchers so much that he was moved behind the plate. There, his work made him one of the stars of the nineteenth century, in a major league career that spanned 20 years and earned the hard-hitting White induction into the National Baseball Hall of Fame. By 1869, half of the Forest Citys were professionals, because directors had no qualms about taking the team to the next level. By 1870, the team became fully professional—inspired, like so many other teams of the day, by the success of the Cincinnati Red Stockings. Cleveland club directors decided to take the game up another notch, and the Forest Citys became charter members of the new National Association in 1871. In that first professional loop's inaugural season, the club compiled a record of 10 wins and 19 losses, but disbanded partway through the following season. By that time, it had become the only "Western" team in a rather shaky league of Eastern cities. Travel was costly and NA clubs were reluctant to travel so far to play Cleveland. Likewise, the Forest Citys' constant travel to the Eastern seaboard proved burdensome on team coffers.[5]

Baseball continued in Cleveland, but on an amateur basis, until 1878, when two businessmen decided to resurrect professional play under the Forest City name. One of them was Ford Evans, a successful retailer of books and stationery, as well as a line of baseball equipment and uniforms from the new Spalding Brothers Company. Evans had been president of the Forest City club when it joined the National Association, and he was described as a "great chum" of William Hulbert, a shareholder in the National Association's Chicago White Stockings of 1871. Hulbert became president of the National League in 1877. Through baseball and business, Evans also knew Albert Goodwill Spalding, the former pitcher for Boston's NA team whom Hulbert lured to Chicago in

1876. Spalding later established a sporting goods empire and became Chicago's president and a power in the National League. Evans desperately wanted back into the big league but his connections with Hulbert and Spalding didn't help.

The other driving force in Cleveland baseball was young businessman William H. Hollinger, a partner in the Standard Steam Laundry. As a young man he had played baseball and frequented pool halls and billiard rooms where he showed great skill, playing for soft drinks and peanuts. He thrived on competition and shared Evans' determination to boost the city and get Cleveland back on the baseball map. Hollinger was named manager of the Forest Citys, the team he and Evans established for 1878. If the club proved successful, Evans and Hollinger hoped to enter one of the two existing professional leagues of the day, either the National League or the International Association. Evans became a hands-on president, acting as a sort of second manager and occasionally travelling with the club on its road trips.[6] Seen as a bit aloof by players, he invariably stayed at better hotels than he booked for them. Decades later one of his long-time players, Jack Glasscock, dismissed Evans as a "high hat man" who knew little about the game itself.

In Detroit by the mid–1870s, the Cass Club emerged as the strongest local team, with some of its best contests against the rival Aetnas. The latter club disbanded after losing to Cass in a big tournament in 1876. Cass kept the struggling sport alive and in 1878 earned 12 wins in a 14-game schedule. Cass and the Aetnas regularly challenged local teams and amateur nines from places like Jackson, Flint, Kalamazoo and Owosso, along with touring professional clubs from Brooklyn and Chicago when they passed through the city. Repeated contests were also held with the strong Tecumseh club from London, Ontario, 125 miles to the east, champions of the International Association in 1877 and still one of North America's top teams in 1878. Cass and Aetna gradually became semi-professional organizations despite the ongoing local prejudice against paid players. One Detroit paper complained in 1878: "Three years ago this city had base ball mania, and the result was that the importation of paid professionals spoiled all interest in the game. Since that time there have been very few games and little interest shown."[7] Despite such comments, as many as 2,000 spectators, known as "cranks" until the mid–1880s when they became fans (for "fanatics"), turned out for the occasional game, suggesting a good core of fans remained in the prosperous city. For the most part, however, Detroiters remained unimpressed with professional teams, and lean times continued for them.

The National Association expired after the 1875 season, immediately replaced by the National League, the driving force for which was Chicago White Stockings club president William Hulbert. This league was led by businessmen who relegated the role of players to that of employees. Business principles were to prevail, respect for contracts instituted, crooked play and player drunkenness penalized, and the game generally cleaned up. Charter members for 1876 were Chicago, Cincinnati, St. Louis, Louisville, Boston, Hartford, Philadelphia, and New York. Cleveland had retrenched after its National Association experience and took a pass. Detroit still wasn't ready to join any professional loop. By 1877, Hulbert was president of the National League.[8]

Late in 1878, things changed. Events in Cleveland and Detroit conspired to give the Forest City another big league team and the City of the Straits its first professional club.

During that summer, the Forest City club scrambled to find dates with other professional and amateur clubs, working around the commitments most of its opponents had with their leagues. Forest City managed to play all six National League clubs of that year—Chicago, Cincinnati, Milwaukee, Indianapolis, Providence, and Boston—winning nine games and losing 18, with one tie. Against the International Association clubs of London, Allegheny (Pittsburgh), Buffalo, Syracuse, Utica, Hornellsville and Rochester, they stood 8–5. Years later it was reported that the club played as many as 111 or 112 games that season, but a complete record cannot be found.[9] The team had been organized under a broad-based subscription plan, but in advance of the 1879 season it was decided to change to the stockholder model, a more businesslike approach favored by the National League. Fifteen stockholders, men who represented the wealthy leadership of the city, put up money for the club, to be renamed the Blue Stockings, often referred to as the Blues. It was generally understood that the team would apply for membership in the International Association, which, following the departure of its last remaining Canadian team, the London Tecumsehs, became known in 1879 as the National Base-Ball Association.

William Hollinger was among the new stockholders in the reorganized club and agreed to act as manager for the following year. As soon as the season ended on October 4 with a 10–2 loss to Cincinnati, Hollinger took to the road to begin signing players for the Blue Stockings' 1879 campaign in the NBBA loop.[10] But while Hollinger was out of town drumming up talent and getting signatures on contracts, Forest City club president Evans staged a coup and took control of the team. He promptly applied for membership in the National League. In mid–October, Evans advised Hollinger that his services were no longer required and ordered him to turn over to club directors the contracts he had signed with players. Hollinger, understandably upset at the treachery of his partner, replied that he had no intention of doing so. The contracts, he maintained, were signed with him personally, not with the club or its president. Hollinger threatened to take his men to another city to play for 1879, if necessary. A struggle ensued, but Evans succeeded in getting players to sign new contracts with him. They preferred to remain in a stable city with solid ownership and the prospect of playing in the National League, rather than take their chances with Hollinger somewhere else.[11]

At the National League annual meeting, Cleveland, Buffalo and Syracuse were admitted as members.[12] The meeting, held December 4 and 5 in Cleveland, was hosted by Ford Evans, and its outcome was a foregone conclusion, Evans working in concert with his friends Hulbert and Spalding. Meanwhile, the loss of three teams to the National League was a serious blow to the International Association, and it expired within two years.

At some point, Hollinger began considering Detroit as a possible new home for his baseball team. His timing couldn't have been better, as it turned out. Hollinger found receptive ears among some leading businessmen who, coincidentally, were quietly developing plans for a new recreational facility in the city of 116,000. Some of the Detroiters with whom he spoke had played baseball as younger men or served as directors of local clubs. They quickly realized that a professional baseball club had the potential to produce additional revenue for them. But the businessmen weren't about to jump at the prospect of a professional club, mindful as they were that the city was fickle about baseball. They knew the professional game still had its critics, including those in the press upon which any team would have to rely for publicity. They were cautious and were not about to establish a team themselves, at least for the time being. But there was much to be considered and discussed when it came to baseball. And Hollinger, still looking for a team to enter a renamed International Association, was willing to talk. To anyone.

Billiards enthusiast Bill Hollinger managed a baseball team in Cleveland, but when he was unexpectedly let go, he took his talents and some of his players to Detroit, where he established the city's first fully professional team in 1879. The Hollinger Nine, as the team was known, was unable to complete a full season. Detroit returned to amateur baseball for 1880, and Hollinger went on to a successful career in billiards and managed a pool hall in the city. This is a newspaper caricature from years later when he was among the top pool players of his day (*Detroit Free Press*/ZUMA Press/ProQuest LLC).

1. Late to the Game

On its January 28, 1879, front page, the *Detroit Free Press* noted the presence of the baseball man in the city:

> BASE BALL—W. M. Hollinger, Manager of the Forest City Base Ball Club of Cleveland, has been in the city several days looking over matters pertaining to the formation of a professional base ball club to represent Detroit in the National [Base-Ball] Association. He has secured the services of several first class players whom he offers to place in the Detroit team if he shall succeed in gaining the necessary encouragement.[13]

The "encouragement" Hollinger was seeking were backers willing to invest in his dream. He was generally optimistic and felt the city could easily support his club. Along with financial support, Hollinger needed a place to play. By the middle of February, it was reported he was still in Detroit and meeting favorable response, it being noted: "His only obstacle apparent at present is the securing of suitable grounds."[14] It was said he was looking at several proposals and sites on Grand River Avenue and Fort Street West. Also considered was the Peninsular Cricket Club, located west of Woodward Avenue between Canfield Street and Forest Avenue. No mention was made of any other potential site at that time.

On the last day of February, a report surfaced about plans some local businessmen had developed for a facility to be known as Recreation Park. An 18-acre site was to be leased on the Brush Farm in the northeast corner of the city for "a sporting park on a grand scale." A company, to be incorporated within days and known as the Recreation Park Company and United Clubs Association, had already sold $6,000 worth of stock for the venture, it was reported. The long and narrow site was bounded on the south by Brady Street and on the north by Fremont Street. It was immediately east of Harper Hospital and a block and a half east of busy Woodward Avenue. The scope of the project was ambitious.

> Facing Brady Street there will be a row of handsome club houses, and just behind these the skating park, which in the summer will be the archery ground. The curling rink will be situated east of the skating park, and this will be used for skating tournaments in the evening, when the building will be brilliantly illuminated. North of the curling rink will be built an open gymnasium shed fully equipped with all gymnastic apparatus. The lease will also include the fine grove of old forest trees in the rear of Harper Hospital and beneath the shade of these there will be croquet grounds, bowling alleys and arrangements for lawn tennis and other summer games. In the middle of the field will be located the base ball diamond and lacrosse grounds and beyond those the cricket grounds. Facing these grounds and the trotting track on the north the grand stand will be placed just under the shadow of the grove. One of the very best half-mile tracks will be constructed, running from Fremont street down into the park in the usual form. Around the entire enclosure will be a fine carriage drive.

The scheme also includes a fish pond, flower garden and some graveled walks, etc., which time along will develop. The building of the fence, which will cost from $1,500 to $2,000, will be commenced so soon as a contract can be entered into, and as soon as practicable a portion of the land will be plowed up and rolled as smooth as a billiard table and on this the ball and cricket grounds will be laid out. Recreation Park, as above outlined, will supply a want long felt in the City of the Straits, and it will, no doubt, become a popular place. The high character of the gentlemen who are at the head of the association assures the public that the park and its adjuncts will be properly managed.[15]

The front-page report in the *Detroit Free Press* also noted that "gentlemen who keep flyers [fast horses]" would be able to use the grounds. This meant such riders would no longer have to travel northeast to the track in Hamtramck or use the half-mile Jennings driving park on Cass Avenue to exercise their steeds. It might also dissuade young men from the dangerous practice of racing each other on city streets, it having been noted a day earlier in the same paper that "Trumbull avenue, north from Michigan avenue, is a favorite driving place for owners of fast horses."[16] The track, described as a three-quarter-mile circuit in all other accounts, was never part of any formal racing circuit and did not supplant the established Hamtramck or Jennings courses. The directors hoped that Recreation Park, by providing a home for baseball, cricket and horse racing, the most popular sports among Detroiters, would become a new attraction and a financial success.

The men behind the new venture were certainly of high character. And holders of large bank accounts. Virtually all were among the movers and shakers of the day in Detroit. Several had played or been supporters or directors of baseball clubs. Others retained a fondness for horses. Nearly all were connected with each other through business. The founding meeting of the Recreation Park Company was held in the offices of the Michigan Car Company, a successful builder of railroad cars. James McMillan, treasurer and manager of Michigan Car, was elected president.[17] McMillan had become a wealthy business leader in his adopted city, a tycoon of transportation. Born in Hamilton, Ontario, in 1838, he was the first-born son of Scottish immigrant William McMillan, a founder and executive with the Great Western Railway. Young James left school at an early age to become a clerk in a Hamilton hardware store, quickly demonstrating a rare flair for business. Not long afterward, the ambitious 17-year-old moved 200 miles southwest to Detroit for a position with a prominent wholesale hardware business, relying on a referral from his employer in Hamilton. He lost his job during the financial panic of 1857, but through more connections (likely his father's), he became a purchasing agent for the Detroit-Milwaukee Railroad, where his abilities attracted increasing responsibilities.[18] He married the daughter of a wealthy grocer and settled into building a good life in Detroit.

The Early Risers amateur baseball club of working men practiced and played before reporting for work on a field beside the Russell House Hotel in downtown Detroit. So many errant balls smashed through the hotel's windows that it established a flat rate to cover the damage. In time, the hotel became the preferred venue for organizational and annual meetings of the professional Detroit Base Ball Club, whose team became known as the Wolverines (Library of Congress).

At his local church, he met John Stoughton Newberry, a noted railroad, maritime and admiralty lawyer, with whom he soon forged a lasting friendship and profitable business partnership.

McMillan and Newberry became involved with a once-troubled freight-car manufacturing firm that began to recover when it started supplying rail cars to the North during the Civil War. Newberry was a well-connected Republican who was named provost marshal of Michigan in 1862 by President Abraham Lincoln. With his extensive political contacts, Newberry won a contract for 2,000 railway cars, and he and McMillan organized the Michigan Car Company to supply rolling stock for the Northern cause.[19] Their highly successful firm acquired the Detroit Car Wheel Company to supply wheels for their cars and to their competitors. They also acquired or established the Fulton Iron and

Engine Works, a foundry and a dry dock company, among other industries. In 1877, they obtained the city's telephone franchise and four years later created the Edison Electric Light Company. McMillan and Newberry were captains of industry by the late 1870s, and thousands of men worked in their firms. They were also what today would be called venture capitalists, using their money to make more for themselves and for others. At one point, McMillan held stock in more than 50 companies, was president of six of them and a board member or officer for 17 others. Aside from their fine downtown mansions, he and Newberry built adjoining palatial "cottages" in exclusive Grosse Pointe on Lake St. Clair, from which they often commuted to work aboard the steam-powered yacht *Truant* they jointly owned. McMillan organized Newberry's successful 1878 campaign for the U.S. Congress, and later McMillan became a Republican senator for Michigan.[20] The two men each donated $100,000 to establish Grace Hospital in 1888, named after McMillan's oldest daughter, Grace McMillan Jarvis.

Aside from business and politics, the two men shared an interest in baseball. A widower at an early age, Newberry lived for a time at the Russell House Hotel downtown and played for the Detroit Base Ball Club, becoming president and captain in 1859. He also played for the Early Risers, a group of less affluent workingmen who found time for the game before going to work. They played and practiced on a field beside the Russell House. So many errant balls from Early Riser games and practices smashed through the hotel windows that it established a flat rate for ongoing damage.[21] For his part, McMillan found time in his busy schedule to act as a director of the Cass Base Ball Club in 1875.[22] Newberry was not a director of the new recreational park, but McMillan likely kept him apprised and sought advice from his close friend with superior baseball credentials.

Vice-president of the Recreation Park Company was Alfred E. Brush, a member of one of the oldest and wealthiest families in Detroit. In 1806, Elijah Brush, a lawyer from Vermont, bought a 138-acre farm from his father-in-law, John Askin, who had opted to return to his home in Canada. Brush was appointed the first attorney general of the Michigan territory, was installed as Detroit's second mayor, and was a member of the territorial army that surrendered Fort Detroit to the British during the War of 1812. His oldest son, Edmund, took over the farm upon Elijah Brush's death in 1813 from unknown causes. The property was one of the most valuable in the small community. Surveyed in the French "ribbon farm" manner, it had a relatively narrow frontage on the Detroit River but extended several miles north along Woodward Avenue into the bush. Today, the Renaissance Centre sits on what was its southern edge, as well as Comerica Park and Ford Field. Brush Park and the Detroit

Medical Center lie just to the north, the latter occupying the land on which Recreation Park was created. Edmund Brush gradually and carefully developed the farm, growing wealthy in the process. From the 1860s to about 1900, Brush Park became one of the city's most desirable and exclusive neighborhoods. Captains of industry and commerce occupied fine, red-brick, three-story Victorian homes within easy walking distance of their downtown businesses. Edmund died in 1877 and his son, Alfred, became a trustee of the Brush estate. It was Alfred who helped arrange the lease for 18 acres at the northern end of the old farm for Recreation Park.[23] As a board member, he could retain some control over how the property was used.

Among the nine directors of the company was George Hendrie, like McMillan a native of Hamilton, Ontario. Hendrie and his older brother William acquired the Detroit City Railway in 1864, with the financial help of McMillan, and turned the horse-drawn street railway into a monopoly. The brothers, partners in Hendrie and Company, originally came to Detroit in 1859 to run cartage operations for the Great Western Railway. The Hendries also opened two Detroit banks, Great Lakes Navigation and other companies. They joined McMillan and Newberry in the Michigan Car Company and, like traditional railroad tycoons, also speculated in property in areas where they planned to extend their rail line, amassing vast holdings. Their base of operations remained in Hamilton, where they operated a large horse-breeding operation and had customers that included the British Army. William Hendrie raced thoroughbreds and trotting horses and was among the organizers of the Ontario Jockey Club.[24] In 1879, George Hendrie was elected president of the newly established Detroit Jockey Club, and he and McMillan were active in horse-racing circles.[25] The Hendries loved their horses and were reluctant to replace them on their street railway while other cities converted theirs to electricity, prompting widespread public criticism that eventually led to Detroit taking over their operation in the 1890s.[26] Their attachment to horses was likely among the reasons Recreation Park included a trotting track.

In April, it was announced that admission to Recreation Park would be $6 for members of the public, allowing year-round access to the park and its facilities. The price was seen as fair because a season's pass for skating rinks was $5. Admission to the track, however, required a separate ticket.[27]

While contracts were being let for work at Recreation Park, William Hollinger was hiring players for the professional team he had been encouraged to create for Detroit. By mid–March, he said the nine was complete, and he listed the names of the players he had retained.[28] On April 3, a public meeting was held at the Russell House Hotel at which Hollinger laid out his intentions, described his players and recounted their playing records. He told his audience that he had not yet found a suitable place to play in the city and that he had received an offer from Toledo to take his team there. It is not known whether Hollinger was bluffing, but that bit of information produced support. Then and there it was decided that his team would play at Recreation Park, suggesting that his audience that evening included directors of the new park company. "This guarantees the Hollinger nine for Detroit," said the *Free Press*, "and to-day and during the next week Mr. Hollinger will visit business men and citizens generally who enjoy base ball, with a view to procuring subscriptions for the support of the club, also with a view to selling season tickets."[29] The Hollinger Nine name would stick, although in the fashion of the day, the "Detroits" was more widely used.

The paper also reported that Hollinger was "much pleased with the liberal spirit the [Recreation Park] company has shown him in his base ball scheme."[30] No terms were released, but they were likely quite reasonable, based on an offer extended by directors to the Peninsular Cricket Club, outlined in the same news article. The cricketers could use the ground at Recreation Park rent-free, but members were required to pay $6 to become members of the park. These fees were expected to produce more than $600 in revenue in the first year. Directors of the facility were anxious to create traffic and believed that membership fees for cricket and baseball teams, expected to be major drawing cards, would generate the sort of income that other activities like impromptu horse racing couldn't.

Work on the grounds was slow getting underway as 60 men with six teams of horses faced still-frozen ground in early April. It had been hoped that 1,500 man-days of labor would have the park in shape within 30 days and allow for a May 1 opening. But it was becoming apparent that mid–May was more likely.[31]

A large drawing showing the layout of Recreation Park was featured on the front page of an April 13 supplement in the *Detroit Post and Tribune*, providing a tantalizing glimpse of what was being created behind the nine-foot board fence that was quickly rising around the property. The three-quarter-mile "driving track" encircled the grounds, and a ball diamond was tucked into the south end of its infield. Also shown were grounds to the north of the diamond that were set aside for ball fields to be "fitted up" in 1880. The skating rink near the park entrance on Brady Street measured 120 feet by 210 feet. Also shown were the house of the resident caretaker, the gymnasium, a clubhouse and a shed for buggies. The newspaper was high in its praise for the facility.

> Recreation Park is destined to become one of the institutions of the city. It will do much to foster and keep alive the keen interest in athletic sports already manifest in this city. It will be a charming resort for young and old, and the public may be

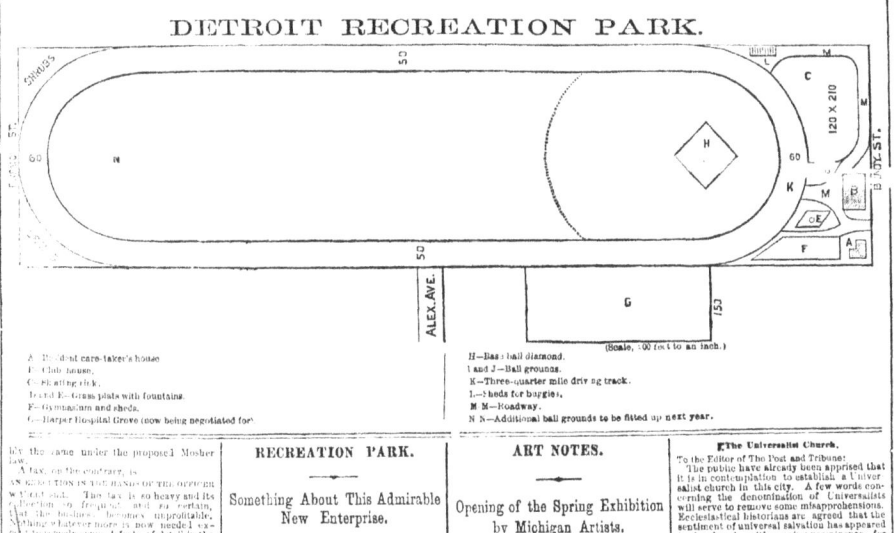

Recreation Park was created on property owned by the wealthy Brush family behind Harper Hospital. The private facility included a three-quarter-mile harness-racing track, curling rink, skating park, gymnasium, fish ponds, archery ground, tennis courts, and cricket pitch. A baseball diamond was located in the infield of the track. The private owners of the park felt that a professional baseball team would draw patrons and ensure success. Recreation Park was home for the Hollinger Nine and later for the Detroit Wolverines. The baseball grounds were considered among the most beautiful in America (*Detroit Post and Tribune*).

> assured that in its management every objectionable feature will be rigidly excluded.[32]

The aim of the venture, the paper said, "is the promotion of healthful outdoor sports and exercises by providing a rendezvous where participants and spectators alike enjoy friendly contests of athletic skill." Aside from baseball and cricket, activities were expected to include "foot-ball, quoits, lawn-tennis, archery, curling, skating, croquet, pedestrianism, etc., [each] in its season." The park was described as 1,750 feet long by 430 feet wide. A two-story clubhouse of 71 feet by 45 feet would feature a tower and flagstaff. The ground floor would include a restaurant, smoking room, reading room, ladies' dressing and waiting rooms, a ticket office and boardroom for directors. The second floor consisted of a parlor, closets and "retiring room." A "spacious gymnasium" was to be equipped with horizontal and parallel bars, flying rings, trapeze, weights and pulleys, "Indian clubs," dumb-bells and other muscle-building equipment. The track, the newspaper noted, was 50 feet wide and 60 feet in the turns. "The right of using this track will be limited to members," it noted. The names of the businessmen who incorporated Recreation Park were listed in the account, with the observation: "They are gentlemen of means and cultivated tastes, occupying prominence in leading social and business circles. Any enterprise they become interested in is certain of success."[33]

While it might appear odd for a ball diamond to occupy the infield of a horse-racing track, it actually made complete sense and wasn't the first time it had been done. Horse racing was a popular diversion at the time, and admission was charged to spectators. Tracks had to be fenced off and entrances tightly controlled to ensure that patrons paid to watch racing programs. As long as baseball was an amateur pastime, there was no need to restrict entry to games because admission was not charged. There had been one notable exception, however. The Great Baseball Match of 1858 was played at the Fashion Race Course in Queens, near the site of today's Citi Field, home of the New York Mets. It pitted all-star amateur teams from New York and Brooklyn in a best-of-three series beginning July 20 to determine bragging rights to baseball supremacy. The clubs decided they needed a neutral site for their games and agreed upon a track in Queens named after a famous racehorse from the 1840s. Because they needed to pay rent for the course and spend money to create a suitable diamond in the infield, the teams decided to charge 50 cents admission (some sources say only 10 cents, plus additional fees). At the end of the series, $71 was left over and was donated to the widows and orphans of firefighters in New York and Brooklyn. Betting was heavy on the games, and the *New York Clipper* estimated the crowd at the first game at not less than 10,000 cranks.[34] Other estimates were as low as 4,000, however. Smaller crowds attended the remaining two games. New York triumphed, twice defeating the favored Brooklyn nine. It marked the first time in history that baseball was played at an enclosed park and that admission was charged.[35] So the plan to combine baseball and horse racing at Recreation Park was not without precedent.

By mid–April, work was well underway on the grounds, with tile drains installed, a water system operational and the field leveled and mostly sodded. The track was partly finished, but work was yet to begin on the clubhouse and grandstands. It had been decided that two baseball diamonds would be created within the racetrack, one for professionals, the other for amateur teams like the Cass Club. The 1,000-seat grandstand was nearing completion when it was announced that the opening day for the new professional team would be May

12, against Toledo.³⁶ After some negotiation, trustees of Harper Hospital granted the use of a grove of trees abutting Recreation Park that would be used for croquet and other activities and to provide much-needed shade on hot summer days.

Hollinger had abandoned plans to join the National Base-Ball Association for the upcoming season, and his club would compete as an independent. The manager was practicing his men every afternoon, lining up games and trying to drum up interest in the coming season. Hollinger, a newspaper reported, "does not hesitate to say that the grounds of the Recreation Park Company will be among the finest in the country, and also that his nine will be the best organization outside of the Base Ball League and one that it will be hard for any League club to defeat."³⁷ For its part, the National League opened its rain-delayed season on May 1. The Detroit club would wear cream-and-chocolate-colored uniforms, with red trim, red belts and red stockings, it was announced, while practice uniforms would be solid white. Until Recreation Park was ready, the Hollinger Nine used the Peninsular Cricket Grounds on Woodward Avenue.³⁸

Detroit's first fully professional team was about to take the field in a new home. The drive and determination of a baseball man from Cleveland had coincided with a recreational initiative by some Detroit capitalists seeking a tenant for their new park. Traditionally, baseball clubs were organized first, then sought a suitable place to play. Here, the venue sought a team to play in it, and William Hollinger was the right man in the right place at the right time. Recreation Park, to be a viable operation, needed a professional ball team as a star attraction. It didn't matter that it came from Cleveland.

Now it was time to see if Detroit's long-standing reticence about professional baseball would continue, or if that page had finally been turned. The connection of the new club with some of the oldest and wealthiest members of the city establishment couldn't hurt.

The prospects seemed promising.

2

The Hollinger Nine

In 1879, the National League was entering its fourth season, strengthened by the addition of Cleveland, Buffalo and Troy, and having shed its bottom-dwelling Western clubs in Indianapolis and Milwaukee. There would be eight teams in the loop, up from six, a return to the number of teams in the League's inaugural season. Historians have referred to 1879 as the last year for player freedom because by 1880 each team was allowed to "reserve" five players from its roster for the following year. The "reserve clause" would be extended to cover all players on team rosters, and despite player protests and court challenges, it wasn't struck down until nearly a century later, in 1975. The reserve system saw players become virtual slaves of their owners. While it brought some stability to the business of professional baseball, it trampled on the rights of players and prevented them from selling their talents to the highest bidder on the open market. So it kept salaries lower than would otherwise have been the case.[1]

The reserve system was introduced by League magnates who had grown angry at players jumping from one team to another, without respecting contracts they had signed. If team owners wouldn't release a player at his request, that player might opt to play poorly in hopes of gaining a release and a fatter pay packet elsewhere. Ten days after being released, a player could be picked up by another team. Some team owners were as guilty of destabilizing teams as were the players, by luring those already under contract. The net effect of "revolving" was that player pay jumped beyond what some teams could afford. Profitability was rare for team owners in the early days of the professional game, and many clubs succumbed to financial reality before their season was over. This forced league officials to recalculate standings by erasing wins earned from teams that had disbanded. The situation was serious, but the medicine administered to cure it for 1880 was draconian with long-lasting impact.

2. The Hollinger Nine

As he assembled his nine for Detroit, William Hollinger dealt with some of those independent-minded players seeking the best deal possible for their services. He was still fighting with Ford Evans, who was signing members of the 1878 Forest Citys for his Cleveland Blue Stockings of 1879. Evans succeeded in hiring five of the men, but Hollinger hung onto four: six-foot-two catcher Emil Gross; hard-throwing pitcher Harry Salisbury; promising young outfielder Bones Ely; and third baseman Charlie Morton, who also played center field. In early March, Hollinger announced all four men as part of his roster during his discussions with potential backers.[2] Ely, however, would not appear in the Opening Day lineup, having opted to go elsewhere. Art Croft, formerly with the St. Louis Browns and the Indianapolis Blues, was announced as the team's second baseman, but he failed to appear in Detroit and was replaced by Sam Barkley, a 20-year-old West Virginian from the Standard Club of Wheeling. Likewise, players Ed Gault, Joe Miller, Clark and Johnson also failed to show. There was much going on behind the scenes. Hollinger had to scramble to sign and then keep players as he wooed backers, conducted practices and kept tabs on progress at Recreation Park. He engaged Trick McSorley, a third baseman from the Cleveland Forest Citys; Isaac Van Burkalow, a pitcher from the Rochester Flour City club; local amateur Tommy Shaughnessy (who had pitched for the Cass Club) who would play shortstop; and Cleveland amateur Ed Swartwood, for right field. McSorley would be named captain. Rounding out the nine was Steve Libby, a first baseman from the Buffalo Bisons of 1878. At one point, Northwestern League president James McKee invited Hollinger to enter his team in that small loop, but Hollinger opted against joining, his hands full as he struggled to assemble his roster.[3]

The battery for the Hollinger Nine was Salisbury and Gross. Van Burkalow, introduced to the public as J. P. Burkalow and invariably referred to as "Burkalow" in press accounts, played mainly center field. He and catcher Doc Kennedy saw their Memphis club disband in mid–1878, so both joined Rochester in the International Association. There, Van Burkalow replaced pitcher Charles Purroy, who was suspected of crooked play. With Rochester, Van Burkalow won 14 games and lost 16, with three ties.[4] Hollinger considered Van Burkalow his "change," or relief, pitcher and only occasionally handed him the ball for a game.

In all, the monthly payroll for the players amounted to a healthy $700, broken down this way:

$125, Emil Gross, catcher
$125, Harry Salisbury, pitcher
$100, Steve Libby, first base

$70, Isaac Van Burkalow, center field, pitcher
$70, J. B. "Trick" McSorley, third base
$55, Ed Swartwood, right field
$55, Charlie Morton, left field
$50, Sam Barkley, second base
$50, Tom Shaughnessy, shortstop[5]

Late signings Libby and Barkley were delayed in getting releases from their clubs, and Hollinger began to fear they would miss Opening Day. Meanwhile, in advance of the May 12 opening game against the Troy Trojans of the National League, the *Detroit Free Press* warned Detroiters to be realistic in their expectations. It noted that Troy was a good team, then standing fourth in the League (actually, League newcomer Troy was a weak link, having lost its first six games). "Too much must not be expected at the start from the Detroit club,

The entrance to Recreation Park was on Brady Street, along the south edge of the park. The two-story main building included a restaurant, smoking room, reading room, "retiring" room, parlor, ladies' dressing and waiting rooms, a ticket office and boardroom for park directors. Some of Detroit's top businessmen were among the managing directors (Burton Historical Collection, Detroit Public Library).

although their daily practice exhibitions during the past week show that they are good general players. They give promise that as soon as they become thoroughly used to the new grounds and to each other, that they will play a strong game."[6]

Game day arrived, but Libby and Barkley still hadn't. Yet again, Hollinger was left to scramble. "Manager Hollinger has suffered much annoyance through the non-fulfillment of contracts by players upon whom he relied," the *Detroit Post and Tribune* noted. "The consequence was that with an incomplete organization but little thorough practice was obtained, and at the last moment he found himself without first and second basemen."[7] So Hollinger improvised. Quickly. Thomas Gillean, a member of the London Tecumseh team, had agreed to act as umpire for the first game and had brought along teammate and fellow Londoner Tommy Smith as company. Smith was a capable outfielder, and Hollinger asked him to join the Detroit club for the day and play center field. Smith agreed, and Hollinger moved Van Burkalow from center to first base. Hollinger then approached the Trojans, explained his need for a ninth man, and obtained Trojan John Shoupe to play second. Hollinger's cobbled-together club was now ready to take to the field in their new cream-and-chocolate uniforms trimmed in red.

Recreation Park was in fine shape for its opening on Monday, May 12, 1879, and the weather cooperated. The track and ball grounds were nicely groomed, and the flowerbeds were full of attractive plantings to greet visitors. The *Free Press* was fulsome in its praise for the facility, describing it as "well done ... there is no city of the same size in the United States where better grounds for outdoor amusements are provided."[8] Scores of gentlemen and ladies began arriving at 1 p.m. for a game that wasn't to begin until 3:45. The racetrack was soon full of parked carriages and other vehicles, and a large number of ladies occupied seats in the grandstand while young boys and men inspected the park and found room to stand beside the track, closer to the ball diamond. The track itself was very dry, however, and passing carriages sent clouds of dust wafting into the grandstand to the dismay, no doubt, of the ladies seated there in their finery. "Small boys with 'score cards, only five cents,' little girls with button hole bouquets, and neat young Frenchmen with fresh waffles, paraded through the throngs with their wares, thus making up what seemed almost a section of some State fair or other great exhibition," the *Free Press* noted. The rival *Detroit Post and Tribune* estimated the crowd at 1,200, a number less than might have been expected, but it was a Monday afternoon, making it difficult for working men to attend. Recreation Park directors Joseph Taylor and Francis O. Davenport appeared at the grandstand about 3:30 to declare the park officially open. In a bit of bad timing, the latter part of Taylor's speech was drowned out by the Great Western Band, which performed on the clubhouse verandah. Ned Russell, a member of the city council, fared better when he congratulated the park company without interruption. Alfred Brush, vice-president of the Recreation Park Company, unfurled a new flag bearing the words "Detroit Recreation Park," and ran it up the flagpole atop the clubhouse. It snapped smartly in the light breeze.[9] With that, it was time for baseball.

Troy and Detroit were anxious to begin the game, and the first pitch was thrown before Taylor's speech was finished and the flag raised. Detroit started poorly, giving up two runs in the first inning to the visitors. Hometown boy Shaughnessy made an error at shortstop that led to one of them. His shaky play was attributed to nervousness in his first professional game. The newspapers said the entire Detroit team seemed rather nervous in the early innings and didn't settle down until four were complete, by which time Troy had tallied seven times and the home nine only once. Smith, the import patrolling center field, had two hits and scored Detroit's only run. His batting in the fourth inning drew "tremendous" applause from the crowd which otherwise found little to cheer about. Troy added three runs in the third inning and two more in the fourth, ending the scoring in the game. Salisbury and Gross worked together effectively, and it was noted that Salisbury "imparts a remarkable curve to the ball." The Detroit bats were largely silent, aside from Smith, with only Van Burkalow, Swartwood and Shaughnessy reaching base. The *Detroit Post and Tribune* said victory had not been expected for Hollinger's men, partly because it was an "incomplete nine." But it went on to praise their effort.

> The Detroits, or the seven who played yesterday, are a stout and solid-looking set of men, and evidently only need thorough organization and practice to make a formidable nine.... The spectators were disposed to regard the Detroits with consideration and make due allowances for drawbacks. There was something about the general appearance of the nine that created a favorable impression, and as manager Hollinger has 49 additional games on his list, his men will have ample opportunity to show improvement, if it is in them.[10]

The *Detroit Free Press* was inclined to finger-pointing in the 7–1 loss. Its account was much shorter than that of the *Post and Tribune,* and it noted that the foreign center fielder Smith made two errors, something it termed "a trifle suspicious." The paper made no mention of his hits or that Smith scored Detroit's only run. It complained that the other "outsider," Shoupe, the player lent by the Trojans, committed three errors at second base and that all but one of Troy's runs were scored on the errors by Shoupe and Smith. "In a summing up of the game the conclusions are that the Detroit Club can play ball all around, their greatest strength, however, being as fielders, while they bat fairly and may do better after a week's practice." The paper found no fault with the umpiring of Gillean, yet another outsider, who performed his duties "very carefully and honestly." The Troy team took home $102.50, and the Great Western Band earned $25 for its performance.[11] It is not known how much was left over for the ball team or the new park.

In Buffalo, directors of the Bisons granted Steve Libby his release on May 13, and he appeared in Detroit the following day to play first base against the amateur Toledo Modocs. Second baseman Sam Barkley still had not arrived from Virginia, so Hollinger moved Van Burkalow to second and installed himself in center field. What was described as a "fair audience" saw Detroit easily handle Toledo by a score of 11–2. Every batter except Salisbury had a hit. Hollinger singled and scored a run, while Gross, McSorley and newcomer Libby each crossed the plate twice. Salisbury struck out 10 Modocs and Van Burkalow took over for the final two innings, recording two strikeouts. It marked the home club's first win. Another game with Toledo the following day was a similarly lopsided affair as Detroit shut out the Modocs, 8–0, in six innings, before the visitors left to catch their train for home. Aside from Salisbury, manager Hollinger also tried McSorley and Shaughnessy as pitchers.

On Saturday, May 17, a large crowd of Detroiters, "a majority being ladies," appeared at Recreation Park for a game against the University of Michigan, whose teams in some years were among the strongest in the state. It was a complete mismatch, however, as the professionals rolled over the error-prone university lads, 23–2. Yet again, the Great Western Band provided musical accompaniment.[12] Home games scheduled for May 21–22 with the South Bend, Indiana, Green Stockings were cancelled when their manager telegraphed May 19 that three of his players were ill. The cancellation was the first of many that Hollinger would face, for a variety of reasons, creating headaches for him and lost revenue for team coffers. Fortunately, in this case, the games were rescheduled for May 27–28. On May 23, Sam Barkley finally arrived and Hollinger's nine was complete. With no games during the week, it was reported the Detroit club was "getting rusty for lack of genuine work," so a game of cricket was played May 24 against the Peninsular Cricket Club on the latter's grounds. As expected, the sometimes puzzled baseballists were easily defeated, 204 to 30.[13]

For its first game on the road, the team crossed the border into Canada and travelled east by train to London to face the storied Tecumseh club on Monday, May 26. London was celebrating the Queen's Birthday holiday, but only a modest crowd turned out to Tecumseh Park. Detroit scored two runs in the first inning and despite a late rally by London, held on to win, 8–7. The visitors complained bitterly about the competency of the umpire in that game and felt his work favored the home club. Afterwards, the team took the train back to Detroit to prepare for the rescheduled games the following two days against South Bend.

The South Bend Green Stockings club included two Detroiters as their battery. Pitcher Mel Kurtz had played for the Cass Club, while his catcher named Parks had played for both Cass and the Aetnas. South Bend and Hollinger's men practiced at Recreation Park under threatening skies while gentlemen raced their horses around the track, ladies exercised their family horses and bicyclists sped by. A crowd estimated at 300 to 400 turned out. Parks reached second on an error by Shaughnessy and scored the first run for South Bend in the first inning. The visitors added another run in the third and kept Hollinger's men scoreless through eight innings. South Bend, ahead 2–0, failed to score in the top of the ninth inning.

In its final at-bat, the home team gave the crowd something to cheer about. Captain McSorley singled, and behind him Libby belted a hot line drive that got him to first and advanced McSorley to third. Local lad Shaughnessy sent a hot one over first base and into right field as McSorley scampered home. On an errant throw by the fielder, Libby also scored and Shaughnessy advanced to second, amid wild cheers. The game was now tied. Swartwood was next up and hit the ball to right field, where the fielder mishandled the ball, allowing Shaughnessy to get home and Swartwood to take second. Under rules of the day, play continued until the inning was finished, even thought Detroit was already ahead, 3–2. The new man, Barkley, came to the plate and immediately proved his worth. He struck the second ball he saw from Kurtz so hard that it sailed over the racetrack in left field for a home run. After he and Swartwood crossed the plate the score stood at 5–2. The rest of the Detroit side struck out, "And thus ended one of the most exciting contests ever witnessed in Detroit," the *Free Press* burbled.[14] The following day, the same teams went at it again and Detroit hammered South Bend, 15–2. Visiting pitcher Kurtz proved easy to solve as he gave up 16 hits, with every batter except the Detroit pitcher getting one, and Swartwood and Shaughnessy three apiece. The players behind Kurtz made 13 errors with their sloppy play, and only four South Bend players were able to hit Salisbury.

The Tecumseh Club from London arrived in town for games May 30–31. Between 500 and 600 cranks showed up at Recreation Park for the first meeting. Rain and hail delayed the start of the game, but a half-hour later as the storm abated, the clubs took the field, with Detroit batting first after the coin toss. Soon the skies opened up again and the game was cancelled. The following day the weather was no better, so the Tecumsehs boarded their eastbound train without ever taking the field. Detroit didn't play again until June 7, when it blanked the Cass Club, 12–0, before a fair-sized crowd. The local amateurs were gracious in defeat, it being reported, "The Cass Club are emphatic in expressing their belief that the Detroits are the best base ball nine in the country and need not fear the Chicago, Boston or other League clubs."[15] Trying to keep his team in game shape, manager Hollinger lined up another game with the Tecumsehs and a nine-day road trip to play three of the four Northwestern League teams later in June, followed by return matches with them soon after in Detroit.

On June 11, a Wednesday, the Tecumsehs returned to Detroit for a game at Recreation Park that was witnessed by several hundred ladies and gentlemen. Unlike the game in London that Detroit won by a single run, this return match saw Detroit score four times in the first inning as the home club romped to an 11–5 victory. Newcomers Libby and Barkley teamed up for a double play, and the Detroiters pounded London pitcher Eustis for five runs in a wild sixth inning. Gross, Swartwood and Shaughnessy wielded the best lumber in the game, Gross with three hits and the others with two apiece. Even pitcher Salisbury joined the hit parade with a single. The Tecumsehs committed 13 errors,

An early game at Recreation Park. The ball diamond was encircled by a three-quarter-mile harness-racing track which was in play. The grandstand would be extended several times to accommodate the crowds who followed the Wolverines. To the left is the two-story building at the entrance to the park on Brady Street. This view looks to the southwest from right field (Burton Historical Collection, Detroit Public Library).

and it was clear the 1879 nine was a mere shadow of the team that had put London on the baseball map in recent years.

That same day, the *Detroit Free Press* carried an item outlining some worrisome problems confronting Hollinger's men. On a positive note, it said the season was about six weeks old and the Detroit team had won nine of its 11 games, outscoring its opponents, 117 runs to 39. The paper said the team was among the best in the country and that Recreation Park was one of the best facilities of its kind. But problems had beset the club as it prepared for a western road trip.

> Being required to build up a name and to revive public interest in the game, they began the season under a cloud. In addition, they have had weather to contend with, all of which has conspired to their disadvantage.... Another disagreeable fact is that every member of nine is in the receipt of two to half a dozen excellent offers to join other clubs, West and East. The receipt of such offers while they are so unfortunately situated in Detroit is very tempting, to say the least, and although the ball-tossers have not as yet complained or made any statement that can be construed as a threat, it does seem as though some scheme could be devised by which the club could command from the hundreds of base ball enthusiasts in Detroit the aid necessary to enable them to go through the season with flying colors.[16]

The assistance sought was not specified by the paper, but it was clearly an appeal for more cranks to attend games. The club was struggling to meet its healthy $700-a-month payroll.

On June 15, Hollinger and his men left Detroit on a Western trip in which they would play three games in each of three cities, beginning June 16 in Rockford, Illinois, June 19 in Dubuque, Iowa, and June 22 in Davenport, Iowa. Returning home, Detroit would play a three-game series against Rockford beginning June 25. Rockford, Davenport and Dubuque were members of the Northwestern League that Detroit had been invited to join. It was repeatedly said in news accounts of the day that Detroit was a member of the Northwestern League, but it was not. In the custom of the day, the four members of the loop all took their names from hosiery: Rockford White Stockings, Davenport Brown Stockings, Omaha Green Stockings and Dubuque Red Stockings.[17]

On June 16, Rockford defeated Detroit, 11–9, but the following day Detroit won, 7–3, boosted by homers from Barkley and Libby, while Salisbury proved hard to hit. Nearly 1,000 fans took in the first game and a "large" crowd the second. The third game went to Rockford, 16–6, as Salisbury struggled. Detroit was still recovering from a grueling, 14-hour train ride that included a three-hour stopover in Chicago. The rough condition of the playing surface, far inferior to their home diamond, didn't help. On June 19 in Dubuque, 600 spectators saw Detroit win, 6–4. The following day, before 800 cranks,

Dubuque turned the tables, winning by the same 6–4 score. Detroit took the rubber match, 6–3, on June 21. Rain wiped out the first game with Davenport on June 23. Davenport would prove to be a watershed for the Detroit nine, in ways beyond weather. A small crowd witnessed the June 24 game when the hometown Brown Stockings took advantage of wild throws by Gross, Salisbury, McSorley and Shaughnessy to win, 9–5. Detroit won the June 25 game, 2–1, in a defensive battle before another light crowd. Staying over another day, Detroit lost 4–3 on June 26, with even fewer spectators on hand.

It was reported following the June 24 game that the finances for the Detroit Club were "pitifully low" because of rained-out games and poor crowds. The team was hoping to earn enough money in Davenport to get to Kalamazoo for a game there to help pay for their trip home.[18] That didn't happen. In a dispatch from Davenport after the June 26 game, a grim picture was painted:

> From the beginning of their Western trip the Detroits have had bad luck financially, and the last straw was put on their backs this evening when it was discovered that the Davenports disbanded immediately after the game, their treasurer going away with the receipts for the three games, and their players scattering to St. Paul, Dubuque, St. Louis and Chicago. The Detroits were thus defrauded of their guaranty of $250, and are here penniless and unable to get home.[19]

The Rockford Club arrived in Detroit on the morning of June 28 expecting to play the game that had been arranged for that day by Hollinger. But the Detroit nine was just leaving Davenport, emergency funds having materialized. So Rockford agreed to play the Cass Club, but it was rained out. Not until June 30 were Rockford and Detroit able to play, and the visitors shut out Hollinger's nine by a score of 3–0. A disappointing 400 fans showed up. Salisbury was unable to pitch, so Van Burkalow replaced him and did a creditable job. Hollinger took Van Burkalow's place in center field but things did not go well for the manager. "Hollinger's weaknesses both in the field and at the bat, undoubtedly had something to do with the final result," the *Detroit Free Press* carped. It blamed two first inning runs scored by the visitors on Hollinger's overthrow to third baseman McSorley. Hollinger also failed to get on base and was among five Detroit players unable to get a hit.[20] Rockford, having missed two games in Detroit when the home club was marooned in Davenport, was unable to remain in town any longer and took the evening train back to Illinois.

After a couple of days' rest, the Detroiters returned to Recreation Park for a much-anticipated July 3 game against the Boston Red Caps of the National League. A crowd of about 800 witnessed the hometown nine's first test against a League team. An impressed Harry Wright, the Boston manager, described the baseball grounds as "the best in the world."[21] He had certainly seen enough diamonds in his long and storied career. The Detroit club acquitted itself well and gave Boston a competitive game. McSorley and Barkley belted triples off Red Caps pitcher Tommy Bond, who surrendered eight hits in all. The bats of the visitors were booming and they pounded three homers off Salisbury and 11 hits. In the field, Detroit committed six errors, while Boston had only two and won the game, 8–3.

Little was seen of the Detroit Club for the next several days, despite its announced plans to play Kalamazoo on July 8, 9, and 10. The silence surrounding the team prompted the *Detroit Free Press* on July 12 to ask on its front page: "What has become of the Detroit Base Ball Club?"[22] The team was reorganizing. It was said elsewhere that the Recreation Park Company had acquired the club and placed the players on salary until the end of the season on October 15.[23] About this time, manager Hollinger quietly resigned his duties.[24]

Recreation Park itself was struggling to become viable and didn't want one of its prime occupants to fail. Directors wanted to see professional baseball become an established attraction in the city, and they were willing to extend a financial lifeline to it. Hollinger had been unable to arrange a game for the July 4 holiday, an ideal date to draw big crowds to Recreation Park, so directors put together a diverse program of amusements and advertised it widely. Admission was 25 cents. At 11 a.m., world-famous navigator Captain Paul Boyton was to stage an entertaining nautical demonstration that included the explosion of a "full-rigged vessel, five feet long, by means of marine torpedoes." At 1:30 p.m., lacrosse teams from St. Thomas and Simcoe, two towns in Ontario, were scheduled to play a game. At 5 p.m., Professor J. W. Hayden would launch his "mammoth balloon," described as the largest ever seen in Michigan. At 8 p.m., Captain Boyton would return with a display of colored ocean signals, fireworks and torpedoes. Professor Rudolph Speil's Opera House Orchestra was to provide a concert from 7 to 10 p.m.[25]

The day did not go as planned, however. Hayden and his balloon failed to show up, with no explanation given. After the lacrosse game, management insisted that patrons without tickets for the Boyton exhibition must leave the park, creating hard feelings among visitors who thought their admission fee covered all activities that day. Managers finally relented, and Boyton went on with his show.[26] In their bid to make the park profitable, directors later that summer booked an all-woman baseball game (that drew 2,000 spectators), demonstrations by sharpshooter Ira Paine, and a balloon ascension by Prof. Walliky Rulison, an "aerial gymnast" from New York who performed tricks on a trapeze suspended from it. Also staged was an "electric promenade concert," in which a band was illuminated by giant lights and "Begin's reflector" attached to the grandstand. The lighting was devised by local inventor Charles Van Depoele, who experimented widely with electric lights, generators and motors.

His lights shone on the musicians, who performed in the center of the diamond. It was said that Van Depoele's lights illuminated them with "a brilliancy equal to sunlight."[27] No one apparently considered using his lights for night-time baseball games, an innovation that was still decades away.

In a bid to streamline management of the park, the executive committee appointed one of the park directors, Francis O. Davenport, a general insurance agent, as managing director. Davenport was given full control of the operation on July 18, his fellow directors confident his energy and ideas could produce better financial results.[28] Among the innovations Davenport introduced were mule races, foot races and a six-day "go-as-you-please" pedestrian race. Sometime earlier that month he had assumed managerial duties for the Detroit Base Ball Club, upon the resignation of Hollinger.

Kalamazoo was paid $111 to come to Recreation Park for games July 15, 16, and 17.[29] Excessive heat was blamed for a disappointing turnout of about 400 cranks for the first game, in which Detroit blanked the visitors, 10–0. The "long period of idleness" of the home team was noted, "and the result only showed that the Detroits, with no financial or other cause to trouble them, can play well."[30] Another small audience watched Detroit defeat Kalamazoo, 5–2, the following day. The final game drew only 200 patrons, but they witnessed what the *Free Press* described as "the best game of base ball ever played in Michigan." The contest remained scoreless for five innings as both nines put on a dazzling display of fielding and throwing. In the sixth inning, Detroit catcher Gross belted a drive that soared over the head of the Kalamazoo left fielder and across the racetrack, to collect a triple. The next batter, right fielder Swartwood, singled, bringing Gross home for the only score in the game. Kalamazoo left the bases loaded in the seventh inning of the tightly contested game. In the ninth inning, the visitors again left two men on base.[31] The final score was 1–0. The Detroit club was playing entertaining ball, but spectators were scarce. The situation couldn't continue.

A rare large audience, including many ladies, appeared on July 18 when the Hollinger Nine welcomed the Woodstock Actives, one of the top amateur teams from Ontario. Having come off the hard-fought win over Kalamazoo the previous day, Detroit was in fine form and after a scoreless first inning began batting the ball all over Recreation Park. The visitors made many costly errors and failed to get a run across the plate. The final score was a 17–0 whitewash. The team's new manager, Davenport, was busy, lining up games for the rest of the month and into August. Dates were arranged with National League nines from Providence and Cleveland, with a return engagement planned for Troy. In a bid to drum up public interest, Davenport also arranged to have telephone reports after each inning of every game posted on bulletin boards along Griswold Street and Jefferson, Woodward and Michigan Avenues.[32] The official scorer for the ball club released his report of the team and the performance of its players up to and including the July 15 Kalamazoo game. It showed Detroit had played 24 games and had outscored its opponents, 213 runs to 114. No win-loss record was provided, however. Gross was the team's top batter, followed by McSorley and Libby.

The game scheduled for July 23 against Providence had to be cancelled when rain halted the Grays' July 21 League game in Chicago, forcing it to rearrange its schedule. Cleveland made it to town for a July 29 game, but only 600 spectators appeared at the park, despite expectations of better patronage. Detroit fielded well and was able to keep the Blue Stockings runners from crossing home plate. Yet again, McSorley wielded a powerful bat, picking up three of Detroit's nine hits. During the fifth inning, Cleveland players complained about umpire Malone, who had awarded four walks to Detroit. They demanded a League umpire. But manager Ford Evans calmed his men, said he saw no unfairness, and had his team continue play. The final score was a 3–0 shutout of the visitors who, with a 14–29 record, were languishing in seventh place in the eight-team National League.

Detroit then embarked on a road trip to Kalamazoo, Grand Rapids, Lansing, Howell and Flint. They drew 1,000 cranks in Kalamazoo on July 31 and downed the home club, 13–5. The following day, they defeated Grand Rapids, 9–2. They picked up easy wins in the other cities and returned home with a slim profit. It was reported that negotiations were underway to bring the Rochester Hop Bitters and Springfield, both of the National Base-Ball Association (formerly the International Association), as well as Providence, to the city for games during August.[33] Although manager Davenport was busy running Recreation Park, he hadn't forgotten the baseball club it now owned. He was trying to arrange a tour to include games in Cleveland and Cincinnati.[34]

On August 9, Detroit defeated Cass, 9–5, at Recreation Park, but no mention was made of the crowd count. Davenport and his fellow park directors must have finally run out of patience as they tried to cover the ongoing costs of their ball club. Four days later, the *Detroit Free Press*, under the headline "Detroit Exits," announced that the end had come:

> After a season of most varied fortunes, the Detroit Base Ball Club was disbanded Monday evening [August 11], and to-day the members are scattered in various parts of the country. The cause of the disorganization is not that the city is not able to support a first-class club, but that such a club cannot be supported here unless it belongs to the regular league or the National League. Not being a member of either league, it was impossible to arrange for games with professional clubs with any certainty that the game would be played.

2. The Hollinger Nine 33

> To keep the Detroits here the Recreation Park Company were at an expense of about $700 a month, and as several of the members had good offers from abroad it was decided to compromise the matter by discontinuing the organization after paying each player his salary up to the 1st of September. That the nine was a thoroughly good one was shown by the game with the Kalamazoo Club when the score was 1 to 0 in favor of the Detroits, and by the game when the Detroits defeated the Cleveland club by a score of 3 to 0.[35]

The paper went on to note that members of the club had quickly found new positions with other clubs, demonstrating the quality of the Detroit talent. Gross went to Providence, Libby to Rochester, McSorley to St. Louis, Van Burkalow and Barkley to Cincinnati, and Morton and Swartwood to Cleveland. Salisbury went home to Racine, Wisconsin, but was lured to Troy, where he won four games and lost six for the Trojans. Shaughnessy simply stayed at his home in Detroit. The newspaper concluded:

> It is probable that hereafter during the season that there will be none but amateur teams at Recreation Park, and it is also probable that next season there will be a first-class club under the management of the Park Company, and that the club will be a league organization, with at least four of this season's club as members of the new nine.

When the club disbanded, its record was 20 wins with nine losses. Fifteen games had been played at home, 14 on the road. Detroit had outscored its opponents, 224 runs to 114, defeated one National League team and lost to another. It was reported that club owners had retained Gross, Salisbury, Libby and Swartwood for the following season.[36]

By mid–September, hope was still being held out for professional baseball in Detroit for 1880, with potential players mentioned, but the *Free Press* cautioned its readers that it was premature to say who would join the team.

> At the time of the disbanding of the Detroit Base Ball Club, there were rumors that next season would see a first-class professional base ball club here, under the patronage of leading wealthy citizens. These gentlemen are prominently connected with Recreation Park, and the new club will be a member of the League. By this arrangement dates with all the prominent clubs can be made, with certainty that they will be kept, and with games regularly played between such teams a profitable interest in the sport will be worked up and maintained in the city.
>
> By the rules of the League, members of League clubs cannot sign for the coming season, and must not be approached by managers of other clubs until the 1st of November. Hence it cannot be said who will constitute the new Detroit nine.[37]

Gross told the paper he enjoyed playing in Detroit and would return next year, even if it meant he'd earn less money than elsewhere. Libby said he would make no plans until he heard from Detroit management.

Directors of Recreation Park continued to consider operating a ball team for the 1880 season. At one point, William G. Thompson, one of the directors, was reported to be "very favorable" to establishing another professional club. Thompson, a lawyer, had close connections to his fellow directors, many of whom were Republicans like him. His former brother-in-law, Alfred Brush, had become vice-president of the park operation. Thompson and Brush were trustees of the Brush Estate and among the men who incorporated Recreation Park. In mid–October, Thompson was reported to be in the East, making inquiries "as to the standing of professional ball players; their salaries and the expense of running a team in the City of Detroit." The *Free Press* added: "it is generally conceded that some such enterprise is needed to revive the fortunes of Recreation Park."[38] Rumors continued to swirl about a new professional club for 1880. The *New York Clipper* reported that the Worcester club "have been offered a bonus of $1,200 to transfer their nine to Detroit, in order that the latter city may enter the League; but the nine will remain in Worcester, Mass., without doubt."[39] As it turned out, the Worcester Ruby Legs joined the eight-team National League for 1880.

By mid–November, it appeared it was just a matter of time before Recreation Park would announce that a professional nine was to become one of its star attractions.

> Ever since the close of the base ball season there has been more or less talk about the subject of organizing a professional club in connection with Recreation Park next season; while persons known to have an interest in the national game and to keep themselves fully informed on the subject have been constantly besieged by anxious inquiries as to whether such an organization is to be had in Detroit.
> Accordingly a thorough and systematic estimate of the expenses for the season, the opportunities for having a successful season and the amount of money necessary to make the beginning has been made. The city has also been thoroughly canvassed with a view to ascertaining whether the necessary cash can be raised.
> The managers of Recreation Park admit that the only attractions—aside from the driving track—offered by them last season and drawing anything like a paying audience were the games of baseball, and they are also of the opinion that a first-class professional base ball club would prove profitable next season.[40]

The paper went on to suggest that by playing in a professional circuit that included Chicago, Buffalo, Cleveland, Cincinnati, Indianapolis and Grand Rapids, a new Detroit club would be guaranteed a set schedule of games. Some leading professional players had contacted local parties to express an interest in playing for Detroit, including hometown boy Daniel O'Leary, known as a heavy hitter and quality outfielder. (O'Leary had played for Springfield and was moving to the League team in Providence.) The cost to operate a team was estimated at between $10,000 and $12,000 for a season of 125 to 150 games, with a profit of $3,000 predicted. The sum of $5,000 was needed to establish the club, and W. G. Thompson, along with John S. Newberry, George Hendrie and W. K. Muir, were prepared to subscribe $500 apiece. Further funds were likely from Recreation Park shareholders, banks, insurance offices, hotels, restaurants and saloons, wholesalers and retailers.

Rumors continued to float in the dying days of 1879, such as one that Buffalo's outstanding pitcher, James "Pud" Galvin, and Rochester manager Joe Simmons were being considered for positions with Detroit for 1880. Despite all the conjecture, when the National League gathered for its annual meeting in Buffalo on December 3, the only application for membership came from a new club in Cincinnati. It was accepted. Not a word was said about Detroit. At that same historic League meeting, the infamous reserve clause was quietly introduced by Boston management and approved.

Meanwhile, in Detroit, Thompson was compelled to abandon his efforts to form a new team. His fellow Republicans were pressuring him to challenge George Langdon, the one-term Detroit mayor, a Democrat. On November 4, despite strong editorial denunciation of Thompson by the *Detroit Free Press*, an organ that favored the Democrats, Thompson was elected to a two-year term as part of a Republican sweep of local offices. He suddenly had more pressing issues on his plate, so he placed the baseball initiative on the shelf.

For his part, William Hollinger decided to remain in Detroit. In September, he was captain of a baseball team that played the Detroit Medical College at Recreation Park. He remained on good terms with the directors of the park and during the winter of 1881 was one of the judges of a skating competition held there.[41] Over ensuing years, he repeatedly drew press attention for his exploits in billiards, becoming one of the top shooters in the city and managing the Normandie Pool and Billiards Room. In 1912, when Hollinger entered a billiards tourney sponsored by the *Detroit Free Press*, his life and career were highlighted in a light-hearted piece accompanied by a caricature of the balding and bespectacled wielder of the cue who was duly credited with bringing professional baseball to the city. His passion, however, had become billiards. "Hollinger is conceded to know about as much about the game of billiards as anyone in town," said the article, in which he attributed his success in the game to a "10-hour beauty sleep" every night. Hollinger maintained his interest in baseball, however, and it was noted that he enjoyed watching the Detroit Tigers play at their home of Bennett Park.[42]

Hollinger's name is forever associated with the first professional baseball club in Detroit. When players he fielded in 1879 went on to become successful in the major leagues, newspapers in the city often fondly reminded readers they had been members of the old Hollinger Nine.

3

Getting Back in the Game

The roots of Detroit's first professional team lay in Cleveland, while another Ohio city played a key role in its second: Cincinnati. The Ohio River city was bounced from the National League for its perceived sins in baseball and immediately replaced by Detroit—another tale of two cities and their baseball. Cincinnati was a far different place than the City of the Straits, 250 miles to the north. Cincinnati's workingmen had embraced baseball and city boosters took it to a completely new level, while Detroit's gentlemen continued to play the amateur game.

Cincinnati was known as the "Queen City of the West" because of its key position on the Ohio River and the beginning of steam navigation in 1811. Hotels, taverns, restaurants and merchants catered to the needs of the flood of travellers heading west, and the city became a key hub for transportation and shipping. Farmers brought crops destined for markets along the Ohio and Mississippi River systems and delivered livestock to meatpacking houses for processing and sale to locals or for shipping to other cities and towns. When it rose to become the pork-processing center of the United States, Cincinnati was dubbed "Porkopolis."[1] Beginning in the 1830s, Cincinnati attracted a large number of German immigrants, who invariably associated beer with their meals and entertainment. Breweries and taverns were ubiquitous and part of the social fabric of the city, which had grown to 216,000 inhabitants by 1870.

The area was a hotbed for early baseball and became home for the game's first openly professional team, the Cincinnati Red Stockings club of 1869–1870. In 1867, Aaron Champion, a young and aggressive lawyer, became president of the amateur club and spearheaded the push to hire outside professionals to make it a winner. By 1869, the Red Stockings had become fully professional, with a player payroll reaching $9,400. Manager, captain and center fielder Harry Wright earned $1,800 a season, as did his brother George, the shortstop. The Wrights, considered the best players on the team, had been lured to Cincinnati from their hometown of New York City. Other members of the club received from $600 to $800. The Red Stockings, consisting of some of the best players of the day, barnstormed 12,000 miles, challenging any and all comers and playing 80 games without a loss. In July 1870, their winning string was finally snapped by an 11-inning, 8–7 defeat at the hands of the Brooklyn Atlantics, before a crowd estimated at 9,000 to 12,000 cranks. By then, Cincinnati had demonstrated to even the skeptics that baseball could be a financially viable proposition. But faced with demands from players for a doubling of their salaries, the club balked and team members scattered. The Red Stockings returned to amateur status and disbanded after the 1871 season.[2]

The success of Cincinnati, however, led to the formation of the National Association of Professional Base Ball Players in 1871, the first professional league. Ironically, Cincinnati never joined the loop that was operated by and for players and lasted five years. In 1876, however, a reorganized Cincinnati club, also known as the Red Stockings, was among the eight founding teams of the National League, an organization established by capitalists rather than players. It succeeded the loosely knit National Association and, tellingly, team owners considered players as mere employees. The Red Stockings finished last that first season, but by 1878 they climbed to second place with a revamped roster that made them the loop's most successful team in the first half of that season. Hopes were high for 1879, but poor defensive play and clubhouse strife led to a slide to fifth place. Star players Deacon White, Ross Barnes and Cal McVey were being paid $2,000 each, a situation resented by the rest of their teammates, who received $800 apiece. Attendance was poor and after team losses surged past $10,000, team president J. Wayne Neff, a leader in the city's pork industry, released the players on October 1 and withdrew from the National League.[3]

Brewing executive Justus Thorner bought the Cincinnati club on October 24 and immediately applied to League officials for reinstatement. Thorner, president of the semi-professional Cincinnati Star Base Ball Association, was a manager with Cincinnati brewer J. G. Sohn & Company, the tenth largest of the more than 40 breweries in the greater Cincinnati area. League magnates accepted Thorner's application despite any misgivings they may have had about his business interests and potential motives. Led by president William Hulbert, League officials were firmly opposed to the sale of alcohol in League ballparks, as well as to Sunday games and gambling. But at the time, they were most anxious to field a western team for competitive balance. Cincinnati's membership was approved at their annual meeting in December in Buffalo, where their major preoccupation was enacting the "reserve clause" that allowed team owners to keep five of their players for the following season.[4]

Meanwhile, Thorner went to work and made wholesale changes to the Red Stockings lineup for 1880. He retained only versatile catcher/infielder/outfielder Deacon White, along with White's younger brother Will, a pitcher, and outfielder Blondie Purcell. Thorner relocated the club from the Avenue Grounds to a new field on Bank Street, much closer to downtown and more accessible for fans. To produce additional revenue, the new club rented out its old park to other teams on dates when the Red Stockings were not playing in town. Those dates included Sundays, when the sale of beer was permitted, a move popular with the city's large German community in a city that had reached a population of 255,000. Both steps were very profitable for the club, but did little to impress the puritanical National League owners dead set against Sunday games and the sale of alcohol. The 1880 Red Stockings were less successful on the field, however, ending in the League basement with a record of 21 wins and 59 losses, leaving them 44 games back of first-place Chicago. In the change of ownership, the team had failed to reserve hard-hitting outfielder King Kelly. He was snapped up by Chicago, where he belted 100 hits and recorded a batting average of .291. For his part, McVey quit the game entirely, while Deacon White sat out half the season in a contract dispute. The team was also wracked with dissension among its directors. Thorner was replaced as president by clothing manufacturer Nathan Menderson, who was in turn succeeded by insurance agent John Kennett.[5]

Cincinnati was an ongoing headache for the businessmen who controlled the National League, and they felt the time had come to bring it in line with the other teams—or get rid of it entirely. On October 4 in Rochester, New York, a special caucus meeting of League magnates was convened, a gathering which included Cincinnati director Kennett. Cincinnati was placed on the hot seat. Delegates proposed amending the League constitution at its upcoming annual meeting to ban liquor and Sunday games in any building owned, controlled, or used by its teams. As expected, only Cincinnati opposed the move. Kennett argued that his city was a unique case, with its large German community that liked beer with baseball, including on the Sabbath. His club, he said, had come to depend on the revenue from beer. League magnates were not moved. Kennett was given a day to contact his shareholders and have them agree to mend Cincinnati ways. When they refused, League directors declared Cincinnati had forfeited its membership and that the decision would be made official and a replacement named at their annual meeting in December in New York.[6] Cincinnati was outraged. In response, the club's directors opted to make a pre-emptive strike, deciding on October 26 to withdraw from the League.[7]

In Detroit, news of the pending expulsion of the Red Stockings was greeted with enthusiasm. It now meant that there was a clear opportunity for the City of the Straits to join the League. "Detroit's only rival for the membership is Washington, which city is not favorably looked upon by the League because of its location," reported the *Detroit Free Press*. The paper said Detroit had received assurances the city would be the League's first choice, provided it raised sufficient capital for the mandatory guarantee fund.[8]

Cincinnati wasn't going down without fight, however. Upon withdrawing from the League, its directors immediately called upon clubs in New York, Buffalo, Albany, and Washington to form a new, independent league "with a liberal policy."[9] In a letter sent to those cities, as well as to clubs in Detroit, Pittsburgh and Philadelphia, Colonel Len A. Harris of the Cincinnati Base Ball Club invited all to a meeting set for November 4 at the Fifth Avenue Hotel in New York City. Cincinnati planned to establish a new organization giving member teams more operating independence and control over the admission fees they could charge.[10] Further talks were held in New York, but nothing concrete emerged in time for an 1881 season. It would take another year before a new six-member circuit, with Cincinnati as one of its pillars, would rise to challenge the League. Named the American Association, it soon became known as the "Beer and Whisky league" because many of its owners had brewing and liquor interests and their product was available during games. Sunday dates and admission fees of 25 cents, half the tariff of the National League, were also adopted by the rebel loop.[11] The AA's recipe for success would prove profitable and eventually worrisome to the League.

Aside from laying the groundwork for a rival league that ultimately would last a decade, Cincinnati's actions opened the door for Detroit to join the ranks of top-flight professional baseball cities. The timing was perfect because the return to amateur status in 1880 had not gone well in Detroit. With a population approaching 120,000, less than half of Cincinnati's, powerful interests in Detroit were eager for the city to compete with other major American centers in baseball, just as it was already doing economically.

The amateur Cass Base Ball Club regained its status as Detroit's top team in 1880, despite some early rumors that a new professional nine was being contemplated and that a professional club might yet be fielded that summer. The *New York Clipper* carried an item saying that Tim Murnane, 28, a Connecticut-born infielder and outfielder who had played with Boston, Providence and the Rochester Hop Bitters, "will most likely manage and play with the professional nine now being organized at Detroit."[12] But nothing came of it, and hopes for a professional team were dashed in mid–April when the Recreation Park Company announced that it would not operate a club and that its park would be home to strictly amateur organizations. Aside from baseball teams like Cass, the Peninsular Cricket Club decided to play all their home games at Recreation

Park. Francis Davenport was again running the facility but would no longer also manage a ball club, a job he had inherited with the departure of William Hollinger. Davenport was joined on the park management committee by newly elected mayor William Thompson, who late the previous year had made preliminary inquiries about establishing a professional team before being sidetracked by winning the mayoralty.[13]

Thompson, 38, was meticulous about many things, including his appearance, his short dark hair carefully parted in the middle and his handlebar mustache neatly trimmed. He carried his "chew" in a silver tobacco box and he dressed well. Thompson may have found the duties of mayor less pressing than he originally expected and was able to continue his active interest in sport. In mid–April, for instance, he was elected president of the Detroit Jockey Club. Wealthy transportation magnate and industrialist James McMillan became vice-president, while Thompson's former brother-in-law, Alfred Brush, was named treasurer and street railway owner George Hendrie became a director. All were among the directors of Recreation Park.[14] Thompson mingled easily with the city's blue-bloods, having married into two prominent Detroit families. He was born in Lancaster, Pennsylvania, and decided to follow in the footsteps of his father, a lawyer. He enrolled in Amherst College in Massachusetts, but the Civil War intervened. In 1861, at age 19, he enlisted in the Fourth Pennsylvania Cavalry and was transferred to Toledo. There he joined a lancer regiment and was posted to Detroit as a first lieutenant. When the regiment disbanded, he returned to Lancaster and was appointed an aide-de-camp with the Sixth New Jersey Infantry. Thompson was severely wounded in the battle of Chancellorsville, a Confederate victory in Virginia, where the South's legendary general Stonewall Jackson was killed.

Thompson was mustered out in 1864, returned to his law studies and

William G. Thompson, a lawyer who was connected with Detroit's leading families and its Republican establishment, took the lead in contacting the National League about membership. Upon his election as mayor, he formally applied for admission under the letterhead of the mayor's office. The Wolverines began play in 1881 (Burton Historical Collection, Detroit Public Library).

settled in Detroit, where he was admitted to the bar in 1867, the same year he married Adelaide Brush, a member of a wealthy land-owning family. She died in 1875, leaving him a daughter, Adele, aged six. Three years later, Thompson married Adele Campau, a member of one of the oldest families in Detroit. By then, he had become deeply involved in city politics, serving as an alderman in 1873 and 1874. He ran for mayor in 1877 but lost to Democrat George Langdon, who occupied the post in 1878 and 1879.[15] Thompson cared deeply about his adopted city and wanted to do what he could to advance its interests. "When I ascended to the roof of the City Hall on a June or August day, it seemed to me as if Detroit was a city situated in the midst of a green forest," he once said. "The trees that line every street and avenue made a most agreeable impression, not only upon strangers but upon Detroiters themselves."[16] He was admiring Detroit when it was known as the Paris of the West.

Thanks to his marriages, Thompson moved freely within the city's top social circles and was also active with the Republican Party, like so many of his friends and associates. Along the way, he had drawn the ire of the *Detroit Free Press*, a Democratic Party organ which tried to paint him as an elitist and no friend of the working man. The paper was the largest in the city, and its support would be essential to his campaign for mayor or to bring a baseball team to the city. The *Free Press* was brutal in its assessment of his character during his campaign for mayor in late 1879. His well-heeled friends felt otherwise. But the *Free Press* minced few words as it listed what it felt were Thompson's many shortcomings.

> With abundance of conceit, he has little judgment; and whatever prominence he has achieved has never been based upon any practical benefit to the city. In possession of money acquired by the accident of inheritance and not earned by his own efforts, it has been his boast in moments of excitation that he would spend thousands of dollars, if necessary, to accomplish this nomination. His native instincts, coupled with his egotistical ambition, have led him into affiliation with the worst elements of the population.[17]

Mere days before the election, the newspaper warned voters about his trustworthiness, despite the sums of money that others had placed with him.

> There is not in the City of Detroit, where he is best known, a corporation doing business to the extent of $5,000 a year whose stockholders would dare to place him in a position requiring business skill and executive ability.... To put the matter in the best possible light for Thompson, the people do not know, absolutely; whether they can trust him or not, and all the evidence they have on the point—most of it from his own supporters—is that it is unsafe to trust him.[18]

His associates in business and sport, men of money—certainly not the "worst elements of the population"—were prepared to trust Thompson. So, too, were voters, as it turned out. As mayor, he would become the driving force in the effort to bring professional baseball back to Detroit.

That season of 1880, Cass played teams from neighboring cities in Michigan—and just across the border in Windsor, Ontario, and the surrounding area—winning a respectable number of games. The club featured Detroit native Dan O'Leary, an infielder with a strong bat who had played with the National League club in Providence. In late June, O'Leary joined the Boston Red Caps for three games, but returned to Cass upon his release. Public interest in baseball was light. In spring and early summer, the Detroit press paid scant attention to the largely quiet local baseball scene, and most coverage of the game consisted of scores from the National League.

A flurry of excitement came in late June when it was announced that the Ruby Legs of Worcester, Massachusetts, a member or the National League, would be in Detroit July 1 for a game against the Cass Club.[19] But the game was eventually rescheduled for August 27, during a western swing by the Ruby Legs to play Chicago and Cincinnati. Given the lackluster season of ball up to late August, the *Detroit Free Press* predicted the Worcester contest would be "the first really interesting game of ball to be played in this city this season."[20] The paper noted that the Worcester club "are first-class players, and are the club about whom there was much talk early in the season, as the representatives of Detroit in the league." Despite its rosy prediction, the newspaper conceded in its subsequent account that "the game was not at all interesting." Worcester clobbered the Cass lads, 12–0, and without much good to report about the play, the *Free Press* took great interest in how loudly umpire George "Foghorn" Bradley made his calls. The volume was high but onlooker comprehension of what he said was difficult because "his only ambition seeming to be to make as loud a vocal exhibition as possible." Bradley, formerly with Boston in the National League and the London Tecumsehs of the International Association, had a nickname that was richly deserved. The *New York Clipper* account of the game noted that "several brilliant plays" were made by Cass, including the work of catcher Ginney and flies caught by second baseman Johnson. The over-matched amateurs managed only three hits off Worcester pitchers Lee Richmond and Fred Corey.[21] The crowd count was 300, a turnout that disappointed managers of Recreation Park who drew scorn for their poor promotion of the event from the *Free Press*. The paper suggested, in an entirely self-serving way, that placards mounted on streetcars were far less effective than newspaper advertising to draw spectators.[22]

By September, talk surfaced about another professional baseball team for Detroit. The *New York Clipper* reported on September 4 that "a strong feeling is manifested in favor of a professional nine for Detroit, Mich., next season, and a number of prominent and wealthy men have signified their willingness

3. Getting Back in the Game 43

to give the enterprise proper backing. With a good nine, properly managed, there is no reason why it should not be self-sustaining."[23] The *Free Press* revealed on September 11 that efforts were underway to raise $6,000 to field a professional nine for the 1881 season, but didn't name the parties who were behind it.[24] Four days later, further information appeared in the paper:

> A prominent gentleman, who is agitating the matter, yesterday said to a reporter of this paper that negotiations are now pending with one of the most successful base ball managers in the country for the organization here of a first-class base ball club. The manager is willing to come to Detroit if a definite engagement is assured him. A preliminary meeting of lovers of the national game in this city will soon be called to take the necessary steps for the organization of a club. The capital stock will be $5,000 of which $2,000 has already been subscribed by men of means.[25]

There is little doubt the "prominent gentleman" was William Thompson, the new mayor in whom the city's major newspaper had placed so little trust. He apparently wasn't holding a grudge and was talking to its reporter. Detroiters with a shared interest in seeing professional baseball return to the city were invited to a meeting September 18 at the Russell House Hotel. That evening, the gathering was called to order by the mayor, who was described as "particularly earnest" about the topic under discussion.

> Mr. Thompson addressed the meeting at length, saying that there seemed to be a general desire on the part of the citizens of Detroit, that a professional base ball organization, and a first class one, should be organized in this city, and with that feeling impressed upon them several gentlemen had taken steps to secure the desired end. According to the requirements of the National Base Ball League a guaranteed fund of $5,000 must be raised by a nine wishing to become a member of the League [to be paid to the League if a team defaulted on its playing obligations]. This fund is not to be paid in immediately, but is subscribed as a guarantee that the nine will play out the schedule of games for the season as arranged by the League. With this understanding the following gentlemen have subscribed $500 each toward that fund: A. E. Brush, John S. Newberry, James McMillan and W. G. Thompson.
>
> Mr. Thompson read a letter from Frank Bancroft, manager of the Worcester Base Ball Club during the past two seasons, with whom he has had negotiations. Mr. Bancroft stated that he had interviewed Presidents Wm. Hulbert, Evans, Sowden [Soden] and Root, of the Chicago, Cleveland, Boston and Providence nines respectively, relative to the admission of the Detroit club to the League, and those gentlemen had assured him that they would work and vote to admit the Detroit club.[26]

Several other proponents of a new club spoke up and "considerable enthusiasm was manifested." Thompson said he was confident about the success of a professional team in a city the size of Detroit. He noted it had more than twice the population of Worcester, which was able to support a team without having to use the guarantee it had established. Thompson was authorized to submit Detroit's application to the League. Two days later, Thompson travelled to Chicago to discuss the Detroit bid with William Hulbert, president of both the National League and the White Stockings.[27] Thompson stayed in the Windy City for a week as he promoted Detroit's bid. Hulbert was impressed with Thompson's presentation and realized it provided him with a golden opportunity to rid the League of a wayward Cincinnati franchise. Hulbert asked Chicago lawyer Abraham Mills to draft a resolution for the upcoming special caucus meeting of League magnates in Rochester, to prohibit Sunday games and the sale of alcohol. Cincinnati was to be the target. Hulbert knew Cincinnati would balk at the move, but he now had Detroit as an ace up his sleeve to replace the Red Stockings.[28] Hulbert had an ally in Thompson.

Frank Bancroft seemed to have close ties with Henry Chadwick, the baseball editor of the *New York Clipper* who wrote extensively about the baseball manager's activities. On October 2, the *Clipper* reported that Bancroft was leaving Worcester and had received offers from several clubs for the following season.[29] A week later, the same publication said Bancroft received "several flattering offers from the West ... and will most likely go to Buffalo, N.Y., next year, and organize a strong League team for that city. The Worcesters have been singularly successful in a financial point of view, thanks to Bancroft's able management and hope to disband on Oct. 4 without spending any of a capital of $4,500 with which they started out."[30] At the time Bancroft was reportedly looking at Buffalo, he was already negotiating with Thompson and lobbying League officials on behalf of Detroit, based on what Thompson told the September 18 meeting of local baseball enthusiasts.

Bancroft, 34, a native of Massachusetts, guided the Worcester Ruby Legs to a fifth-place finish in the National League in 1880 with 40 wins and 43 losses. His club in Worcester, population 58,000, was the first of seven major league teams he managed during a 22-year career. He was an early advocate of spring training in the South to ensure his teams were ready for Opening Day.

Detroit Mayor William Thompson was barely back from his week in Chicago when he travelled to New York in early October 1880 for further talks with Hulbert and Harry Wright, the manager for Boston. Thompson assured the pair that there would be no difficulty raising $5,000 for the guarantee fund, but pointed out that shareholders were reluctant to hire players until Detroit's place in the League was secured.

> In return, Messrs. Hulbert and Wright assured Mr. Thompson that they had no doubt that the Detroit club would be admitted to the league, as they had but one city (Washington) as a rival, and that city, by reason of its great distance from other base ball centers, would be, beyond doubt, the second choice of the league.[31]

3. Getting Back in the Game 45

Detroit City Hall was occupied by Mayor William G. Thompson from 1880 to the end of 1883. One of his first pieces of business was to seek membership in the National League, and he directed operations of the Detroit Base Ball Club from his office desk. At the time, Detroit was an attractive, bustling and vibrant city, known as "The Paris of the West." The city had a diversified economy, and its leading industries included paints, solvents, pharmaceuticals, stoves, steam engines, railroad cars, bridges, and iron works (Detroit Historical Society).

Meanwhile, in Detroit, it was said that two-thirds of the $5,000 guarantee had already been raised, and on October 26, the *Free Press* quoted Bancroft as saying that if he was hired to manage the Detroit team he could bring four first-class players and expected no difficulty in attracting five more of the same caliber.

At the *Clipper*, baseball editor Chadwick fired salvos at the National League for the "tyranny" of the reserve clause and for its treatment of Cincinnati. He had never liked the exclusive approach and tight control of baseball by the small group of businessmen who ran the League. He preferred a more liberal, broadly based approach to the game, such as that shown by the International Association/National Base-Ball Association that in 1880 breathed its last. Chadwick said the reserve clause would prompt players to consider forming a new league in protest. And he sympathized with Cincinnati for running afoul of Hulbert and his cronies.

> The moral ground assumed by [the] League as the ostensible cause of its action against the Cincinnati Club is untenable. The Chicago Club entertained no such scruples against Sunday games when it sent its team to California; nor was there any strenuous objection against beer when the sale of it "paid" on the old Chicago field. The whole matter seems to be governed by a desire to get rid of a club whose official action is far too independent and uncontrollable by the powers that be to admit of their being allowed to remain in the League.[32]

Chadwick was ignored by Hulbert and his cronies, and on October 26, Cincinnati directors voted to withdraw from the National League. A few days later, the *Clipper* reported that Frank Bancroft had "resigned" from the Buffalo club and had decided to manage in Detroit. But there was a hitch. "The officers of the Buffalo Club have refused to accept Bancroft's resignation and it is probable it may be withdrawn," the paper said. Meanwhile, it was also reported that Bancroft planned to go to Detroit and take with him Worcester's outfielder and captain, Lon Knight.[33] The matter was resolved on October 30, however, when the directors of Buffalo agreed to release Bancroft.

On November 11, Thompson travelled to Chicago to meet yet again with Hulbert about Detroit's application coming before the National League's annual meeting on December 8. The four-page application was written on the letterhead of the City of Detroit Mayor's Office, signed by Thompson, and dated November 17. It was personally submitted by Thompson, the club's majority owner, to Hulbert and League secretary Nick Young. A cover letter included the requisite fee of $10 and indicated, as an aside, that the Detroit Base Ball Club was "liable to have some trouble with Providence over a player by the name of Bradley." The application listed Thompson as president—although he was not yet formally elected—with directors including Alfred Brush, George Hendrie and James Thompson, all of whom signed it. The capital stock of the club was listed at $10,000, with plans to issue all but half of that sum. On the fourth page, beneath the word "Favorably," the signatures of Hulbert, Boston owner A. H. Soden and Cleveland owner J. Ford Evans were affixed. The application still exists. It was retrieved from the estate of League secretary Young in 2005. Robert Edwards Auctions put it up for bids that year, billing it as the "Magna Carta of Detroit City Major League baseball." It fetched $16,240.[34]

Meanwhile, Bancroft had already signed catcher Charlie Bennett and outfielder George Wood, both of whom had been released by Worcester. Worcester outfielder Lon Knight was already on board, and Ruby Legs third baseman Art Whitney also agreed to contract terms. Providence pitcher George Washington "Grin" Bradley was signed once Providence agreed to release him. Bancroft also spoke about his effort to sign an unnamed, young and promising amateur pitcher from Canada, and other players, including Detroit's own Dan O'Leary, who had planned to retire.[35] Ned Hanlon, the talented left fielder for Cleveland, was signed, and Bancroft said he was also looking at outfielder Sadie Houck of Providence and infielder Joe Gerhardt of Washington. Chick Fulmer, a member of the Buffalo Bisons from 1878 to 1880, was mentioned, but the manager opted to withdraw the offer and instead engage Gerhardt for the infield. For his part, Fulmer opted against playing anywhere during 1881 and became manager of a traveling troupe of performers who staged a production of "Uncle Tom's Cabin."[36] In 1882, he was back in baseball in Cincinnati. Meanwhile, Bancroft was said to be organizing a southern trip for Detroit during the winter months, to include games in Cuba and New Orleans.[37]

On November 29, 1880, a "large and enthusiastic meeting of gentlemen" convened at the Russell House Hotel to talk about baseball. Mayor Thompson acted as chairman again and announced that under state laws the articles of incorporation of the new ball club had to be signed in the presence of a notary public. William Sheeran, a notary public, witnessed Thompson, George Hendrie, James McMillan, Alfred Brush and six others place their signatures on the document. Thompson read the constitution and bylaws for the new organization, borrowed largely from the Chicago club with the blessings of its president Hulbert, no doubt. A nomination committee was struck to propose directors of the Detroit Base Ball Club, and its report was adopted. Thompson was named president and Eugene T. Barnum, owner of a wire and iron works company, became vice-president. Thompson and Frank Bancroft were appointed the team's representatives to the National League. "During the meeting President Thompson stated that the necessary $5,000 stock had been raised, and that without doubt the Detroit Club would be admitted to the National League at the meeting to be held in New York City on the 8th of December," reported the *Free Press*. The nine-man roster proposed by manager Bancroft was approved. An observation from the Sunday edition of the *Buffalo Courier* was appended to the paper's report about the organizational meeting: "Mr. W. G. Thompson, the Mayor of Detroit, is the greatest base ball enthusiast in that city."[38]

In the days that followed, some roster changes were announced and Bancroft said he had decided to delay the southern tour of his new team until January. It had been expanded to include stops in Memphis, St. Louis, Louisville, and Cincinnati on the club's return trip home. League officials apparently got wind of Bancroft's plans and learned to their dismay that some of the New Orleans games were scheduled for Sundays. Quick to appease the League magnates on the eve of their important vote, Thompson penned the following letter, dated December 6, to the editor of the *Free Press*:

> The professional base ball players under contract with the Detroit club are required to report here in the spring, and until then we have no authority over them. I learn from the *Boston Globe* that Mr. Bancroft proposes to take them South to play a series of games in New Orleans on Sundays. If this is so, he will do it on his own responsibility. When they come under the control of the Detroit club they will not be permitted to play ball on Sundays. The rules of the National League prohibit playing ball on Sundays, the sale of intoxicating liquors, pools and betting on games on the ball grounds, and those rules will be strictly enforced by the Detroit Ball Club.[39]

The newspaper dutifully printed the letter but couldn't resist taking a shot at the man it said earlier could not be trusted. It took note of Thompson's expressed opposition to pools and betting and reminded its readers that the previous summer he had "vigorously defended" those who had violated rules against those same activities at the Hamtramck racetrack. Regardless, Thompson's message seemed to head off potential trouble. His target audience had been the directors of the National League and likely Bancroft, who cancelled the tour.

The fifth annual convention of the League was spread over three days, beginning December 8 at the St. James Hotel in New York. After preliminary matters, such as confirming the Chicago White Stockings as winners of the League pennant for 1880, and acknowledging that Cincinnati had withdrawn as a member, delegates went behind closed doors. The first order of business there was to determine whether to add Detroit or Washington to fill the spot vacated by Cincinnati. On the first ballot, Detroit edged out its rival, a result then made unanimous by Boston, Worcester, Cleveland, Buffalo, Chicago and Providence. The delegate from Troy was absent. Mayor Thompson was then added as a delegate for the remainder of the convention. He and his fellow magnates approved constitutional amendments to ban any team from League membership that allowed Sunday games, the sale of beer or spirits, or open betting or pool-selling on their grounds. There was no opposition, and the measures were adopted without controversy. William Hulbert's move to replace an independent-minded Cincinnati franchise with a more amenable one from Detroit was paying immediate dividends.

A minor dust-up involved Cleveland and Washington, the former asserting the latter owed it money and urging Washington's expulsion from the League

3. Getting Back in the Game

Alliance, a group of teams loosely affiliated with the League. Washington replied that it needed to consider the matter further but claimed a hidden agenda was at work to help Detroit enter the League. It argued that Detroit manager Bancroft had signed its pitcher, George Derby, while Washington was still a member of the Alliance, a move that was clearly against the rules and which applied to both the League and the Alliance. With Washington expelled, Detroit would be in the clear. Further consideration of the matter was deferred to a meeting scheduled for March, a move which did little to placate Washington. League magnates weren't going to let any fly in the ointment spoil their backing of Detroit. In other business, Hulbert, who initially declined to serve, was persuaded to assume the League presidency for another year. Detroit's Thompson was appointed to the executive committee.[40]

The men who controlled Recreation Park and the Detroit baseball team had reason for optimism as 1880 drew to a close. Skating at the rink in the park was described as "superb" and more than 700 Detroiters donned skates there on Christmas Day. On December 28, Mayor Thompson filed the ball club's articles of incorporation with the Wayne County clerk's office. In so doing, he took time away from preparing his first annual address on the state of the city under his leadership.

To celebrate New Year's, Recreation Park was illuminated with calcium lights as part of a gala event that included public skating to the music of the ubiquitous Great Western Band and an exhibition by champion skater Captain John Miner.

The weather was particularly cold that first day of 1881, and baseball may have seemed a long way off in Detroit. But the city would soon be playing the big league game, and the first pitch was eagerly anticipated. It was just a matter of a few months away.

4

A Fine Debut

Detroit entered the National League at a time when the game of baseball was still being refined. For 1881, the number of balls for a walk was reduced from eight to seven, and the pitching distance was increased from 45 to 50 feet, although pitchers were still restricted to an underhand delivery. In another change, batters would no longer be warned by the umpire if they failed to swing at a third pitch in the strike zone and get another chance. The first two tweaks favored batters, the third helped pitchers. The effect of the first two, it has been noted, was to add 15 points to the batting average of League hitters and to increase walks by 40 percent.[1]

The Detroit team was christened the Wolverines, but in the custom of the day, it was most widely known as the "Detroits," even by the local newspapers. Likewise, the teams from other baseball cities were generally referred to as the Buffalos, Chicagos, Bostons, Clevelands, Troys and Worcesters. Team names would become important to end potential confusion when a league to rival the National League was established and some cities were home to two professional clubs. The Wolverine name was widely used in Michigan, which is known as the "Wolverine State," although the largest member of the weasel family has never been named the state animal. For good reason. The wolverine is not a native species, and until 2004 a wild one had never been found in the state. Several theories abound as to how the animal became associated with Michigan, including the popular one surrounding the 1835–1836 border dispute between Michigan and Ohio over the "Toledo Strip." Michiganders became known as wolverines, the carnivores known for their ferocity and tenacity. It is unclear whether the Ohioans first used the name disparagingly because of the animal's gluttonous habits or whether Michiganders themselves adopted it with pride to sow fear in the enemy. Years later, the University of Michigan adopted the wolverine as its school mascot.[2] Today, the name that was once commonplace in the state is associated almost exclusively with the university.

By 1881, building a new team had suddenly become more difficult. For a newcomer like Detroit, the introduction of the reserve clause for the 1880 season made it difficult to find quality players. With the seven surviving National League teams each reserving five players for the next season (Cincinnati was out), it meant 35 of the top professionals of the day were off-limits. So manager Frank Bancroft faced the challenge of assembling a roster by finding players that other clubs had overlooked or released, or by luring second-stringers and taking chances on untried talent. He had developed good connections in New England baseball and his many friends included Henry Chadwick at the *New York Clipper*, whose refinement of the box score and his relentless push to improve and promote the game earned him the sobriquet "Father of Baseball."[3] For his part, Chadwick opposed the reserve rule, but the capitalists who ran the League were determined to control their salary costs and paid no attention to him. Bancroft tapped all his contacts to find baseball talent and was willing to innovate to assess and improve player performance. He was an early proponent of spring training games in Southern states, although his travel plan before the start of Detroit's inaugural League season had been suddenly short-circuited.

A native of Lancaster, Massachusetts, Bancroft opened the Bancroft House Hotel in 1877 in New Bedford, a prosperous whaling port and textile manufacturing center of about 25,000 people. Early that same year, he and other business leaders invested in a professional team that entered the new International Association, a rival for the one-year-old National League. The IA consisted of smaller cities overlooked by the League, and it crossed the border to include successful Canadian teams in London and Guelph, Ontario. Bancroft's fel-

Frank Bancroft, a New England hotel owner and manager of the Worcester baseball team in the National League, came to Detroit to manage the Wolverines for the 1881 and 1882 seasons. In its inaugural year, Detroit placed fourth in the league. After Detroit, Bancroft moved on to several clubs, including Cincinnati, before returning to the hotel business in the East (Library of Congress).

low investors persuaded the hotelier to act as manager of the club for two seasons, during which he quickly earned the respect of club directors and players. His efforts were noted 70 miles to the northeast in Worcester where, for 1879, that city of 58,000 fielded the Worcester Brown Stockings in the same professional loop as New Bedford. By then, the upstart league had been renamed the National Base-Ball Association to reflect the loss of its Canadian teams. Worcester hired Bancroft, hoping he could help the city gain admission to the National League. Bancroft did his best and began the hunt for top-notch players. He recruited Toronto-born shortstop Art Irwin and university pitcher Lee Richmond, a lefty from Ohio, both of whom were embarking on successful careers. In Richmond's Worcester debut on June 2, 1879, he held the powerful Chicago White Stockings hitless and recorded eight strikeouts for an 11–0 exhibition victory. Richmond and Irwin helped vault Worcester into prominence, defeating other National League clubs while compiling a season record of 26 wins and 31 losses.

For 1880, Worcester, renamed the Ruby Legs, was admitted to the League. In preparation, Bancroft took the club to Cuba for exhibition games during December to keep his players sharp. Among them were catcher Charlie Bennett, outfielders Alonzo "Lon" Knight and George Wood, shortstop Irwin, and third baseman Art Whitney. For financial reasons, the ground-breaking tour was cut short after several games. During Worcester's debut season in the League, the Ruby Legs began strongly but faltered toward the end, finishing fifth with a record of 40 wins and 43 losses. Richmond won 32 games but lost the same number. After the season, Bancroft crossed swords with members of his board of directors and resigned. Not long afterward, following his brief flirtation with Buffalo, he joined the new Detroit organization.[4]

The first player signed by Detroit's manager, Frank Bancroft, was catcher Charlie Bennett, a Pennsylvanian who had played for him in Worcester in 1880. A crowd favorite in Detroit and one of the top catchers of his era, Bennett remained a Wolverine throughout the team's entire eight-year existence. The ballpark where the later Detroit Tigers first played was named in his honor (National Baseball Hall of Fame Library, Cooperstown, New York).

4. A Fine Debut

Bancroft built the Wolverines around a nucleus of four players from his Ruby Legs of 1880, starting with outfielder Knight, 27. A Philadelphian, Knight had played for the Athletics in that city before joining Worcester in 1880. Charlie Bennett, 26, from New Castle, Pennsylvania, played in Philadelphia and Milwaukee before landing in Worcester. Sure-handed behind the plate and wielding an excellent bat, Bennett's background included a short stint with the amateur Detroit Aetnas. Hard-hitting outfielder George Wood, 22, a Canadian from Prince Edward Island, had migrated south to join Worcester and Bancroft in 1880. Agile infielder Art Whitney, 23, a Massachusetts native, began his professional career when Bancroft signed him for 1880 in Worcester. Once the signing dispute with Providence was resolved, George "Grin" Bradley, 28, was engaged to pitch. Bancroft continued to hint that he had found a promising young pitcher in Canada and hoped to sign him. The new manager persuaded Ned Hanlon, 23, of Connecticut, a strong center fielder with great hands from Cleveland's 1880 team, to agree to terms. Hanlon would become a pillar of the Wolverines' roster and a future captain. Washington-born infielder Joe Gerhardt, 26, also signed and would become a reliable fixture at second base. Lew Brown, 23, of Massachusetts, formerly with Boston, Chicago and Providence, was added to play first base. Versatile Charlie Reilley, 25, a native of Providence who had played with Troy and Cincinnati, was retained to patrol left field, cover shortstop and act as a backup catcher. Bancroft soon signed George Derby, 23, a promising young pitcher from Webster, Massachusetts. Derby had put an exclamation mark on his two seasons with the National Base-Ball Association's Washington Nationals with an October 16, 1880, defeat of the League champion Chicago White Stockings, 5–4 in 10 innings.

Bancroft was not afraid to experiment as the season went on, signing several players to short trial contracts to see if they had the right stuff to become Wolverines. In the course of the season, 26 men donned the Detroit uniform, six of whom were pitchers. That was seven more players than tried by Worcester, the next most hiring-happy club in the League. By early March, Bancroft's roster was complete and his handiwork was drawing comment. Asked if he thought Detroit would be as good a city for baseball as Cincinnati had been, National League president William Hulbert replied: "Yes, better; they have got a weak team for this year, but they do not expect it to do much toward winning the championship."[5] Hulbert and others would be surprised at how well Detroit would do in its inaugural campaign, largely because of Bancroft's ability to identify talent, develop it, and manage it.

Optimistic that the Wolverines would be a good draw, directors of the club voted in late March to build a new, 1,200-seat grandstand directly behind home plate rather than relocate the existing one that lay farther to the south and just outside the racetrack that circled the playing field. The capital cost of $400 was quickly approved, and it was agreed to keep the old stand, but given its less-than-ideal location, no extra fee would be charged spectators who occupied it during the club's 42 home games.

The Detroit players were told to report for work on April 1 in Princeton, New Jersey. Upon arriving, they learned that manager Bancroft had arranged a busy schedule of spring training games, many of them to be played before they saw their home field in Detroit. It was almost as if Bancroft was compensating for being barred from taking that Southern trip. The following day, Detroit played its first practice game against Princeton, the United States champion college nine of 1880 and considered one of the strongest non-professional teams in the country. The well-practiced Princeton club lost, 7–2, to the rusty professionals for whom Bradley pitched and Reilley caught on a bitterly cold day. Despite playing together for the first time, Detroit fielded surprisingly well, committing only five errors, and outhit the university lads. After this first performance, club president Thompson predicted "that Detroit does not rank lower than fourth at the close of the season."[6] He was far more upbeat than League president Hulbert. It seemed a tall order for a club assembled from leftovers, second-stringers, and relative rookies, especially before the Wolverines played their first League team. But Thompson was confident.

While in the East, Detroit played a series of games against the non-aligned New York Metropolitans. The first clash came on a bitterly cold April 4 when George Derby was called on to pitch mere minutes after arriving by train and being introduced to his catcher, Bennett. Derby had little prior practice and, chilled to the bone, threw seven wild pitches. The home team downed the Wolverines, 6–3, before a frozen crowd of 200. A game planned for the following day was cancelled because of biting wind and snow, so Bancroft held practice indoors, likely wishing he'd been allowed to have his club working in sunnier climes.[7] The two teams met again April 7, with the weather still cold and raw. Detroit's batting was weak with only three hits, and the Metropolitans prevailed, 4–1. The Wolverines found their bats on April 8 and 9, however, to defeat New York by scores of 17–7 and 4–3.

Having split their four-game series with one of the top non–League clubs in the country, the Wolverines headed northwest to Detroit in anticipation of their May 2 home opener. It was soon discovered that pitcher Bradley was acutely ill with pneumonia, apparently contracted during one of his outings in frigid New York, and was confined to a hospital bed. The team continued to pay Bradley's salary and his hospital bill, and his fellow players visited his bedside when allowed to do so. He gradually rallied after several weeks and insisted he was fit to play, but his doctor didn't agree. For a time, Bradley was given a job manning a Recreation Park entrance turnstile, at half pay. Bancroft finally relented to Bradley's demand and put him at shortstop for one game on May 11. But Bradley fared poorly, so weak he fell down while running to first base, and went hitless in four at-bats. Bradley didn't return to the lineup, and 10 days later Doctor James Book advised club president Thompson he didn't think it "wise" for his patient to play again during the season. Bradley immediately demanded his release from the team and it was granted.[8]

A few weeks later, he signed on with the Cleveland Blue Stockings, where he played 60 games, 54 of them at shortstop. The man who wasn't supposed to play at all ended the 1881 season with a batting average of .249 and 60 hits. Bradley also pitched in six games, earning two wins and four losses. After all the time, money and effort spent helping him recover his health, Bradley was not remembered fondly by the Wolverines or by the Detroit press. Did he have miraculous powers of recovery, or had he cleverly orchestrated things to pursue a better opportunity in Cleveland? Detroit opinion favored the latter notion.

Back in Detroit, Bancroft planned to practice the team four hours every day, from 9 to 11 a.m. and again from 2 to 4 p.m. Wet grounds at Recreation Park delayed things for several days, however, and Bradley's illness created an unexpected headache for his manager, who used several pitchers without success. Meanwhile, practice games continued against the Cass Club, the University of Michigan, and teams from Kalamazoo, South Bend and Akron. Bancroft managed to slip away to Chicago to purchase uniforms of light gray trimmed in cardinal red, with gray caps, red belts and red stockings.[9]

Late in April, Bancroft's much-heralded young Canadian pitcher showed up. Amateur James "Tip" O'Neill, 22, a native of Woodstock, Ontario, 175 miles to the east, was touted as an accurate thrower and heavy hitter. He debuted April 29 in an exhibition game against the University of Michigan played in Ann Arbor. Detroit won, 17–4. O'Neill was so wild, however, that Bancroft took the ball from him in the fourth inning, even though he had allowed only a single run. O'Neill was replaced by Will White, who in turn gave way to Derby before the Wolverines left the field in the seventh inning to catch the train home. The following day at Recreation Park, O'Neill was given the ball again to face a semi-professional team from Cleveland, the White Stockings. He fared much better this time, with better control, allowing three base hits as Detroit walloped the visitors, 15–2. In a second game against the Cleveland nine, O'Neill played center field, recording one hit and one error in a 24–10 Detroit victory. O'Neill, however, failed to live up to Bancroft's lofty expectations and was gone before the season began. He appeared with the Detroit-based Hiawathas, a barnstorming team for part of 1881, as well as back home in Woodstock.

Bancroft could spot talent but should have been more patient with the young Canadian hurler who went on to great things in baseball. "Tip" O'Neill's major league debut came in 1883 with the National League's New York Gothams, where he won five games while losing 12. The following year, he joined St. Louis in the American Association, where his pitching arm gave out after winning 11 games and losing four. O'Neill switched to the outfield, and his outstanding hitting kept him in the game through 1892. His career batting average stood at .326 and he was consistently among the hitting leaders, reaching .435 in 1887, his best season. His slugging average that year was .691, with an AA-leading 225 hits, including 14 home runs. O'Neill is the only player in major league history to lead his league in doubles, triples and homers in the same season. He led St. Louis to four American Association championships from 1885 to 1888. Decades later, he was dubbed "Canada's Babe Ruth" and was inducted into the Canadian Baseball Hall of Fame. To this day, the Hall has an annual award in O'Neill's name, which is bestowed on a player who has excelled in individual achievement and team contribution while adhering to baseball's highest ideals.[10] Detroit missed a good one.

Baseball's usual Opening Day was May 1, but for 1881 that was a Sunday and the League opposed Sunday games. So Detroit's inaugural game at Recreation Park was delayed one day. The visitors were the Buffalo Bisons, in for a series of three games. An expectant crowd of 1,265 was on hand for the opener, not bad for a workday Monday. Derby took the ball. Detroit lost the coin toss and batted first, scoring their first two runs in the second inning when long flies brought home Knight and Hanlon. Buffalo replied with three runs in the bottom of the same inning, capitalizing on fielding and throwing errors by the Wolverines. Detroit managed seven hits off Bisons pitcher Jack Lynch, including a ninth-inning home run belted over the fence by catcher Charlie Bennett. But eight errors marred Detroit's game and Buffalo won, 6–5. The following day's game drew 1,500 spectators and produced a happier result. Derby pitched well, Detroit's fielding was sharp, and they lashed eight hits off Bisons pitcher Pud Galvin in a 4–2 win. The third clash of the opening series came May 4, when Buffalo batters were hot, ringing up 13 base hits off a sore-armed Derby in a 4–3 Bisons win. The teams travelled the length of Lake Erie for three more games in Buffalo. On May 5, Will White, Deacon White's brother, signed to a trial contract, was handed the ball by Bancroft but struggled. Buffalo bats recorded 13 hits in an 8–1 Bisons victory while Galvin held Detroit to five hits. The next day, Detroit scored single runs in the first two innings and was ahead 2–0 going into the ninth, with Derby pitching well. Sloppy defensive work allowed Buffalo to score three times and take the game, 3–2. The sixth and final matchup came on May 7 when the Bisons triumphed again, easily solving

Derby and taking advantage of errors behind him to score five runs in the eighth inning and break open a 1–1 tie for a 6–1 win. Having lost five of its first six games, the Wolverines were off to a rough start.

Back at Recreation Park, Bancroft's revolving-door policy continued. Dan Stearns, a native of Buffalo, was brought back from that city for a tryout at shortstop. But he was error-prone and managed only one hit in three games before his release. Despite the difficult opening days of the season, directors of the ball club were encouraged by the interest the city had taken in the team and decided to add additional seating. The new grandstand would be reserved for ladies and children and their escorts.[11]

Bancroft's old team, the Worcester Ruby Legs, arrived in town for a three-game series and on May 10 administered what the *Free Press* described as Detroit's "worst beating" to date. "The play of the Worcesters was the finest ever seen in this city," the paper opined.[12] Lefty hurler Lee Richmond puzzled Detroit batters

Outfielder Ned Hanlon was the second player to become a Wolverine. He became team captain and, like Charlie Bennett, would remain with the team for its entire history. After his playing days were over, he became a very successful manager for several teams (Library of Congress).

with his curves and they managed only four hits. Meanwhile, the home team committed nine errors behind Derby, who recorded seven strikeouts. Detroit was blanked, 6–0. The following day, with the ailing and soon-to-be-released Bradley at shortstop, Worcester belted 14 hits, sending Derby and his mates to a 5–3 defeat. On May 12, with Will White pitching for Detroit, Worcester completed its sweep with a 10–4 win, breaking open a fairly close game in the eighth inning with four runs. The *Free*

Press blamed the loss on Detroit pitching: "White, who is an old-fashioned, straight-armed pitcher, not a modern, underhand thrower, is not the man for a pitcher's position. The Worcesters had no trouble in batting him, and the only wonder is that they made no more base hits and runs."[13] White was soon released.

The butter-fingered Stearns had barely left when Sargent Perry "Sadie" Houck was hired to fill the void at shortstop, just in time for a three-game series against the Troy Trojans. Houck, 25, a veteran from Washington, D.C., had played with Providence, Washington and Boston. It was hoped he could fill the need to improve infield play. Meanwhile, the *Free Press* counseled its readers that the poor start of eight losses in nine games for the Wolverines shouldn't come as a surprise. The paper noted that the reserve rule made it difficult for a new club to find top-quality professional players, of which there were probably fewer than 100 in all of the United States.

> The managers of the Detroit Club ask the public to recognize the fact that it is an impossibility for a new organization to compete, in base ball, with an old one, but hope to strengthen the club year by year until it takes a place in the front rank. Meantime they ask the public to look upon the game as an exhibition of skill, and to place it with other amusements.[14]

The May 14 game against the Trojans was rained out after several innings had been played, with Detroit ahead by three runs and seemingly in control. A blast of wind toppled the new grandstand, where about 50 men had sought refuge. They all scampered to safety upon hearing the loud groan that preceded its collapse. The following day, Detroit resumed where it left off. Houck proved himself a valuable addition by belting three hits as Detroit managed a rare victory, downing the Trojans, 12–2. Detroit bats had little trouble with pitcher Mickey Welch, piling up 21 hits. The next day, the Wolverines won again, this time 4–0, with Derby allowing only two hits and striking out seven Trojans. Troy bounced back for a 7–2 win on May 18, scoring five runs during a bad second inning for Derby.

A large crowd filled Recreation Park on May 20 for the first of three games against Providence. Detroit led the Grays until the ninth inning, when Derby tired and the visitors put four runs across the plate to win, 5–4. Derby was particularly effective on May 21, however, allowing only three Providence hits in a 16–0 rout. Weak bats combined with 11 errors by Providence produced the lopsided result in which 47 Detroit batters faced the usually tough, but sore-armed John Ward. Detroit won the rubber game on May 23, 5–2, scoring three runs in the eighth inning to produce a rare loss for Hoss Radbourn. Things were looking up for Detroit as the club welcomed Boston to town for three games on the eve of a three-week road trip to Eastern cities. All started well on

4. A Fine Debut

May 25 with a 9–0 shutout in which Red Caps pitcher Tommy Bond struggled with Wolverines hitters, who pounded out 16 hits. Derby helped himself with a home run, while Houck, Gerhardt and Brown dazzled the large crowd with their fielding. On May 26, about 1,400 spectators saw Detroit win, 4–2, as first baseman Lew Brown hit a home run deep into the woods behind Harper Hospital to score two runs in the fourth inning. Houck and Whitney had base hits and scored in the seventh to give Detroit the win. The Wolverines completed the sweep on May 27, with an 11–2 shellacking of Boston pitcher Jim Whitney. Detroit smacked 17 hits to put a satisfying cap on a home stand that had started so poorly. Cranks responded to the improved fortunes of the home club, and total attendance for the Boston series reached 4,000. After the game, every member of the club, as well as umpire Dick Higham, was presented with a basket of flowers by admirers. Crowd favorite Bennett also received an "immense floral ball." Hours later, as they left for their extended road trip, a crowd gathered to send off the Wolverines.

> The Detroit Base Ball Club was serenaded previous to their departure last evening by the Detroit Opera House orchestra, lead by Prof. R. Speil, which accompanied them to the depot. Before leaving, Mayor Thompson, President of the Detroit Base Ball Club, made a farewell speech, and the nine was given three rousing cheers and a "tiger" by the citizens assembled who wished them a successful trip and victory wherever they went.[15]

The Wolverines had captured the fancy of Detroiters, putting a smile on the faces of the mayor and his fellow directors whose gamble seemed to be paying off. After a shaky 1–8 beginning, the team was now playing well, winning seven games while losing two, for a record of 8–10 as it left town.

The *Detroit Free Press* acknowledged that the Wolverines had become a great addition to the city. "The large attendance at the games of base ball which have been played in this city shows that people here take a deep interest in the pastime," it said. It lauded the efforts of directors to preserve order on the grounds and ensure compliance with rules against rowdyism and brawling. The paper noted that the park was pleasant and the sport had been "at all times interesting and frequently very exciting." But it complained that there was insufficient room in the grandstands and that directors ought to add yet another to accommodate fans and increase revenue. "Indeed, if the Detroit club meet with a fair degree of success in their present tour, the stand will be sorely needed on their return, and the public will expect to see it on the grounds," the *Free Press* said.[16] Meanwhile, the owner of a home near Recreation Park was doing a brisk business selling vantage points on his roof for 20 cents; however, on May 27, during the last game with Boston, it was damaged by the weight of spectators. The following day, the homeowner called club president Thompson to demand $20 in compensation. "The Recreation Park people think it a very rich joke," observed the *Free Press*. "It's no joke, however, to the roof proprietor, unless he can get money enough to make his rafters doubly stout, in which case he'll smile. So will President Thompson, too."[17] Issues of public safety and revenue loss for the ball club were apparently of little interest to the *Free Press*. In years to come, other enterprising property owners tried to capitalize on the proximity of their roofs to Wolverines games, only to be met with tarp screens and legal action. It was an unexpected side effect of the team's popularity.

The 24-day road trip kicked off with three games against Bancroft's old team in Worcester. The first game, on May 30, drew 3,653 spectators, a testament to the strong following the Ruby Legs had developed in a city half the size of Detroit. Lefty Lee Richmond pitched, and while Detroit managed eight hits, they committed eight errors to produce an 8–4 Worcester victory. Jack Leary, who Bancroft took on trial as a backup pitcher to Derby, arrived for the June 1 game, played center field and managed three hits in a 10–3 win. The following day, the Detroit bats came alive to victimize Worcester's other pitcher, Fred Corey, for a 6–1 win. Detroit took two of the three games played in Troy before small crowds, though Bennett was hurt.

A three-game series with Boston began June 13 with a 2–0 Derby shutout. The next day, in a game marred by 11 Detroit fielding errors with 10 unearned runs for Boston, Derby went 10 innings but lost the game 10–9. Detroit had 14 hits. Boston scored a 7–1 victory on June 15 when Derby replaced an ineffective Leary, who would soon be released. First baseman Lew Brown followed Leary out the door, let go for his drinking that Bancroft blamed for the second Boston loss. Brown had signed a pledge to abstain, at the manager's insistence. Several weeks earlier he was caught drinking, fined $10 and warned not to repeat. His expulsion was used as a reminder to all Detroit players that "sobriety, honesty and morality" would be strictly enforced.[18] Bancroft moved quickly to replace Brown at first. He hired lanky, left-handed hitter Martin Powell, 25, a native of Massachusetts, who began the season with the Washington Nationals. Powell brought sure hands and a powerful bat. The six-footer would become an invaluable addition to the Wolverines. Powell's 1881 batting average of .338 would be second only to Chicago captain Cap Anson's .399. Providence was the last stop on the trip, for three games, and Detroit picked up two wins. The Wolverines ended their road trip of League games with seven wins and five losses, alone in fourth place with 15 wins, one back of Worcester.

Before heading home, Detroit played two exhibition games against the New York Metropolitans that attracted large crowds, and won both. In a 9–0 shutout on June 21, Martin Powell showed he could also pitch, unveiling a good curve and nice speed in allowing only five hits. He was beginning to make manager Bancroft seem very shrewd. While Leary was formally released for poor play and a failure to remain sober, Frank Mountain, 21, a freshman pitcher from Union College in Schenectady, New York, was brought on board through the manager's revolving door. An inch short of six feet tall, Mountain showed promise, pitching both games against New York before the road-weary Wolverines headed for home.

Back in Detroit, the players would have noticed that the seating capacity at the Recreation Park grandstands had been doubled to more than 2,000. A crowd of about 1,500 was on hand on June 24 for the start of a three-game set with Troy, in which circumstances conspired against the home team. Derby was given permission to visit his parents, who lived 20 miles from a New York Central Railroad stop the Wolverines passed through. But Derby missed a connection and was too late arriving in Detroit to pitch in the Troy game. Meanwhile, during morning practice, the new backup, Mountain, sprained his knee and was forced to pitch the entire game even though he could barely walk. The fourth-place Wolverines fell short in a late-game rally to lose, 9–8, to the fifth-place Trojans. A disappointing 900 spectators watched Detroit blank the Trojans, 8–0, on June 27 when the hometown batters found that future Hall of Famer Tim Keefe provided little challenge. Troy repaid the favor the next day with a 5–1 rout in which Detroit's other newcomer, Martin Powell, compensated for going hitless by making 14 putouts. Hobbled by injuries to Wood, Reilley and Mountain, Detroit next welcomed last-place Providence to Recreation Park and lost all three games of the series, dropping to fourth-place.

The four-game losing streak was snapped on July 4 when Detroit defeated Worcester in both games of a doubleheader, 11–8 and 7–3, the wins propelling the club into a tie with the Ruby Legs for third place in the tightly bunched League standings. Best of all, the fans were coming back to the ball park. The two Independence Day games attracted a total of 5,600 cranks. Three days later, Detroit beat the visitors again, 7–3, to occupy third place by itself, three games back of second-place Buffalo. Intense heat on July 9 kept the crowd to about 800 for the opener of a series with Boston. After a five-run first inning, Detroit cruised to a 12–3 victory, helped by eight errors from the Red Caps. Detroit defeated Boston, 8–3, on July 13 in an error-filled game. Bennett homered and tripled for the home team in a game played before 781 spectators. Detroit bats struggled with Boston pitcher John Fox on July 14, and the visitors earned a 3–2 win. As the series wrapped up, it was noted where Detroit's real challenge lay ahead in its remaining League games. The western teams were much stronger than those in the east and the Wolverines faced six games with first-place Chicago, six with fourth-place Cleveland and three with second-place Buffalo.

Cleveland was first up, and Detroit played a three-game series there beginning July 16. Former Wolverine George Washington Bradley appeared at shortstop and third base for the Blue Stockings, with whom he had signed late in June. The *Cleveland Herald* reported that Bradley appeared in "such a nervous state" for the opening game, noting "of course, he wanted to flay the Detroiters alive. Players take an especial pride in defeating a club to which they formerly belonged."[19] Detroit, anxious to send a message to the illness-faking Bradley, won the first game, 8–5, lost the second, 5–2, but took the third, 8–3. Derby allowed only four hits and tripled to help his cause in the final game when Detroit belted 11 hits. In the meantime, Buffalo was on a roll, sweeping a three-game series from faltering Chicago. Poor play continued for Chicago and it dropped games in Detroit on July 22 and 23, 6–4 and 3–2. In the first game, catcher Charlie Bennett threw out three White Stockings who attempted to steal second base. Detroit was losing, 4–0, until its bats woke up in the four-run sixth inning. For the second victory, the Wolverines clung to a one-run lead during a nail-biting ninth inning. Chicago won the third game, 9–4, as Derby, Detroit's ace, was greatly distracted by his wife begging him to go home to Pennsylvania where she was about to give birth. The White Stockings scored five runs in the seventh inning. Meanwhile, Derby's wife delivered a 10-pound boy, but it is not known if the pitcher arrived in time to witness it. The Chicago series had attracted about 9,000 spectators to Recreation Park who came away pleased at how well the League's youngest team fared against one of its founding members.

The red-hot Buffalo Bisons were next into Recreation Park, for a three-game series to finish the month. With the absences of Derby and Whitney, who was ill with bilious fever, the Wolverines lost the first game, 15–4. Mountain struggled with the visitors, who touched him for 16 hits, and 16 errors were made by Detroit in what was described as the "worst game of the season."[20] The only bright spot was Bennett's bases-loaded homer, which scored all the Detroit runs. Mountain recovered for a better outing on July 29 when Detroit won, 9–3. New father Derby was back pitching the next day, and the Wolverines fended off a late Buffalo rally to win, 7–6. By the end of July, Detroit was breathing down the neck of the second-place Bisons. One more home field series was scheduled before a two-week road trip to Chicago and Cleveland. The guests were the Blue Stockings, and Detroit took two of three games from them to move into second place past Buffalo, which lost three straight to Chicago. For their part, the White Stockings were shaking off some early-season troubles and reasserting themselves as the class of the League. In the third game with Cleveland, the Blues hit Derby hard and prevailed, 10–3, but the Wolverines held onto second place with its record of 29 wins and 25 losses.

4. A Fine Debut 63

Meanwhile, the play of the surging Detroit club was attracting attention in other cities. The *Cincinnati Enquirer* said that Detroit had closed to within five games of Chicago and if its winning ways continued, Detroit might capture the League pennant.[21] For its part, the *New York Clipper* noted the parity among League teams and liked Detroit's chances of toppling powerhouse Chicago. In July, it noted, Chicago had won eight games and lost eight, while Detroit had won 11 and lost only five. "The Detroit Club, under the efficient management of F. C. Bancroft, is looked upon by many as the 'dark horse' that will win the race for the League championship."[22] The *Clipper* also reported that the season was a success financially, with Detroit expecting to have $8,000 in its treasury by season's end. Meanwhile, on the home front, the club was determined to maximize its returns during its inaugural season. Directors of Recreation Park had decided to help by seeking a court injunction to stop "the private stand speculators from plying their trade on base ball days."[23] The offending scaffolding was just beyond the right field fence. When the court postponed a decision on the matter to late August, the scaffolding grew, but so did the fence—by three or four stories.[24]

Detroit's challenging road trip kicked off with losses on August 9 and 11 in Chicago, 5–3 and a 17–0. Detroit errors lost the first game. Pitcher Fred Goldsmith was nearly invincible in the second, surrendering a single hit to George Wood, while Frank Mountain struggled mightily with Chicago batters lighting him up. Detroit made 10 errors while Chicago had 16 hits, 10 unearned runs, and played error-free ball. Catcher Silver Flint went five-for-five at the plate and completed his ninth straight game without a passed ball. This was the most lopsided victory of the season, helping Chicago regain lost ground and dropping Detroit to third place. On August 13, the Wolverines shut out the home team, 2–0, on the strength of Derby's pitching. It was the first time the White Stockings were shut out on their own grounds that season. Captain Cap Anson did his best to avoid the whitewashing with a triple, but when he tried to go home on a short fly to Ned Hanlon in center field, Hanlon fired the ball to Bennett, who tagged Anson out.

A three-game series in Cleveland started poorly with losses of 8–5 and 6–5 on August 16 and 17. Frank Mountain was released, his pitching record at three wins and four losses. He hung around for a few more games, however, amid some confusion about his status. Mountain would be replaced by Tony Mullane, an Irish-born, 22-year-old rookie from Akron, who could pitch from either the right or left side. Also added to the roster was Will Foley, who took over at third base for the ailing Whitney. On August 18, Detroit rebounded to shut out Cleveland, 3–0. The road trip then returned to Chicago, where it began. The Wolverines lost on August 20, 10–3, with Chicago scoring six times in the eighth inning, and on August 23 went 12 innings before succumbing to the White Stockings, 8–6. To that point in August, Detroit, battling injuries and illness, had four wins and seven losses, to hold onto third place. With 31 wins and 31 losses, the nine was two wins behind Buffalo. On August 25, Bancroft found something to cheer about when his club salvaged a 7–5 victory before heading home. In its account of the lone victory in the Windy City, the *Detroit Free Press* referred to the club as the "Wolverines" for the first time. The Western road trip had produced only three wins and six losses.

Detroit resumed hostilities with the White Stockings at Recreation Park for three games beginning August 27. Nearly 2,000 cranks turned out for the first contest, which marked the debut of Tony Mullane, pitching for Detroit. The first ambidextrous pitcher in major league baseball history proved effective and the Wolverines won, 9–1. It is not recorded from which side(s) the hurler pitched that day. A natural right-hander, he taught himself to pitch from the left side after an early-career injury to his right arm. Newcomer John "Dasher" Troy, 25, of New York, played well at second base, replacing Gerhardt, who was attending his father's funeral in Washington. With Buffalo losing to Cleveland, the win put Detroit back into a second-place tie with the Bisons. Chicago won the next two games, 12–8 and 10–3, with the bats of Anson and Flint particularly effective against Derby and Mullane, respectively. On August 30, Flint went five-for-five and Anson four-for-four against Derby. The losses dropped Detroit to fourth place.

With that, the Wolverines left for a three-game series in Buffalo beginning September 2. Derby's shoulder was sore and he was sidelined. In the first game, pitcher Pud Galvin gave up 13 hits but belted a single, a double and a triple in a 14–6 Bisons win. Mullane struggled, giving up 16 hits. Buffalo took the second game, 5–3, with Detroit trying out pitcher George "Stump" Weidman, a Rochester native who played for Buffalo in 1880. The Bisons swept the series on September 5 in a hard-hitting game, 6–3. Weidman pitched again, Wood was playing poorly, and Reilley was released. Detroit fell to a tie for fourth place, and because crowds were so light in Buffalo the gate was insufficient to cover team expenses.

The Wolverines returned home for their last three games at Recreation Park to play host to Cleveland. Detroit took the first game, 5–2, to give Weidman his first win, lost the second game, 5–3, because of sloppy fielding and came back to win the third, 6–4, when the home team batters found their old mate Bradley easy to solve. Weidman pitched again while Derby was expected to rejoin the team on its final road trip. Detroit's new backup catcher, Sam Trott, had four hits. Crowds were light for the final home stand, with a total attendance of 2,000. The *Free Press* reported that the team had more than $12,000 in its treasury after its 42 home games. Manager Bancroft surprised everyone when he announced he was done with baseball and next season would focus on managing his hotel in New Bedford.

Detroit was swept in a three-game series in Providence that began September 13, due to sloppy play, despite the return of Derby. Next stop was Boston, which for a short time in August had slipped past Detroit in the League standings, but was spiraling downward in September. Detroit lost the opener, 6–4, on September 17, its fourth defeat in a row, but bounced back to win, 8–1, on September 20 and defeated the Red Caps, 9–4, the following day. On September 23, the Wolverines took on Worcester and lost, 12–6, largely due to poor fielding. Weidman's pitching was described as "elegant" the following day, however, when Detroit downed the Ruby Legs, 8–3. The ambidextrous Mullane was released from his trial contract after winning one game and losing four. The error-bug infected Worcester in the series finale that Detroit won, 11–6, before a crowd of only 200. The share of the gate for Detroit was a paltry $31, not enough to cover expenses.

Detroit travelled west to Troy for a season-ending series before tiny crowds. Wolverines errors contributed to a Troy win, 4–2, on September 28, but the following day Detroit recorded its 40th season win to edge past the Trojans, 4–3. The final game was a 7–0 shutout for Detroit and gave the club fourth place in the standings—exactly where president Thompson had predicted it would finish. Chicago captured the pennant, as expected, 15 games ahead of Detroit. Providence was second and Buffalo took third place.

It had been a strong season for a newcomer club touted as a potential pennant-winner at the beginning of August. Manager Bancroft likely had writer's cramp after signing 26 players to Detroit contracts throughout the season, but only six players remained from the starting roster when play ended. The Detroit record was 41 wins and 43 losses. Pitcher George Derby pitched 55 complete games, third-most in the League, winning 26 and losing 26. He recorded a League-best 212 strikeouts and the third-best earned run average of 2.20. He had been a workhorse as potential backups came and went, but his arm had become sore. The next best Wolverines pitcher was late-season addition Weidman, who won eight games and lost five.

The *Detroit Free Press* was high in its praise of the club as it looked back on the season:

> The Detroits have done more than well. It is true that some affect to grumble at them for not taking a higher place in the league, but such grumble [is] without good cause. But little was expected of the club, and it has accomplished much. How different from the clubs of which so much was expected and so little realized. The management can now retain five of its best players for next season … the public can rest assured that the Detroit club of 1882 will be a stronger one in many respects.[25]

On September 30, National League directors convened a special meeting at which they expelled several players whose behavior was deemed inappropriate. Detroit's Sadie Houck was banned from play for insubordination and drinking. Mike Dorgan, who played eight games for Detroit, was ejected for insubordinate behavior in Richmond before he was tried out by Bancroft. Both were blacklisted by the League, which stiffened its rules for player behavior. The Wolverines played some exhibition games in Philadelphia, New York, and Richmond during October. At the latter venue, manager Bancroft donned a uniform to play left field, while Detroit-based umpire Dick Higham played right. Management announced the five players it was reserving for next season: the battery of Derby and Bennett, infielders Powell and Gerhardt, and outfielder Hanlon. Wood, Knight and Weidman had already signed, so it appeared the team would remain largely intact for another campaign.

As the players scattered to return to their homes in late October, they had no way of knowing how much the baseball landscape would be changed by the time they took to the field the following spring.

5

A Wild Ride

Even before the 1881 season ended, several large cities were agitating for a new model in baseball, unhappy at the tight control and exclusivity of the National League. Chief among them was Cincinnati, still smarting over its expulsion/resignation from the League for allowing Sunday games in its old park and permitting the sale of alcohol. Former Red Stockings owner Justus Thorner teamed up with O. P. Caylor, a baseball columnist for the *Cincinnati Enquirer*—who had also worked in the front office of the club—along with several other local businessmen, to bring top-notch professional baseball back to the Queen City. In Philadelphia, "Hustling" Horace Phillips, manager of the non-aligned Athletics and former manager for Troy, Baltimore and Rochester, was upset there was no major league team in that city or in other major population centers, including New York and St. Louis. Caylor met Phillips at a Philadelphia hotel one September night and the pair decided to act. The following day, they sent telegrams to baseball men in other cities advising them that a new league was being established and inviting them to a preliminary meeting October 10 in Pittsburgh.

The gathering was convened by Denny McKnight, president of the Allegheny Base Ball club, which competed in the International Association in 1877 and 1878. More than a dozen men from several cities agreed to hold a founding meeting for the American Association three weeks later in Cincinnati. Phillips was not among them, however, having just been fired by Philadelphia. The peripatetic and erratic bundle of energy had yet again clashed with the backers of a team. Phillips was not done with baseball and would soon manage AA teams in Columbus and Pittsburgh. The AA decided to let each club set admission prices (usually 25 cents, half that of the National League), play games on Sundays (where permitted by law), and sell alcohol in their parks. Because so many team owners and directors were involved in the beer or liquor business, the new loop would become known as the "Beer and Whisky League." McKnight was elected president, and franchises were granted to Cincinnati, Philadelphia, Pittsburgh, Louisville, St. Louis and Brooklyn (replaced by Baltimore). New York manager Jim Mutrie declined to commit to the rebel association, fearing the potential loss of lucrative games against League teams with which his Metropolitans had a busy schedule. New York, the country's largest metropolis with a population of 1.2 million, delayed its entry into the major leagues until 1883, when Mutrie's Metropolitans entered the American Association while the New York Gothams joined the National League.[1]

Detroit found itself caught in the crossfire that developed between the two leagues, which initially seemed willing to get along. During spring training, 21 exhibition games were played between teams of the two organizations. But trouble soon developed. Dasher Troy had played 11 games with Detroit in 1881 and Samuel Washington Wise only one. Neither infielder was on the reserve list established by the Wolverines for 1882, so Troy signed with Philadelphia and Wise with Cincinnati, both Association clubs. The National League viewed this as some sort of transgression by the upstart loop, even though the AA contracts were valid. In response, both players signed contracts with National League clubs, Troy returning to Detroit and Wise going to Boston. The war was on. The dispute demonstrated that League teams had little use for the newcomers. When Philadelphia complained to Detroit about Dasher Troy, Wolverines president William G. Thompson was dismissive: "I know nothing about your association, or your claim that Mr. Troy has previously signed with you; if he wronged you in any respect, of course, as you say, you may expel him, and have the courts open to you for redress."[2] Troy was not on Detroit's reserve list, but when management learned that Sadie Houck was blacklisted for 1882, Troy was needed to play shortstop. Then Troy, to escape his commitment to Philadelphia, said that when he learned Philadelphia played on Sunday, he sought his release from Philly—but it was refused. In retaliation, AA president McKnight declared in May that Association teams would no longer play League clubs and would ignore the League's reserve list. The AA also paid the legal costs to challenge the contract-jumping by Troy and Wise. Neither case was successful, and the pair found themselves blacklisted by the new league, Troy the first to be so designated.[3] He played 40 games for Detroit before a season-ending injury, while Wise appeared in 78 games for Boston. The angry Association retaliated further before the 1882 season was over, persuading 13 National Leaguers to sign "options" to play for AA teams in 1883. They included Detroit's Charlie Bennett. In early August, the Pittsburgh Alleghenys gave Bennett $100 for signing such an option and promised him a salary of $1,700 for 1883. When the 1882 season ended, the Alleghenys sought to bar Bennett from playing for Detroit in 1883, but a judge ruled their option was not a binding contract and Bennett returned to Detroit.[4]

Then there was the case of Joe Gerhardt. The solid second baseman was on the Wolverines' reserve list for the 1882 season and, having signed a valid contract, was expected to return to Detroit. So it came as a surprise when the *Cincinnati Enquirer* reported in early March that the popular Gerhardt had retired from the game to accept a "lucrative position" in Louisville. The native of Washington, D. C., it was said, had accepted a "most flattering" offer for his services.[5] Gerhardt sent a letter to the Detroit club at the same time, saying he had "retired from the baseball arena, and is going into business with a friend in Louisville."[6] The news created an infield vacancy for Frank Bancroft, who had agreed to return to manage the Wolverines for another year after accepting what was also termed a "flattering offer."[7] Bancroft replaced Gerhardt with Mike McGeary, a veteran second baseman who at 31 was one of the oldest players in the National League. Among other clubs, McGeary had played for Troy, Providence and Cleveland.

The plot thickened when Gerhardt sought his release from Detroit, an unexpected move if he had retired as claimed. Bancroft, however, refused to grant it, still hoping to persuade Gerhardt to return. At the end of March, the *Louisville Sunday Argus* reported that Gerhardt had taken a position as a barkeeper in the New Orleans Saloon in Louisville. The paper said of Gerhardt: "The ball field will know him no more."[8] But Bancroft suspected his star infielder wanted to play for the Eclipse, Louisville's entry in the American Association. Why else would Gerhardt seek a release? It certainly wasn't required to tend bar. In early April, Bancroft made a quick trip to Louisville to check out the situation and warn Gerhardt that if he didn't return to Detroit, he'd be blacklisted from playing anywhere. Upon returning home April 5, Bancroft was buttonholed by a *Free Press* reporter. The conversation went this way:

"Hello Frank! When did you get home?"
"This morning."
"Did you see Joe?"
"Oh, yes."
"Is he coming?"
"That's uncertain."
"What did he say about it?"
"Nothing much."
"It would be safe to gamble that he won't come wouldn't it?"
"I'll just bet you $10 he will be here by the 1st of May!"[9]

When Gerhardt failed to report for spring training on April 1 as required in his Detroit contract, Bancroft moved to have him blacklisted. About a week later, Detroit president William G. Thompson was also asked about Gerhardt, and didn't mince words. "It's all moonshine about his quitting baseball and going into other business," he said. "He has been practicing with the Louisville club ever since he went there, and was trying to get his release so that he might play with them." Thompson insisted Gerhardt would be expelled from the League for failing to honor his Detroit contract.[10] And he was. In May, suspicions about Gerhardt were confirmed when directors of the Louisville club asked the American Association to ignore his blacklisting by the League and let him play for the Eclipse.[11] As it turned out, Gerhardt didn't play baseball anywhere in 1882, but joined Louisville for its 1883 campaign. Had anyone taken up Detroit manager Frank Bancroft on his wager about his wayward player, Bancroft would have been $10 poorer. The cases of Detroit's Troy, Wise, Bennett and Gerhardt demonstrated that peaceful coexistence between the National League and the American Association would be unlikely.

On January 30, the annual meeting of Detroit directors and shareholders featured a spirited debate about whether to pay dividends to shareholders from the club's successful operation. A total of $12,410 was in the bank and, after subtracting the initial outlay of $5,000 to get the team in operation, $5,000 to $6,000 was available for distribution. Operating expenses for the team were

An early game at Recreation Park. Note the advertising sign for Garland Stoves, one of the leading industries of the day. Also visible is a sign promoting Hudson's, which became a leading retailer in Detroit. Aside from contributing to revenue, advertising signs and tarps were often used to block the view from abutting properties where owners erected stands on their roofs to lure customers with cut-rate admission (Detroit Historical Society).

reported to be $41,105. Several directors insisted it was best to leave the money in the team kitty, partly because the upcoming season was to begin with a costly Eastern tour. When others sought a dividend, the matter was deferred to a committee for study. The money stayed put until May of 1883, when directors decided to pay a dividend of 25 percent, based on the amount the club had earned in its first two seasons of operation.[12] Meanwhile, Thompson soon returned as president and said the only new face on the Wolverines for 1882 would be third baseman Joe Farrell, 25, a strong hitter from Brooklyn making his League debut.[13] But when it became clear that Gerhardt was not returning after all, the well-traveled McGeary was hired to play shortstop.

In late March, Bancroft announced he had arranged a series of 10 exhibition games in April against the new American Association teams in Pittsburgh (the Alleghenys), St. Louis, Louisville and Cincinnati, with the latter appearing in Detroit on the eve of the League season. Spring training began April 1, and games were scheduled in Ann Arbor, Flint and Stanton. The Wolverines arrived in good shape, it was noted, and the team was expected to be stronger in the coming season. For 1882, all League players would be required to wear silk jerseys that were color-coded to their position. Only stocking colors would distinguish the teams, Detroit's being an "old gold" hue. Catchers, it was decreed, would wear scarlet jerseys, pitchers light blue, first basemen scarlet with vertical stripes, second basemen orange and black vertical stripes, third basemen blue and white vertical stripes, shortstops maroon, left fielders white, center fielders red and black vertical stripes, and right fielders gray. All players were required to wear white pants, white belts and white ties. The uniforms proved to be confusing and unpopular for both players and spectators alike and were abandoned midway through the season and did not return for the following season. Players resented being compared to jockeys or clowns and the silk jerseys were intolerably hot. Supplied by Albert Goodwill Spalding's new sporting goods firm, the uniforms were intended to compete with some of the colorful new outfits worn by American Association teams. It was an experiment doomed to failure. In another bid to pursue elusive profitability, the League shifted some operating costs onto the backs of players. For the 1882 season, players were required to carry their own bats and rainbow outfits during road trips and maintain and launder two complete uniforms.[14]

Spring training had barely begun when William Hulbert died on April 10 of a heart attack. The president and founder of the National League and president of the Chicago White Stockings had just begun to wage war on the upstart American Association, remarking high-handedly at one point: "The League does not recognize the existence of any Association of ball clubs excepting itself and the League Alliance."[15] Had he lived, Hulbert would have seen a new loop that was a success from the outset and lasted a decade in what became known as the "Golden Age" of baseball. In its first year, all six AA clubs turned a profit, something only Chicago in the National League had been able to do with any degree of consistency. And its six teams drew more cranks to their parks, collectively, than all eight NL teams.[16] Hulbert, having worked so hard to create and build a sustainable baseball league, would not have been amused to see the upstart challenger thrive and prosper—especially when it played games on Sundays and sold beer in its ballparks. Hulbert was replaced as president on an interim basis by penny-pinching Boston owner Arthur Soden.

Detroit left for its Southern trip and games with American Association teams on April 9. Because of Dasher Troy's blacklisting by the AA, Bancroft wisely opted not to play him against AA teams to avoid needlessly antagonizing the opposition. In 11 games against Louisville, St. Louis, Cincinnati and Pittsburgh's Allegheny club, the Wolverines won every one. Shutouts were recorded against Louisville and St. Louis, with the closest games being 4–3 and 7–6 wins against each club, respectively. The most lopsided victory came April 25 in Cincinnati when Detroit clobbered the Red Stockings, 15–1.

Detroit's 1882 season opened on May 1 with a series in Cleveland, where they swept the Blue Stockings, 5–4, 7–1 and 1–0. The National League schedule called for four series with each team, two three-game series at each team's park. The Wolverines travelled to Buffalo, where they lost, 4–3, on May 5, but won the next two clashes. Optimism was high as the Wolverines returned home for the first game at Recreation Park on May 15, riding a 5–1 record, good for second place. They manhandled the Buffalo Bisons, 8–1, before 3,000 Detroiters who braved a chilly wind. The following day, Cleveland fell, 8–3, pitcher George Washington Bradley giving up 10 hits. Cleveland won the May 17 game, 9–3, but Detroit bounced back for a 3–2 win a day later. By beating Buffalo, 14–11, on May 19 the Wolverines vaulted into first place with a 9–2 record. Bancroft was methodically alternating George Derby and Stump Weidman, and the pitching rotation was working well. The Wolverines clung to first despite losing two out of three games in Chicago, but after a 7–3 defeat by the White Stockings on May 26 at Recreation Park, slipped to second behind Providence.

Success on the field was mirrored at the box office. In five games ending May 26, the Wolverines drew 9,000 spectators. For a May 29 exhibition game against Philadelphia's AA club in that city, Bancroft adroitly sat AA-blacklisted Dasher Troy and replaced him with William Reid, formerly of the Tecumseh Club of London, Ontario, who had signed a trial contract. A huge crowd of 7,185 turned out in Providence for the Detroit game on May 30, the largest to ever to witness a game in that city. First-place Providence held a half-game lead

5. A Wild Ride   73

on Detroit and its supporters were anxious to see the Grays stay on top. The Decoration Day holiday throng saw the home club capitalize on errors by the Wolverines to blank them, 4–0, producing a 1½-game lead. The next day, Detroit won 6–4, but lost by an 8–7 score on June 2. The Wolverines would trail Providence until late June, when they recaptured the lead for about a week. Of 13 road games played in Providence, Boston, Worcester and Troy, Detroit took seven of them and tied one, the latter a 14-inning, 4–4 battle with Boston on June 3 that was called on account of darkness. In an exhibition game on June 8, Bancroft again sat Troy so as not to antagonize the AA Metropolitans. Reid from London was again tried in the infield, taking shortstop while McGeary moved to second to cover Troy's position. Detroit won, 4–3. Five days later in a return match, Bennett replaced Troy in the infield as the Metropolitans were downed, 8–3. Detroit ended the trip by sweeping Worcester in three games and taking two out of three from Troy. Reid was released.

Chicago was off to an uncharacteristically slow start, sitting fifth in the League standings when they appeared at Recreation Park for a single game on June 19 to replace a May 27 rain out. The White Stockings pounded Stump Weidman hard, collecting 18 hits on their way to a 12–0 rout of the Wolverines. Chicago's Fred Goldsmith scattered six hits to earn the shutout, much to the disappointment of the 1,500 spectators that day. In their six clashes so far in the season, Chicago had taken four.

For its Eastern trip, Detroit took along umpire Dick Higham, who was informally posted to the city and was a League-approved umpire for the second year in a row. Club president Thompson, however, grew suspicious of Higham, feeling he ruled against Detroit on too many close calls. For his part, Higham, 30, had developed close ties with the Wolverines, occasionally joining them as a player in exhibition games. Born in England, he had grown up in New York, where he broke into professional baseball in 1871 with the New York Mutuals of the National Association. An outfielder, catcher and second baseman, Higham also played for a time with the Baltimore Canaries. He served as a substitute umpire in the NA, as did many players of the day. For part of the 1875 season, Higham was captain of the Chicago White Stockings, but was expelled from the team for associating with gamblers and throwing games. He was hired by Hartford for the inaugural 1876 season of the National League and was the club's best hitter. In 1877, Higham was captain of the Syracuse Stars in the International Association, moving to Providence the next year, then to Albany and finally to Troy, where he finished his playing career in 1880.

His reputation for questionable conduct was well known and may have curtailed his career in the League. Inexplicably, the League included him on a list of approved umpires for 1881. He had previous umpiring experience and was willing to take on the thankless job that often drew abuse from every quarter. Higham worked 58 games that first season and was moved from Providence to Detroit, to Troy and then back to Detroit.[17] Thompson was so sure something shady was going on with Higham that he hired a private detective to investigate. The detective found a letter addressed to well-known local gambler James Todd and apparently signed by Higham. It outlined a code that Higham would telegraph to Todd, advising him when to bet on Detroit.

Dated May 27, 1882, in Detroit, it read:

> FRIEND TODD: I just got word we leave for the East on the 3 p.m. train, so I will not have a chance to see you. If you don't hear from me play the Providence Tuesday, and if I want you to play the Detroits Wednesday I will telegraph in this way: "Buy all the lumber you can." If you do not hear from me don't play the Detroits, but buy Providence sure—that is, the first game. I think this will do for the Eastern series. I will write you from Boston. You can write me at any time in care of Detroit B.B. Club. When you send me any money you can send check to me in care of the Detroit B.B. Club, and it will be all right. You will see by that book I gave you the other day what city will be in.
> Yours truly,
> DICK.[18]

Thompson wasted no time in filing a complaint of crookedness against Higham. The umpire was brought before a group of League owners who gathered in Detroit on June 24 to demand an explanation. Higham denied he had written the letter. Samples of his handwriting from receipts and letters persuaded the League officials that the letter to Todd had indeed come from Higham's hand. They sent a report calling for his expulsion to League secretary Nick Young.[19] Higham became the first, and only, major league umpire to be banished forever from the game for dishonesty. The *Detroit Free Press* printed the letter to Todd in full. The paper noted that despite Higham's insistence that he did not even know Todd, manager Bancroft learned that Higham had left a letter at the Brunswick Hotel with instructions that it be delivered to Todd. "It would be interesting to know in what degree the "lumber" market affected the three games at Providence and the three at Boston, of which the Detroits won two and lost four," the newspaper wondered aloud.[20] For his part, Higham never umpired again. He became a bookkeeper in Detroit before moving to Kansas City and Chicago, where he died in 1905. In 1882, the League enacted a rule that barred players, managers and umpires from betting on games, and by the end of the season, the League adopted the AA's practice of not allowing umpires to have any sort of affiliation with any particular team. Umpires became full-time, salaried officials of the League itself, rather than have them rely for their pay on teams who chose them.[21] The case of Dick Higham no doubt contributed to the change.

5. A Wild Ride 75

Meanwhile, back on the field Detroit played host to Providence and lost two out of three games with the front-running Grays before welcoming tailenders Worcester for a series that began June 26. As expected, the Wolverines swept the Ruby Legs who had won only nine games compared to Detroit's 19. The third win tied Detroit with Providence for first place, a position they retained until July 8, when a resurgent Chicago claimed the lead. After beating Troy twice in a three-game series, on July 4, Detroit won the first game of a doubleheader with Boston, 2–1, but was shellacked in the second game, 14–1. Derby had a bad outing and gave up 22 hits. Boston won, 10–4, on July 6, and when Chicago downed Detroit, 8–4, on July 11, the Wolverines fell to second place. For their part, the White Stockings had a very good June, winning 12 of 18 games and with their July 11 victory returned to their customary position atop the League. Detroit edged the home team, 2–1, the following day, but would never regain the lead. The rubber match was a blowout for Chicago. Nearly 6,000 spectators saw Derby pounded again, this time for 20 hits, in a 23–4 Chicago win. Detroit committed 15 errors to three for the White Stockings. Backup catcher Sam Trott was called upon to play shortstop, an unfamiliar position, and was responsible for a third of Detroit's muffs. Trott replaced Dasher Troy, who was spiked during the first Chicago game and was described as seriously injured. As it turned out, Troy was gone for the remainder of season, and his loss would be keenly felt.

Cleveland traveled to Recreation Park on July 15 and Detroit lost two of three contests, slipping to a tie for second place. Buffalo arrived for a rare four-game series on July 21, and the Wolverines dispatched them three times. The last series on the eve of another Eastern road trip was with Chicago, which took two of the three games, the final win by an embarrassing 17–1 score. Bancroft, faced with several injuries, had been trying new players in his infield, but Troy was hard to replace. Stump Weidman was the victim of Chicago bats, which pounded out 21 hits that day. Meanwhile, Larry Corcoran didn't surrender a hit until the eighth inning, when Detroit's Lon Knight tripled and came home on a double by Trott. By August 1, Detroit was solidly in third place, with 31 wins, behind Providence with 34 and Chicago with 33.

The Eastern swing began with a series against lowly Worcester on August 4. Although the travellers were plagued with injuries, illness, rumors of squabbling and a poor attitude from Derby, the Wolverines took two out of three games. In Troy, they lost two games before shutting out the Trojans, 6–0, on August 14. Providence enjoyed a three-win lead over Chicago in the pennant race when Detroit appeared at the Messer Street Grounds for an important set beginning August 16. In the first game, Derby gave up 14 hits, the men behind him committed eight errors, and the Grays won easily, 13–4. The following day, August 17, the two teams played an entirely different game, one that would become known as the most remarkable game in major league history.

About 1,200 spectators were at the ballpark for the hot Thursday afternoon to watch the League's first- and third-place teams go at it. Bancroft gave the ball to Stump Weidman, who was proving a more reliable performer than Derby and on his way to 25 wins, a career high. Derby would register 17. For Providence, John Montgomery Ward took the ball. He had been showing signs of arm fatigue and was gradually being supplanted by Charles "Hoss" Radbourn, the often ill-tempered hurler who won 33 games in 1882 to 19 by Ward. Radbourn was placed in right field for this game. The first three innings were scoreless. In the fourth, Detroit center fielder Ned Hanlon capitalized on two throwing errors to advance to second. The speedster was off like a shot when his first baseman, Martin Powell, singled to center. Hanlon barreled his way home and it looked like he would score, but center fielder Paul Hines made a perfect throw to Grays catcher Sandy Nava, who tagged Hanlon out. Goose eggs were registered inning after inning in a defensive battle that featured several remarkable fielding plays by Providence third baseman Jerry Denny.

After nine innings, the teams played on with no change in pitching, as was the custom. Inning followed inning in the nail-biting contest. In the 15th inning, with two out, it appeared Hanlon could win it for the visitors. He advanced to third after singling off Ward. Detroit catcher Sam Trott connected for a hit to deep right field and Hanlon started for home. The trajectory appeared to take the ball over Radbourn's head,

Stump Weidman was one of the first pitchers signed by Detroit. He was with Buffalo in 1880, where he toiled in the shadow of future Hall of Famer Pud Galvin. The durable Weidman carried the Wolverines to early successes during his five years with the club (Library of Congress).

but he had a bead on it. He sprinted hard toward the outfield fence and managed to make a bare-handed catch to the delight of the crowd. In the bottom of the inning, it seemed the Grays would finally end the marathon. George Wright, the Providence shortstop and manager, belted a Weidman offering to left field. The ball shot through a half-open gate used by fans with carriages who parked along the outfield fence. The ball continued through a maze of spectators and onto an adjoining street, with Detroit left fielder George Wood in hot pursuit. Wood caught up to the ball and fired it over the fence to Charlie Bennett, who was playing third base. Bennett relayed it to catcher Trott, who tagged the charging Wright out at home. Critics said later that umpire George "Foghorn" Bradley should probably have declared a dead ball once he could no longer see it.

Darkness was gathering as the struggle continued into the 18th inning. Detroit failed to score in the top of the inning. The leadoff batter in the bottom of the inning was Radbourn, appearing at the plate for the seventh time and held hitless by Weidman up to that point. But this time Radbourn connected for a majestic fly to left field, toward the same carriage gate that was now closed. The ball soared over the fence just inside the foul line to give the future Hall of Fame pitcher a home run. The park erupted in joy at the dramatic finish, with gentlemen throwing their hats in the air and spectators streaming onto the field. The *Providence Evening Telegram* dubbed it "the most beautiful base ball game in the history of the League," while the rival *Providence Journal* predicted it was "one long to be remembered by those so fortunate as to be present."[22] Back home, the *Detroit Free Press* referred to it as "the greatest game of ball ever played … unrivaled in the history of the league."[23] The game was talked about for years. And for good reason. The irony was that a hard-fought pitching duel with dazzling defense was won by one of the all-time pitching greats who didn't pitch at all that day.

Detroit lost its third game in a row to Providence the following day and then three to Boston, including a 4–0 shutout on August 24, to fall to fourth place in the standings. Back in Detroit, the Wolverines defeated Troy three times and tied the Trojans once, before winning two out of three from Boston. After losing two out of three to cellar-dwelling Worcester, Detroit slipped to fifth place as its late-season swoon continued.

Derby's play began to alarm manager Bancroft. He complained about soreness in his pitching arm and asked Bancroft to use Weidman in two games of every three-game series. During a 5–2 loss to Worcester on September 14, the one-time ace showed little speed in his delivery and was unusually wild. Derby was pulled after four innings and suspended by Bancroft for poor play. Weidman was left to carry the load for Detroit's final home stand of the season against Providence. In the September 16 game, he was helped by a George Wood home run, one of 10

Detroit hits, to down Providence, 2–1. He lost the next two to the Grays before the Wolverines hit the road for a six-game road trip to close out a very disappointing season. Detroit was swept in all three games in Buffalo and slipped to a tie for fifth place. In the first game, September 22, Derby returned, gave up eight hits, and lost, 4–1. The following day, with Weidman ill, Derby pitched again and was shelled for 17 hits. The Bisons won, 15–1. Derby was sent home by an exasperated Bancroft, and third baseman Art Whitney took the ball in a 7–4 loss. Derby, the promising young pitcher, had strained his arm from overwork and would not return to Detroit. The season was barely over, however, when he was scooped up by Buffalo. With the Bisons in 1883, he recorded two wins and 10 losses before retiring at age 25, his arm gone. Derby had played a key role in the early success of Detroit, but he had paid the price of Bancroft's inability to find a reliable and regular backup during his first season.

The three losses in Buffalo prompted the *Free Press* to complain:

> Disaster has overtaken them, and the rapidity with which they tumbled from first to sixth position in the league has been startling. Their hard luck overtook them on their last Eastern trip, and it will hold on to the close of the season, now, happily, near at hand. Three games at Cleveland and the season's agony will be over.[24]

In Cleveland, the Wolverines won the first game 4–2, relying on Stump Weidman, who left a sick bed to assume the pitching duties. He allowed only four hits and "his presence seemed to inspire the rest of the nine with confidence."[25] Weidman returned the next day, but he and Whitney were pounded for 16 hits and the Blue Stockings blanked the Wolverines, 9–0. The final game of the season was halted in the eighth inning by umpire Foghorn Bradley because of darkness, with the score tied at 7–7.

Detroit's 1882 season ended with a whimper. With 42 wins and 41 losses, the Wolverines tallied one more win than during their inaugural season, when they finished fourth. But after spending several weeks at the top of the League standings, their fall to a tie for fifth place was hard to accept. Chicago took the pennant for the third year in a row, three wins ahead of Providence. The Wolverines were 12½ games and 13 losses back of Chicago. The only teams with worse records than Detroit were the Troy Trojans with 35 victories and the woeful Worcester Ruby Legs with 18. Among the few bright spots for Detroit had been several of its hitters. George Wood was the League's home run leader with seven, while Hanlon and Bennett were tied for fourth with five apiece. On the pitching front, Derby, who won 17 games and lost 20, ranked third in strikeouts with 182. Weidman pitched 411 innings, to tie Worcester's Lee Richmond for fifth. Over in the American Association, the Cincinnati Red Stockings claimed the loop's first pennant, winning 55 games and finishing 11½ games ahead of the second-place Philadelphia Athletics.

5. A Wild Ride 79

Anxious Detroiters turned to Wolverines president Thompson with questions about his plans for the 1883 team. He was cautious when a *Free Press* reporter wanted to know how the roster was shaping up. His answer was revealing about the nature of his dealings with players and contracts.

> "There is really but very little to be said at the present time, for the entire team has not yet been determined upon, and until the contracts are signed, it is foolish to announce the engagement of any player. If there is a ball player in the country in whose promise you can place reliance, and not be disappointed, I have not met him."[26]

Thompson cited the case of Troy Trojans center fielder Roger Connor, who promised to join Detroit. Terms were agreed upon, but then he balked and insisted that three of his teammates be included in the deal. All four players signed with the inaugural NL New York Gothams. Thompson confirmed that he had contracts with seven players for the 1883 Wolverines: Bennett, Weidman, Trott, Farrell, Wood, Hanlon and Sadie Houck, whose one-year blacklisting was about to end. As Detroit played post-season exhibition games in New York and elsewhere, first baseman Martin Powell agreed to a contract, as did rookie pitcher Dick Burns, 19, of Holyoke, Massachusetts. Tom Mansell, 27, formerly of Syracuse and Troy, was engaged to play right field while White Stockings infielder Joe Quest, 30, was signed for second base when it appeared that an effort to bring back Dasher Troy was fruitless. Meanwhile, manager Frank Bancroft was being wooed by several teams with "tempting offers."[27] The Wolverines were also able to make tempting offers. It was later revealed the club finished the 1882 season with $18,000 in the bank, nearly $6,000 more than a year earlier. However, shortly after the season ended Bancroft agreed to become manager of the Cleveland Blue Stockings for 1883. He had done a fine job during his two years in Detroit with an 83–84 record, and directors were anxious to find a suitable replacement.

Directors of the Detroit club thought they had their new manager in Herman Doscher (sometimes spelled Doescher). Doscher, about to turn 30, had just completed his 11th year as a professional, most recently as a substitute infielder with Cleveland. The New Yorker was in the twilight of his professional playing career, which began with the 1872 Brooklyn Atlantics of the National Association. Primarily a third baseman, he moved to the NA Washington, then played two years with the London Tecumsehs, helping them win the International Association pennant in 1877, before jumping to the National League's Troy and Chicago nines. Doscher umpired League games during 1880 and 1881 before joining Cleveland for five games in 1881 and 25 more in 1882. At the end of the Blue Stockings' 1882 season, it was generally expected that he would become the club's new manager, and he began scouting players for the following season. In late October, the *New York Clipper* carried a snippet that caught the attention of Cleveland directors, who were paying Doscher: "The Detroit and Cleveland clubs purpose [sic] exchanging managers, Frank Bancroft going to Cleveland, where he will have full control of the team—something he did not have this season. Doscher has already been engaged as manager of the Detroits for 1883."[28] Doscher had already assigned himself the third base position on the Wolverines roster for 1883 that he submitted to the National League.[29]

When the directors in Cleveland discovered that the man they were paying to find new players was also working for Detroit and suggesting that recruits and existing Cleveland players sign with that team, they charged him with "embezzlement and obtaining money under false pretenses."[30] Doscher was expelled by Cleveland and, on November 8, National League secretary Nick Young issued a notice to all League clubs that Doscher was suspended for the balance of the year and for the entire 1883 season for "insubordination and dishonorable conduct."[31] The annual meeting of the League in December rejected Doscher's appeal and upheld his banishment. He was not reinstated until 1886.

Detroit's efforts to find a new manager resumed, and Thompson was determined to land a no-nonsense man who had high moral standards and demanded the same of his players. He was growing weary of dealing with people whose word could not be trusted. In early March, after a long search, directors authorized Thompson to hire veteran Jack Chapman. Chapman, 39, had a long history as a player and manager that dated from before the creation of the National Association and through the founding of the National League. A native of Brooklyn, Chapman had played with both the Atlantics and Eckfords of that city, and also with Philadelphia. A right fielder, he was a member of the Atlantics team that defeated the Cincinnati Red Stockings on June 14, 1870, ending that famous club's winning streak of a season and a half. Chapman was one of two players of his day to pick up the colorful nickname "Death to Flying Things," because of the apparent ease with which he tracked down fly balls. The sobriquet was also applied to infielder Bob Ferguson, who toiled for several teams including Troy. Chapman played for Louisville in the National League in 1876 before becoming manager. He remained as manager for the fateful 1877 season when four Louisville players sold out to gamblers, earning each a lifetime ban from the game. Chapman was unaware of what was going on beneath his nose, however, and he maintained a first-rate reputation among both players and fans.[32] Chapman later moved on to Milwaukee and Worcester and announced he was going into business in New York before catching the attention of the Detroit club. He wasn't much of a talker, but he was known to be good at controlling players and getting the best out of them.[33] Upon his arrival in Detroit, Chapman's managerial record stood at 87 wins and 136 losses. He inherited a team whose roster was already set.

The National League had plenty on its plate when delegates gathered for their seventh annual meeting in Providence on December 6. President Thompson was the only representative from Detroit. Troy and Worcester, the smallest cities and weakest links in the League, reluctantly agreed to "resign," immediately replaced by New York and Philadelphia. This gave the League a foothold in two major population centers where the American Association was making inroads and also rid itself of two small cities with difficulty drawing crowds. A. G. Mills, president of Chicago, was named president, replacing interim president Soden of Boston. The delegates decided to hire a full-time staff of four umpires and pay them $1,000 apiece, plus traveling and hotel expenses, for a five-month season. The move mirrored one already made by the AA. Thompson was particularly outspoken about the need for better umpires, at one point describing the existing men as "broken down by dissolute [drink], vicious habits of life; [they] are a lot of tramps." He said they should be League employees, and neither the opposing clubs nor spectators should know in advance which umpire would officiate until game time.[34] The latter provision was no doubt intended to prevent pre-game collusion between umpires and gamblers. The magnates also ended the use of multi-colored uniforms based on playing position and reinstated players who had been disqualified a year earlier for various transgressions. They included Sadie Houck, already signed by Detroit in anticipation of such a ruling. Delegates upheld Cleveland's suspension of Herman Doscher and rejected his appeal. Finally, a three-member committee was struck to meet with three members of the Association to see if the two loops could find a way to honor contracts signed by the other.

In February, representatives of the National League, the American Association and the revived Northwestern League met in New York for the first time ever in a bid to find common ground. They agreed to respect each other's contracts and blacklists and to increase the reserve rule to cover 11 players on each team, in what became known as the Tripartite (later, National) Agreement. They couldn't agree on standardized rules, however. Among other provisions, the AA retained the old rule that a batter was retired if a ball he hit was fielded on the first bounce. The League had just eliminated it. The rule differences were not major and would have to be worked out when teams from the two leagues met.[35] The AA dropped its ban on playing NL teams that its president Denny McKnight had angrily imposed in May when friction between the two circuits first erupted. A sort of truce had been achieved, largely because of the passing of William Hulbert, the National League's founder and an ardent scrapper.

6

Thompson and the Tail-enders

After their fifth-place finish in 1882, the Wolverines hoped for a better showing in 1883 with veteran Jack Chapman at the helm. The annual meeting of Detroit shareholders was held March 27, when it was disclosed that nearly $18,000 remained in the club treasury and was available for distribution. This year there was no great debate about whether dividends should be paid, with shareholders apparently willing to wait until directors felt the time was right. Pursuing success on the ball field was the first priority. In the interim, one season ticket was issued for each share of stock. William G. Thompson and his railroad and business friends James McMillan and George Hendrie were among the directors chosen to manage club affairs. Returned as president, Thompson reported on the Tripartite Agreement, which brought peace to professional baseball. He said it would make recruiting more difficult because every club in the National, American and Northwestern loops could reserve 11 men, tying up the elite players. A lower-rung team like Detroit would have to struggle to improve its roster, relying on rookies and castoffs. Thompson suggested that a tournament for amateur teams be held at Recreation Park during the Michigan State Fair to help Detroit identify and cultivate local talent. The notion found ready support and was referred to the directors for study. Newly hired manager Chapman was introduced, and he was immediately questioned about just-signed pitcher Dick Burns, a highly touted amateur right-hander from Holyoke, Massachusetts. Chapman assured directors that Burns was a hard-thrower who could bat from either the left or right side and was a speedster on the base baths. He said the 19-year-old had excellent habits and was bound to develop into a "desirable" pitcher.[1]

Spring training began April 2 in Detroit, but because the ground at Recreation Park was in poor condition with lingering ice and snow, Chapman practiced his men twice each day indoors at the Detroit Music Hall. Sadie Houck seemed happy to be back in the game after serving his one-year suspension. As nimble as ever, the shortstop was full of fun and said he felt like a 16-year-old. Newcomer Tom Mansell, 28, of Auburn, New York, who had played with Troy and Syracuse, was the only player who seemed out of shape. He was described as "very fleshy" and immediately set about to lose weight. Another new face was Joe Quest, a 30-year-old second baseman who had played with Chicago for four years. The veteran would be named Detroit captain. A close watch was kept on Burns, who needed to become a strong and reliable backup for Weidman. Burns impressed observers with what was termed an "in-shoot" fastball and changeup.[2]

Chapman also showed he meant business in the upcoming season when he handed each of his players a code of conduct. It included bans on "kicking" (loud complaints directed at the umpire or others during games), drinking or "carousing" at any time, card-playing, and smoking while in uniform. An 11 p.m. curfew was to be respected, and gamblers were to be avoided. Players were expected to be gentlemanly in their behavior and to clean and mend their uniforms at their own expense. Fines of $10 to $50 would be imposed for infractions. Chapman explained that he had the full backing of the board of directors to enforce the code.[3]

While other teams held spring training and exhibition games in Southern states, the Wolverines continued to practice indoors because of poor weather through much of April. They travelled to Indianapolis for games April 19 and 20, but the first contest was rained out. On their way home, they played in Fort Wayne, Grand Rapids and East Saginaw. Overall, Detroit saw precious little preparation time for a season that would open with a home-and-away series of six games against powerhouse Chicago, a team that was conducting its spring training in the sunny South.

The weather cooperated for Detroit's home opener on May 1, and a crowd of about 2,000 turned out to see the Wolverines face the reigning League champion White Stockings. Weidman took the ball for Detroit, while Fred Goldsmith pitched for Chicago. Crowd favorite catcher Charlie Bennett homered in the fourth inning, much to the delight of the fans. Fielding was sharp by both teams, but Chicago benefitted from some timely hits to take the game, 7–4. The following day, cold and windy weather kept the crowd to about 600 and Chicago won again, this time 5–3, with Larry Corcoran besting Weidman. Burns debuted for Detroit on May 3 and was hit hard, surrendering 12 hits in Chicago's 10–1 win and a sweep of the series.

The two clubs met again in Chicago's newly upgraded Lake Front Park for three games beginning May 5. This time, Detroit spoiled Chicago's party. A crowd of 5,000 saw Detroit take Chicago's home opener, 3–2, the winning run crossing home plate in the ninth inning when Hanlon hit the ball over the right field fence. Under local ground rules it was only a double because the fence was short. Weidman scored on the play and registered eight strikeouts, while Detroit batters touched up Corcoran for eight hits. Uncharacteristically, Chicago was guilty of sloppy play, committing eight errors. Weidman pitched a one-hitter the following day when Detroit blanked the White Stockings, 7–0. Goldsmith surrendered 10 hits in the losing cause. It was the first time Chicago had been shut out on its home grounds since Detroit's 2–0 win on August 13, 1881. The final game of the series was on May 9, and Weidman returned to pitch, disappointing the 1,500 spectators who braved cold, wet conditions only to see the White Stockings hammered, 17–7, in a slugfest. This marked the first time in four years the powerful Chicago club had been swept in three games at home.[4] Every Wolverine had at least one hit, with triples recorded by Bennett, Houck, Mansell, Quest and Wood. Home field had produced no advantage for either team. Detroit, with three wins and three losses against the defending champions, found itself tied for second place.

The Wolverines returned to Recreation Park and downed New York's Gothams, 12–1 and 9–5, but the third game of the series was rained out. In the 9–5 game, Burns recorded his first major league win despite 10 fielding errors behind him. On May 12, because of optimism produced by the strong start, directors of the Detroit club declared a dividend of 25 percent for shareholders, to be paid from funds accumulated during the team's first two years of operation. Philadelphia was next in town for a series beginning May 15, and the Quakers took the opener, 4–3, tagging Burns with the loss. The following day, Detroit needed 11 innings to defeat the visitors, 11–10, in a sloppily played affair with newcomer Frank McIntyre picking up the win in his only appearance for Detroit. He replaced Weidman, who attended his brother's funeral. The rubber match with Philadelphia was May 17, when Detroit pounded Jack Neagle for 14 hits to take the game, 12–6. On May 18, the rained-out game from May 14 with New York was played, with the Gothams winning, 11–6, in what the *Free Press* described as an "appalling and indescribable" contest because of sloppy fielding.[5]

After the three series against Chicago, New York and Philadelphia, Detroit had seven wins, good for fourth place. The Wolverines won four out of their next five home games, taking two from Providence and then two out of three from Boston, renamed the Beaneaters this season, and rose briefly to a tie for first place. During the Boston series, Detroit signed a young pitcher named George Radbourn, 27, a cousin of Providence ace Hoss Radbourn. The cousins never faced each other, however. Detroit's Radbourn won in his first appearance, a 5–2 victory on May 30 over the Gothams in New York. But he lost by large scores in his next two outings and was released. His major league career consisted of three games. That was 524 games fewer, and 308 wins shy of cousin Hoss, who was inducted into the Hall of Fame in 1939.

As they embarked on a lengthy Eastern road trip, the Wolverines were tied for third place with Providence, both clubs with 11 wins and six losses. The trip was a disaster and dropped them to sixth place. Boston swept them in a four-game series, as did Providence. Then Cleveland and Buffalo each took two out of three games played in their cities. On June 9 in Boston, the Beaneaters clobbered Weidman and his replacement, Mansell, the pair giving up 29 hits in a 30–8 mismatch in which Detroit made 11 errors. Weidman was batted hard by both Boston and Providence, and Burns had a bad outing against the Beaneaters. On June 12 in Boston, Burns allowed 19 hits, at least one to each Beaneater, and Boston walloped Detroit, 20–9. Quest sprained a leg, Burns was benched briefly, and Weidman was granted a brief leave of absence because of a sore and badly bruised arm and shoulder.

The downward slide continued. Manager Chapman began looking for another pitcher, disappointed in the play of Burns and concerned about Weidman's performance. He considered signing a promising young Canadian, Billy Mountjoy, who was attracting attention with his success in Port Huron, just north of Detroit, but Chapman found an interesting lefty instead. He was Boston-area amateur Fred "Dupee" Shaw, 24, who could also play right field. Shaw made his pitching debut on June 22 when Cleveland edged Detroit, 9–8. Detroit committed 13 errors behind him, prompting the *Free Press* to note the "wretched fielding game yesterday, which must have made poor Shaw wish he had never learned to pitch."[6] He gave up five hits in his second start three days later when Detroit was blanked, 2–0, by Buffalo's Pud Galvin. In the last game on the road trip, June 26 in Buffalo, Shaw notched his first victory when the Wolverines won, 8–3. The *Free Press* enjoyed the victory over George Derby of the Bisons, Detroit's underwhelming pitcher from 1882, and praised Shaw, "who seems to be the man Chapman has been hunting for, and who is certainly doing phenomenal work in the box for an amateur of the most pronounced description, [and] proved as much a puzzler to the Bisons as on Monday [the 2–0 shutout]."[7] Meanwhile, right fielder Mansell was released for poor play.

Back in Detroit, the Wolverines played host to Chicago on June 27 and lost, 6–2, in yet another bad outing for Weidman. The loss dropped Detroit to seventh place in the standings, with a record of 17 wins and 23 losses. However, the Wolverines remained comfortably ahead of the tail-ender Philadelphia Quakers, who had managed a mere nine wins and 32 losses in their miserable first season in the League. Only 900 cranks attended the game, far fewer spectators than Chicago-Detroit clashes traditionally attracted. The *Detroit Free Press* noted that the team was greeted with applause that was "neither very tumultuous or prolonged."

> The tumble the club has taken from the top nearly to the bottom of the league ladder since it left home, has noticeably cooled the ardor of their admirers, who would much prefer to see them win a wretched game than lose a brilliant one. The late President [William] Hulbert reflected Detroit sentiment when he once said, "I don't care anything about the base hits and errors. If we win the game, it is a good one; if we lose it, it is a poor one."[8]

There would be plenty of poor ones ahead for Detroit. It lost 16 of the 28 games in its home stand before hitting the road again. The team, mired in seventh place, might have dropped to last if Philadelphia hadn't been playing even worse. By the end of July, speculation was rampant that two or three Wolverines would be released for playing poorly on purpose, hoping to be released so they could accept attractive offers from other clubs. But Chapman was wise to such things. He declared: "I shall release no one; but shall suspend them instead."[9]

Cleveland swept four games from Detroit, including a July 2 drubbing, 15–5, in which Burns allowed 18 hits. From June 6 to July 4, the Wolverines managed only two wins against 19 losses. Later in the season a similar stretch of futility was recorded. Providence swept a four-game series in the middle of the month, just after captain Quest was suspended for poor play by Chapman. Detroit shut out New York twice, 1–0 and 2–0, on July 25 and July 26, with Weidman and Shaw earning one victory apiece, rare bright spots in what had become a tough month. Another noteworthy win came on July 28, when Detroit defeated New York and its rookie pitcher, "Tip" O'Neill, the Canadian who wasn't deemed quite ready for the big time two years earlier when he tried out for Detroit. O'Neill would win five games and lose 12 in his debut season with the Gothams. Detroit also earned three victories from the struggling Philadelphia Quakers. At the end of July, some ominous news came when the team's guiding light, William G. Thompson, let it be known he did not "yearn" to return as club president for another year.[10] Even the team's most ardent booster was becoming disillusioned with its performance.

On August 2, Jack Jones appeared as Detroit's pitcher in a 6–2 win over Philadelphia. The 22-year-old hurler for Yale University would appear in 12 Wolverines games, winning six of them and losing five with one no-decision. Two days later, with Weidman pitching, Detroit was embarrassed by cellar-dwelling Philadelphia in a 6–0 shutout. This gave the Quakers their 13th win of the season, compared to 27 for the Wolverines. Three games with third-place Chicago capped Detroit's home stand, and the Wolverines surprised by taking two of them, including a 6–0 shutout August 7 when Weidman allowed the powerful White Stockings only five hits, while Goldsmith gave up 12. The next day, Shaw led Detroit to a 5–1 win, helped by 18 fly ball outs and 11 Chicago errors. Despite 10 Chicago errors on August 9, Chicago won, 6–3, while Bennett and Powell sat out with injuries.

As the ball club left town for games in Cleveland and Buffalo, directors expressed their confidence in manager Chapman, despite the team's poor showing. They decided to renew his contract for another year, it being noted that he "has handled the team with excellent judgment, and has made many friends. He is well-liked by players, and is known among them as a square, upright manager."[11]

The Wolverines took three out of four games in Cleveland, which had risen to first place, with Jones throwing a 5–0 shutout on August 14. But they followed that up by losing four in a row to fifth-place Buffalo before returning home for their final home stand of nine games against the same two teams. Detroit defeated Buffalo twice, took one game from Cleveland, and tied one game with each. Crowds were small, with several games drawing only 800 spectators. The Wolverines seemed as dispirited as their supporters, committing 14 errors in a 6–4 loss to Buffalo on August 30. Weidman was again complaining that his arm was sore from overwork, while Quest, whose play was lethargic after returning from his leg injury, was released and signed with St. Louis of the American Association. The last game of the season at Recreation Park was a 12–4 loss to Buffalo, when Shaw pitched poorly and Bennett remained out of the lineup with a hand injury. The *Detroit Free Press* seemed relieved: "So far as Detroit is concerned, the season of 1883 is over. So far as the Detroits are concerned, there yet remain four weeks in which to close their inglorious career."[12]

In Chicago, the White Stockings walloped Detroit four straight times, by scores of 13–1, 14–1, 26–6, and 12–8. In the 26–6 game on September 6, Chicago belted 29 hits off Weidman and Burns. A major league record 18 runs crossed home plate in the seventh inning alone. The statistics apparently overwhelmed the Western Union Telegraph operator, drawing the ire of *Detroit Free Press* sports editor Charles Mathison, who complained bitterly about the "very ludicrous deformity" of the "bob-tailed" game report transmitted to Detroit.[13] With its sweep of Detroit, Chicago reached first place in the League standings, a position it would have trouble retaining. Providence swept Detroit in a three-game series, with the Wolverines still plagued by sloppy fielding. Another three-game sweep followed at the hands of the Beaneaters, which solidified Boston's hold on first place. Detroit defeated the still-dreadful Quakers in Philadelphia, 9–3, on September 21, to snap a losing streak that had grown to 12 games. Detroit then won four of its last six games, tying one with Philadelphia and losing the final game of the season on September 29 to sixth-place New York by a score of 7–2.

Detroit ended 1883 in seventh place, 23 games back of pennant-winner Boston, but a comfortable 23 games ahead of the Quakers. While the 40 wins and 58 losses meant Detroit had recorded only two victories fewer than in 1882, the schedule had been increased from 84 games to 98. Its winningest pitcher, Weidman, had 20 wins and 24 losses, double the victories of Shaw. Detroit announced it was reserving 10 players for the following season: Weidman, Shaw, Burns, Bennett, Trott, Powell, Houck, Farrell, Hanlon, and Wood. Two of them would soon be gone; shortstop Sadie Houck signed with Philadelphia in November, and catcher Sam Trott was released in December and signed by Baltimore's new Union League team. The season was considered a financial success, however, despite poor weather in the early going and poor play later on, both of which had hurt attendance.

In a post-season interview, manager Chapman expressed optimism for 1884, when he would start spring training in the South to ensure that his men were ready for the season. He conceded he had received three "very good offers" to manage in other cities, but he had opted to stay put. "I like the city and it suits me to stay."[14]

At the National League meeting in November, the constitution was amended to allow players to sign contracts with new clubs 10 days after the release notice from their previous club was received by the League office. Much discussion centered on the aggressive pursuit of League players by other organizations, but no consensus emerged on how to deal with it. It was hoped that some good would come from the peaceful coexistence pact known as the National Agreement, an update of the Tripartite Agreement, that had been signed in late October between the League and the American Association. Aside from those issues, a major rule change was approved. The last restriction on arm motion by pitchers was removed, which meant an overhand delivery was now permitted. But the pitching distance remained at 50 feet. At one point in deliberations, Detroit's president Thompson stormed out of the meeting, upset at a proposal to pay League president Abraham Mills a salary of $4,000 annually. Thompson said he could not support such pay for comparatively little work. Despite his protest, his fellow magnates returned him as a director.[15] Thompson had not sought a third term as Detroit mayor, and he had already indicated that he wasn't anxious for another term as president of the Wolverines, so it wasn't expected that he would remain a director for long.

The cozy relationship that appeared to be developing between the National League and American Association led to the creation of yet another professional baseball league for 1884, the Union Association. The driving force behind it was Henry Lucas, a 26-year-old member of a prominent St. Louis family. A millionaire because of his shipping and real estate interests, he detested the reserve clause and sought the acclaim of being a ball team owner. Lucas cultivated player dislike of the reserve clause and helped establish teams in St. Louis, Chicago, Cincinnati, Baltimore, Boston, Washington, Philadelphia and tiny Altoona, Pennsylvania (which lasted only six weeks). Lucas once famously intoned: "I am the Union Association. Whatever I do is right."[16] The Union Association did not recognize the reserve rule and openly raided other teams for players. The St. Louis Maroons, owned by Lucas, won the one and only pennant before the new loop, which was characterized by shifting franchises and instability, went out of existence when the National League accepted Lucas and his Maroons for 1885.[17] Historians, strangely, consider Lucas' vanity loop of one-year duration as a major league, a status withheld from the more successful International Association of 1877–1878, which was renamed the National Base-Ball Association for 1879–1880.

Jack Chapman signed most of his 1883 players to new contracts for 1884 and pursued some interesting prospects, few of whom would pan out. They included a couple of young men from Hamilton, Ontario, shortstop Arthur "Addie" Richardson and catcher Fred Wood, Massachusetts native and second baseman Charles Maxwell, and right fielder Walt Walker of Berlin, Michigan. The most promising of the group, Wood, saw service in 12 games, while Walker played once and Richardson and Maxwell didn't make the cut. Meanwhile, the *Cincinnati Enquirer* reported that first baseman Martin Powell refused to return to Detroit because he didn't like team president Thompson. The *Detroit Free Press* suggested it was a case of sour grapes and Powell wasn't wanted because of his excessive salary demands.[18] Powell, like many other disgruntled players of the day, jumped to the new Union Association. He signed with the Cincinnati Outlaw Reds for $2,500. To replace Powell, Chapman hired Milt Scott, 23, who had played with Fort Wayne of the Northwestern League in 1883 and with Chicago in 1882. Scott would become a reliable fixture for Detroit at first base. Another Fort Wayne player, Bill Geiss, 25, of Chicago, was signed to become a change pitcher, but his work at second base was so good he pitched in only one game, a no-decision. Also signed was Frank Meinke, 20, of Chicago, to play third base, shortstop, and right field. But Meinke also pitched, circumstances calling him to do so in 35 of the 92 games he played, posting eight wins and 23 losses. With the team mostly set, the Wolverines settled on two uniforms for 1884, one of them gray with red trim, the other white with brown trim.

On the eve of the new season, the fourth annual meeting of the Detroit Base Ball Association was held on March 30, and Thompson was back as pres-

Jack Chapman (in street clothes) managed the Wolverines to a last-place finish in 1884. To his immediate left is Ned Hanlon and to his immediate right appears to be pitcher Pretzels Getzien. At the far right, the player is likely catcher Charlie Bennett, and second from left may be outfielder George Wood. Given the quality of the image, it is difficult to identify the remaining players with certainty. They include Frank Meinke, Dupee Shaw, Milt Scott, Joe Farrell, Stump Weidman and Bill Geiss (National Baseball Hall of Fame Library, Cooperstown, New York).

ident, despite some earlier indications he had tired of the job. Total receipts for the club in 1883 had been $53,595.48, and after all expenses had been paid, including improvements to Recreation Park, the net profit for the year amounted to a modest $34.57.[19] It was fervently hoped that greater success on the field would boost that bottom line.

As instructed by Chapman, the Wolverines reported for spring camp April 1 in Richmond, Virginia. By the end of the first week, exhibition games began, first with Richmond, and then it was on to Washington, Baltimore, Allegheny (Pittsburgh), Indianapolis, various Pennsylvania clubs, Trenton, New Jersey, and Brooklyn, before the season opened. Detroit proved a good draw during its exhibition tour and the club was reported to be "away ahead financially," despite some poor weather and cancelled games.[20]

The Wolverines began League play on May 1 in Philadelphia. Three thousand spectators were pleased when the former doormat Quakers pounded Detroit's Stump Weidman for six runs in the first inning and four more in the second on their way to a 13–2 romp over the visitors. Detroit committed 14 errors, suggesting that not all the club's rust had been shaken off down South. The Wolverines lost 10 more games against Philadelphia, New York, Providence and Boston before Dupee Shaw led them to a 4–2 win over the Beaneaters on May 16. In their tenth loss of the season, on May 14, Hoss Radbourn allowed only five hits and belted five himself as the Providence Grays won, 25–3. In their worst loss in history, Detroit committed 18 errors, including five by newcomer Fred Wood in right field. He was released after two more games. Joe Farrell, playing third base, also made five errors, but kept his job. The victory was the most lopsided result of the entire National League season.

The last four games of the season-opening road trip closed out May in Chicago, where Detroit lost, 15–5, 11–10 and 12–2, before taking the final game, 12–6. In the May 29 series opener, which was Opening Day in Chicago, five White Stockings batters launched the ball over the short, 180-foot left field fence. Under new ground rules this year devised by Chicago captain Cap Anson, they were to be considered home runs instead of doubles, as in the past. After the 1884 season, likely in response to the situation in Chicago, the minimum distance to outfield fences in League parks was set at 210 feet. In the meantime, Chicago capitalized on their hit-friendly confines at Lake Front Park with 142 home runs compared to 13 in 1883.[21] After a tough 11–10 Wolverines loss on the morning of May 30, Decoration Day, Ned Williamson, the White Stockings' third baseman, pounded three home runs in his team's 12–2 second win of the day. For the season, Williamson would hit 27 round-trippers, a total not exceeded until Babe Ruth of the Red Sox hit 29 in 1919. All but two of them were hit in Lake Front Park, while Ruth received no help from short fences. On May 31, Detroit salvaged a rare win when Chicago pitcher Larry Corcoran allowed 17 hits, including two home runs by Wolverines left fielder George Wood.

The 1884 season was looking like a repeat of 1883, with Detroit dropping 20 of 24 games before its first appearance at home. Leaving Chicago, the Wolverines were dead last, 16 games back of League-leading Providence and 3½ games behind seventh-place Philadelphia. The *Free Press* conceded the race for the pennant had been "disastrous" to date, but observed that finding top-notch players had been difficult with three major professional leagues competing for talent.[22] For the June 2 home opener, the Wolverines attracted 1,500 spectators to Recreation Park, despite competition in the city that day from Adam Forepaugh's Circus and Menagerie, featuring a white elephant. The visitors were Cleveland, now widely known as the Blues. The Wolverines put on an entertaining show of their own at their freshly scrubbed park on a warm, sunny afternoon. Wood homered in the first inning and Hanlon did the same in the eighth in a 9–2 Detroit win. Detroit took only one more game in the four-game set before welcoming Buffalo to town. After defeating the Bisons, 11–5, on June 6, Detroit dropped the next two to the visitors. A four-game series with Chicago began with an 8–4 loss on June 11. Weidman and Shaw each picked up a win before Weidman lost, 9–4, on June 14, giving up 13 hits with 11 errors made behind him. Afterward, he complained of a sore arm and was relegated to right field for nearly two months before he was able to pitch again.

Detroit remained in last place, two games behind Cleveland and Philadelphia, and the loss of a pitcher didn't help manager Chapman's state of mind. Within days he signed amateur Frank Brill, 20, who had been pitching with the Monitor Club in New York. Brill's first appearance was a 4–3 loss to Providence on June 23, and he proved a disappointment for the season, with only two wins and 10 losses for Detroit. Pitching would prove to be an ongoing headache for Chapman. Shaw had been pitching poorly and making uncharacteristic errors, at one point his delivery described as "very feeble" in a July 8 loss of 11–4 to Philadelphia.[23] Suspicions arose about the hurler. The next day, he was fined $30 for his listless play. That night, Shaw boarded a train for his home in Boston, where it was soon learned that he had joined the Reds club of the Union Association. With Detroit, his record had been nine wins and 18 losses, but he would lead the Boston pitching staff with 21 wins and 15 losses. He would be blacklisted by the League for jumping his contract.

In a rare bright spot for the season, Detroit hammered visiting Chicago, 14–0, on July 15, but only 500 cranks witnessed it. It was the worst drubbing the White Stockings suffered all season. Brill was sharp, allowing only five hits to earn the shutout. Chicago may have been guilty of treating Detroit like the League doormat it had become when it fielded a rookie pitcher. He was Mike Corcoran, 25, an older brother of the White Stockings' reliable hurler, Larry Corcoran, 24, who rotated pitching duties with Fred Goldsmith. He walked seven Wolverines and gave up a homer and 16 hits. The newcomer's performance earned him a release after just the one game. His sibling would hold the family bragging rights in baseball, playing for eight years, pitching 277 games and winning 177.

Weidman's arm was better, and he returned to pitch on August 2 against Buffalo in Recreation Park. Bisons hurler Pud Galvin was particularly sharp that day, however, and allowed only a single to Bennett. Meanwhile, Dan Brouthers and Jack Rowe, two of Buffalo's "Big Four" batters, both homered off Weidman to produce a final score of 2–0. Weidman could thank his lucky stars he didn't appear in the next game on August 4, when Meinke took the ball and surrendered 22 hits to the hard-hitting Bisons. Galvin completely dominated Detroit batters and set them down, one-two-three, for eight innings. In the ninth, with one out, new Detroit shortstop Henry Buker hit a grounder to third baseman Deacon White, who made a perfect throw to Brouthers at first base. But the big man muffed the ball on what should have been a routine out, giving Detroit its first base runner. Galvin then struck out the next two batters to end the game with a no-hitter. He came within a whisker of pitching a perfect game, facing 28 batters instead of the minimum 27 because of Brouthers' error. The final score was 18–0. Luckily, only 800 fans were there to witness the spectacle. Buffalo shut out Detroit and Weidman again, 9–0, on August 7, and won 14–2 the next day, with Galvin throwing a three-hitter to extend Detroit's losing streak to eight games. In the second game that day, the Wolverines, with Weidman pitching, downed the Bisons 1–0 in 12 innings to salvage one win in the

Charles "Pretzels" Getzien was a reliable pitcher for the Wolverines. The German-born right-hander could be relied upon when other hurlers failed. His surname, originally Goetzien, was often misspelled as Getzein, and in this instance as Getzin. His nickname came from the twist he imparted on his curveballs. He learned the game as a boy in Chicago, where his family settled (Library of Congress).

five-game series. The win ended Galvin's impressive scoreless-inning streak at 38. After picking up a win from Cleveland, a 12-game losing skid ensued, during which Chapman found yet another pitcher. Charles Getzien (often misspelled Getzein) made his debut on August 13 when Detroit lost, 1–0, to Cleveland. The 20-year-old was born in Germany, but his family had moved to Chicago and he had pitched with Grand Rapids in the Northwestern League. He picked up the nickname "Pretzels" because of the twist he imparted on his curveballs. Getzien lost his first eight starts with Detroit before winning his first game on September 20, a 7–1 win over Hoss Radbourn and Providence. He was stellar on October 1, when he didn't allow a hit as Detroit shut out Philadelphia in a rain-shortened, six-inning game. Getzien's record for 1884 was five wins and 12 losses, but after that inauspicious first season he would become a mainstay in Detroit for years to come.

As the season wound down with Detroit still mired in last place, manager Chapman tried several new players, but none showed any particular promise. At one time or another during the season, 26 players donned the Wolverines uniform, and several more were released before they had the chance to do so. With three major professional leagues fielding 34 teams, available players were in short supply, especially good ones. Losses continued to pile up. After a nine-game losing streak in mid–September, Detroit went .500 until the end of the season for an overall record of 28 wins and 84 losses. That left the Wolverines seven games back of seventh-place Cleveland and a whopping 56 games behind pennant-winner Providence. The Grays went on to defeat the New York Metropolitans of the AA three games to none in the first "world's series," taking full advantage of their ace hurler, Hoss Radbourn. The best Detroit pitcher had been the departed Shaw, with nine wins, while Meinke managed only eight.

Meanwhile, faced with small crowds at Recreation Park, directors of the club were growing concerned about its continued viability. At a meeting on September 22, directors and shareholders decided to reorganize the team and remain in the League, putting new directors and management in place. A concerted effort would be made to find better players, a move made somewhat easier in coming months with the collapse of the Union Association, whose players flooded the market. Adding to the supply, the American Association cut back to eight teams from 12. Detroit directors decided to increase the capital stock from $5,000 to $10,000 and appointed local businessman Frederick K. Stearns and lawyer William J. Gray to find buyers. The pair received subscriptions for $600 on the spot, it was reported.[24] Within days, nearly three-quarters of the new shares had been sold, Stearns told the *Free Press*, which went on to discuss the need for change:

The present Board of Directors, while still taking a lively interest in the club, and ready to assist it at all times, do not longer desire to take an active part in its management. They feel that they have done their share in that respect, and also that it may be for the best interests of the club to intrust [sic] its fortunes to younger men who are, or have been, players. It is believed that men who have a practical knowledge of the game will infuse an interest into it that has been lacking of late.[25]

The paper suggested that Joseph A. Marsh, president of the Cass Club, and Fred Stearns, a former infielder with the University of Michigan nine and the Detroit Aetnas, would likely be among the new directors to assume leadership of the club. Marsh was manager of the Detroit News Company, a wholesale purveyor of periodicals, books, and stationery supplies. Stearns was the son of Frederick Stearns, president of Frederick Stearns and Company, a leading pharmaceutical manufacturing firm that was shipping its medicines around the world.[26] The younger Stearns was being groomed to take over the family firm.

On October 7, a week before the season ended, the Detroit club held its annual meeting and announced that the organization was $700 in debt. President Thompson noted that it had started the season with $9,000 worth of property it still owned and $6,200 in cash, which now was all gone. He said poor attendance was responsible for the red ink and that the team needed an average attendance of 1,000 at its home games to turn a profit. Stearns and Gray reported they had little trouble raising $5,000 in new capital, but that two directors were resisting the reorganization of club affairs.[27] A new effort would have to be launched.

The Wolverines, fittingly, lost their final game of their dreadful season to New York, 4–3, prompting the *Detroit Free Press* to pronounce: "At last the long agony is over; the base ball season of 1884 is closed, and the Detroit club stands in the league where stands the fool in his class." It blamed poor behavior by the players, primarily late-night carousing, showing up drunk for some games and playing like "chumps," thereby losing patronage from Detroiters. It urged the new board to ensure that management would fine all players who flouted the rules, noting that manager Cap Anson in Chicago kept his players in line with steep financial penalties.

The newspaper then turned to club president Thompson for his views on the just-closed season. Clearly, he was fed up, and he pulled no punches with a frankness that was brutal.

> Four years ago, it seemed to me that Detroit ought to have a professional base ball club. I interested Mr. Hendrie, Mr. McMillan, Mr. Newberry, Mr. Chittenden, Mr. Brush and other capitalists in the scheme, and was assured of abundant funding. I spent my money and my time in incorporating the association and securing its admission to the league. We engaged the best players we could get, and paid them larger salaries than they ever before received, and from time to time since then we

have advanced the pay of those we have reserved. Every honorable means has been resorted to in endeavors to strengthen the team, and yet in spite of all our efforts we have been unable to keep pace with the other clubs. In 1881 we finished fourth in the race, in 1882 sixth, in 1883 seventh, and this year we are at the tail.

To what causes do you attribute the poor success?

To the dishonesty and ungratefulness of players. They contract with us, at a salary larger than the income of a large majority of professional men, to remain sober and play the best ball of which they are capable. We have kept our faith with them, but they have not with us. I do not believe there is a league team in the country that has not among its members two or three who will not throw a game at any time in the interest of the pool box [betting]. The rest are honest, but are powerless to win games if the two or three, or even one of them, play to lose. They are not honorable enough to keep their contracts, and if any one speaks to them about it, they reply as impatient as a bootblack. Only two or three months ago I said to one of them, who hadn't made a hit in six weeks, "What's the matter with you? You are not batting as well as you ought," and he instantly responded: "If you do not like the way I play ball you can give me my release. I can get more salary elsewhere!" and that very man's salary has been nearly doubled since he came here.

As a class, always excepting those who are worthy and honest, I believe them to be in the most ungrateful set of men I ever met, and I am done with them. Just as soon as the stockholders elected a new Board of Directors I shall retire from base ball, and I shall never again, directly or indirectly, employ a man I cannot discharge. Imagine a cashier, book-keeper, reporter or employe [sic] in any other walk of life, saying to his employer, "If you don't like my style, you can do the other thing!" And yet these fellows want the earth for their services and then violate every provision in their contracts and give no adequate return for the money they are paid. They are paid from $12 to $25 each per game they play, and then go and sell the games to the pool-box gamblers. I'm done with them![28]

That was quite a parting shot from the man who had founded the team and invested so much time and energy in it. On November 16, the Detroit directors met and authorized Thompson to attend the National League's annual meeting on November 19 and 20 in New York, on the understanding it would be his last. In New York, Thompson declined to continue as a director of the League, so a position was reserved for a director from Detroit to be named later. Abraham Mills stepped down as League president, replaced by Nick Young, its secretary. Delegates rejected an appeal by players, including Dupee Shaw, for reinstatement. Shaw and others had been blacklisted for jumping to the Union Association while still under contract to League clubs. In business relating to rules, a bid to outlaw overhand pitching failed, but a compromise was reached requiring the pitcher to keep both feet on the ground at the start of his delivery to moderate the speed the new technique could produce. It never occurred to anyone to increase the pitching distance from 50 feet in a bid to help batters. That move was delayed until 1893, when the 60-feet-six-inches of today's game was introduced. In yet another change, the League directed home teams to provide separate benches for the visiting team, ending the practice of sharing a common bench.

In late December, the financially shaky Cleveland team folded. Its Kennard Street Park was small and inadequate, and after losing three of its stars to the Union Association team in Cincinnati it drew poor crowds. An 8–1 loss to Providence on October 11 was the Blue Stockings' final game in the National League after a six-year run. Cleveland was the only League casualty in the three-way fight between the League, the National Association and the Union Association. Henry Lucas, the driving force behind the Union Association and owner of St. Louis, bought the Cleveland franchise for $2,500 so his Maroons could replace the Blues in the League.[29] The deal didn't include the players, who were scooped up by Brooklyn. Partly to appease Lucas, the League in April reinstated the blacklisted players who had jumped to the Union Association and imposed fines on them instead. The players included Dupee Shaw, formerly of Detroit, and McCormick, Briody and Glasscock, formerly of Cleveland, all of whom had to pay $1,000 apiece.[30]

January 1885 was a month of uncertainty for baseball in Detroit. Amid rumors of Lucas buying Cleveland so he could enter the League, another surfaced that Thorner in Cincinnati was planning to buy several Detroit players— or perhaps the entire franchise. "This Rattles Us," the *Detroit Free Press* said in its headline, reporting a *New York Times* story about the plan, which *Free Press* sources seemed to confirm.[31] On January 7, Detroit shareholders made it clear that the team would remain in the League and raised the last of the $5,000 in new stock. Hotel proprietor William Chittenden, a new director, was named the League director on behalf of the club. At a special National League meeting on January 10 in New York, St. Louis was admitted and directors voted to keep Detroit. A director of the Boston Beaneaters had been in Detroit, ready to scoop up catcher Charlie Bennett and other players if Detroit disbanded. He went home.[32] On January 19, Detroit shareholders met again and accepted the resignation of president William Thompson and all other directors, pending election of their replacements. The affairs of the club would be reorganized with new directors at its helm. They included Joseph A. Marsh and Frederick K. Stearns. At the end of the month, directors elected Marsh as president, and the hunt for a new team manager began in earnest. The Thompson era was over. He sold all his stock and donated $100 to the club treasury before walking away. The former mayor would confine his interest in sport to horse racing, and a few months later he became vice-president of the Detroit Driving Club.

Thompson, and many Detroiters, were disappointed that the Wolverines' fortunes had had slipped so much during their four years of League play. The new directors were determined to turn things around and within days found a familiar face to replace manager Jack Chapman, who went to Buffalo in 1885 to take over managing duties from Pud Galvin. The new manager was 29-year-old Charlie Morton, a member of Detroit's Hollinger Nine in 1979, who played outfield and third base. After that season, Morton had moved to Cleveland but failed to make the roster there. He became a journeyman player for AA clubs in Allegheny (Pittsburgh), St. Louis and Toledo. A player-manager in Toledo, Morton would fill the same role in Detroit. In his first newspaper interview, the new manager praised the quality of players in Detroit, the fine grounds at Recreation Park, and Detroit as a baseball city. He said spring training would be conducted in the South. "I think the prospects are growing brighter every day, and I look forward to a prosperous season," Morton said.

The Wolverines, their directors and supporters all had reasons to be hopeful. After occupying the basement of the National League, there was nowhere to go but up.

7

Retooling

Joseph A. Marsh, the new president of the Detroit Base Ball Club, upped his game when he moved from leading the Cass Club amateur nine to assume the same post with the Wolverines. He had played baseball but was more of a supporter of the game than an athlete. Considered an intelligent man with sound judgment, Marsh hoped to turn around the fortunes of the Wolverines, about whom many Detroiters had grown apathetic. His predecessor's outburst about players left a pall of negativity surrounding the club, and rumors that the National League might still want to replace it didn't help. As a businessman, Marsh knew the way to turn a profit was to give the public what it wanted. In baseball, that meant a winner. He was already winning in business after establishing the Detroit News Company, a branch of the American News Company of New York, in 1876. This was three years after James Edward Scripps published his first edition of the *Detroit News* daily newspaper to compete with the *Detroit Free Press,* founded 45 years earlier. Sharing the same name, the firms operated by Scripps and Marsh were sometimes confused. Marsh's company was a wholesaler of books, daily, weekly and monthly periodicals, stationery and business supplies. He did business throughout Michigan, Ohio, Indiana and Illinois, with a network of travelling salesmen. By the mid–1880s, his downtown Detroit operation on West Larned Street had grown to about 30 employees.[1]

While Marsh was the titular head of the baseball club, its driving force was another new director, Frederick Kimball Stearns. He would replace Marsh as president a bit more than 18 months later. Stearns, a major shareholder, also had access to enough money to transform the Wolverines from a woebegone basement dweller on the brink of extinction, to the very top of the professional baseball world. He certainly had the desire to do so. More than 100 years later, the New York Yankees were driven by a free-spending activist owner named

George Steinbrenner, who did everything in his power to get his team to the top of the baseball heap—and keep it there. For the Detroit Wolverines, beginning with the 1885 season, Stearns became their Steinbrenner. Stearns had excelled at the game himself and knew it well. And he was determined to make Detroit a winner.

Stearns was born in Buffalo on December 6, 1854, to Frederick and Eliza (Kimball) Stearns, and within months the family moved to Detroit, where the senior Stearns established a drug business with a local partner. Southeastern Michigan had large deposits of chemicals and salt, which gave birth to a thriving pharmaceutical industry, and Stearns was among its leaders. The new firm won many contracts to supply Michigan troops during the Civil War, and it prospered. Stearns took full control of the operation whose "non-secret" medicines clearly indicated their components, unlike most of its competitors, who shrouded their concoctions in secrecy. The popularity of these "non-secret" medicines saw them stocked by most retail pharmacists across the United States and Canada. Stearns was not all about business, however, and at some point developed an interest in baseball in his new home. In 1865, the Michigan State Base Ball Association was formed and plans were laid for a state championship to be held during the Michigan State Fair in late September in Adrian. A Detroit jeweler created a silver goblet to be presented to the champions, valued at $80. It featured three miniature bats, a silver ball, and bases. The impressive trophy was displayed during that summer in the window of Frederick Stearns' drugstore at 71 Woodward Avenue.[2]

Frederick K. Stearns had a passion for baseball and played the game when he attended the University of Michigan in the 1870s. He connected with the Detroit Base Ball Club, where he became a major shareholder and president. His drive and determination to produce a winner in the City of the Straits paid dividends (from *Detroit in History and Commerce* by James J. Mitchell, Detroit: Rogers and Thorpe, 1891).

7. Retooling

Frederick Stearns played second base for the University of Michigan baseball team. He appears at the bottom left in this photograph of the 1875 nine. During the summertime, Stearns and several of the players joined the amateur Aetnas in Detroit. The son of a leading pharmaceutical manufacturer, Stearns became president of the Detroit Wolverines and led them to the pennant of the National League and the world's series championship in 1887 (Bentley Historical Library, University of Michigan).

His 10-year-old son Freddie was no doubt among the many admirers of the goblet, which would be awarded to the amateur Detroit Base Ball Club.

The young Stearns attended Philo M. Patterson's private school, known as the Detroit Classical and Mathematical School, on Griswold Street. The school, founded in 1860, fielded its first baseball team in 1869, the Hunkidori Club, and played its inaugural game in June on a lot at Second and Bagg Streets. The Hunkidoris defeated the Velocipedes, 27–14. The following summer, boys at the school established the Nobby Base Ball Club (later to become the Aetnas). Among their founding members was Frederick Kimball Stearns, aged 15. Their home field was a vacant lot on Fort Street near Tenth Street, and their first game, on April 15, 1870, was a 78–11 victory over another local club, the Actives.[3] Three years later, Stearns enrolled at the University of Michigan, by which time interest in baseball had dwindled for reasons that are not clear. Stearns recounted the grim situation that he and other players faced in Ann Arbor in a story published years later by the university's alumni association:

> I remember in '73 when we started to revive interest in baseball, that we had no uniforms. So I stood in line at Van Amberg's Circus, with another boy, and collected ten cents apiece from those we could who were going in. I think we raised about $80, which bought us stockings, knickers and caps, but we had to play in our own shoes and undershirts. Still we 'got there' in good shape, and [we] had one of the two best teams in the state—the Aetnas of Detroit being the other.[4]

The image of the son of a leading Detroit manufacturer begging for loose change outside a circus to clothe his baseball team is rather startling. Stearns, a second baseman, didn't see action until the 1874 season and was named team captain. Rather than play other universities, the Michigan team found opponents in several Michigan cities and became quite successful. The team didn't have a formal name, but students at the university had been calling themselves "wolverines" since about 1861, adopting the nickname from the state's unofficial symbol. Today, all University of Michigan teams are known as the Wolverines, and so linked is the name to the school that its use elsewhere has virtually disappeared.

After the school year ended, Stearns and his fellow players joined local clubs in their hometowns. Stearns hooked up with the Aetnas as an infielder. Regular opponents for the Aetnas included the Cass Club, the Mutuals of Jackson, Unas of Kalamazoo and, across the border in Ontario, the Tecumsehs of London and the Maple Leafs of Guelph. On September 2, 1875, Stearns played first base when the Aetnas lost, 7–4, to the touring Chicago White Stockings. It was his first taste of playing ball at its most competitive level, and he would remember the thrill. His 1876 season was his last at the university, but he couldn't get baseball out of his blood and continued to play whenever he could. A fierce competitor, he watched with frustration and growing impatience in the years to follow as the professional Wolverines struggled and nearly expired.

At age 29, Stearns became a director of the club and brought his formidable energy to bear in a bid to make it successful, first by selling shares to raise capital. His influence on club affairs would soon grow along with his shareholdings. When Stearns wanted something, he did what he felt was necessary to get it. A thumbnail biography published several years later shed some light on his character, noting that he "certainly has all the assurance, the force of character, and the consciousness of power necessary to dominate men ... he is argumentative, aggressive, and ... he will see to it that Frederick K. Stearns is not ignored wherever his interest lies."[5] Yet another biographer described him as a "hustler" in business. "On the theory that nothing succeeds like success, Mr. Stearns may be fitly called a successful man, as whatever he has ever interested himself in, in business or outside, he has always made a success."⁶ Shades of George Steinbrenner! Stearns was a man of action and wasted no time placing his imprint on the Wolverines.

By late March, manager Morton's roster was complete when he hired a familiar face to play second base and act as captain. Joe Quest, now 32, was back. He had been released by Detroit toward the end of the 1883 season for indifferent play after returning from a sprained leg. He joined the American Association club in St. Louis for the rest of that season and part of the next before catching on with the Pittsburgh Alleghenys. The aging infielder, once known for his sparkling play and leadership abilities, was anxious to prove he could still play the game in the League. Detroit directors were willing to gamble on the veteran. A question mark was Joe Farrell, the reliable Wolverines third baseman since 1882. His legs had swollen and he could barely move with what was later deemed to be a rheumatic condition. Morton wanted him back but realized Farrell's illness was serious. The manager knew it would take some time for Farrell to get better, so he decided to play third base himself. Morton worked out just as hard as the other players in the pre-season gymnasium work that began in March. Catcher Charlie Bennett was back, as were pitchers Stump Weidman, Pretzels Getzien and Frank Meinke. Also returning were center fielder Ned Hanlon, left fielder George Wood and first baseman Milt Scott, along with utility player Ed Gastfield, 19, of Chicago, who had appeared in 23 games in 1884. Newcomers included Jerry Moore, 30, from just across the Detroit River in Windsor, Ontario. He was a catcher and outfielder. Also new was Frank Ringo, 24, a Missourian who could catch and play infield and outfield, along with Jerry Dorgan, 29, from Connecticut, yet another catcher who also played outfield. Both Ringo and Dorgan had short stints with League or Association teams before landing in Detroit. Marr Phillips, 28, of Pittsburgh, a shortstop formerly with Indianapolis, was also new. That made for a roster of 14, excluding Farrell but including Morton. Some of the men would be around for a handful of games, others for a couple dozen. Meinke and Gastfield were gone after one appearance each, and few players would remain for the entire season, a revolving-door campaign in which 28 men donned the Wolverines uniform.

The season opener was scheduled for April 30 in Detroit with the Buffalo Bisons as guests, but the contest was rained out. The following day, 830 shivering cranks in overcoats watched the Wolverines win, 8–3. Weidman held off the big Bisons batters—Dan Brouthers, Jack Rowe, Deacon White and Hardy Richardson—which was no small feat. The foursome had earned the nickname the "Big Four" because of their success at the plate, Brouthers in particular. The previous season his average was .327, fifth best in the League, and his slugging average was first, at .563. Weidman allowed only four hits, while Buffalo's ace Pud Galvin surrendered 13. The following day, Detroit won again, 10–4, with Getzien pitching. On May 4, the Wolverines needed 11 innings to down the Bisons again, also by a 10–4 score, with Weidman again defeating Galvin. Detroit bats were working well, while the fearsome Buffalo hitters tended to hit the ball directly into the hands of the home team. A fourth game, scheduled for May 5, was also rained out, and the Bisons left town. The next opponent was St. Louis, but the weather was the real enemy. The first game of a three-game series on May 7 was washed out. Conditions were better the next day, and the Maroons delivered Detroit its first loss, 10–3. The final game, set for May 9, was also postponed because of rain. Detroit had played only four of the seven games of its opening series, with a record of 3–1.

A 16-game road trip began May 11 in Philadelphia with a 10–3 loss at the hands of the Phillies. The swing through Philadelphia, New York, Boston and Providence brought the Wolverines back to earth with a thud. Their only win came on May 27 in Boston, and few of the games were even close. Manager Morton began releasing players in an attempt to improve the fortunes of the club. By the time Detroit returned home for a four-game series against Chicago beginning June 1, its record was four wins and 16 losses, good for last place, a half-game back of Buffalo. Things didn't improve with home cooking. The White Stockings swept all four games. Detroit hit poorly, and after its 7–4 loss to end the series, the *Detroit Free Press* had harsh words for the club.

> With a few exceptions they are not playing good ball. Why this is so management should ascertain without delay. They have not come upon the diamond this week and showed by their actions that they intended to win. On the contrary, their actions would convey an impression that they had come out to perform the duty of being beaten again; an unwelcome task, but one that must be done. There has been no vim or snap in their movements and very little in their play. Yesterday's exhibition was the worst of all, and should never be repeated.[7]

The disastrous eastern trip at the start of its latest campaign echoed Detroit's 1883 and 1884 seasons. Former club president Thompson could be forgiven for heaving a sigh of relief, having washed his hands of the team. However, based on what lay ahead, it was clear that new president Marsh and director Stearns were not prepared to sit back and merely hope for better results. On June 13, when the *Free Press* reported a 17–9 trashing of Detroit at the hands of the White Stockings in Chicago, it also carried a snippet saying that the Wolverines were being eyed by Indianapolis of the Western League for possible purchase. Indianapolis manager Bill Watkins was in town after reading an Ohio newspaper account saying that Detroit was in trouble, and he was looking to buy the franchise and players. His Hoosiers were by far the strongest team in the shaky Western League, which Watkins had helped to organize. But the league's collapse seemed imminent because of its weaker links. If Watkins' successful club could buy Detroit, the reasoning went, it could gain entry to the National League. The *Free Press* tracked down a Detroit director who dismissed the notion of any sale, claiming it was a bit of mischief perpetrated by the rival *Detroit Post*. The unidentified director was unequivocal when asked what message Watkins received when he asked about buying the Wolverines: "That we have no intention of disbanding our team, or selling our franchise, neither now, at the end of the season, nor any other time. We are going to strengthen up the club at every opportunity and keep right along, for we know that a winning club here would be liberally patronized."⁸ It sounded very much like the kind of thing Frederick K. Stearns would say.

A flurry of background activity ensued, and the very next day, Detroiters learned that the situation had reversed: Indianapolis was now negotiating to transfer its club and players to Detroit. Members of the Hoosiers had promised to join Watkins in Detroit. President Marsh declined comment, saying he might have something to reveal the following week.⁹ On June 16, the *Free Press* reported that Watkins had proposed merging the two clubs after

Bill Watkins was nearly killed when he was struck in the head by a pitch while playing in Indianapolis. He recovered and became manager of the club. At the urging of Frederick Stearns, Watkins relocated to Detroit along with Indianapolis players when that club folded in 1885. He managed the Wolverines to a second-place finish in 1886, his first full year at the helm. Watkins had a penchant for fining players for poor play, and he eventually alienated them, resigning during the 1888 season (National Baseball Hall of Fame Library, Cooperstown, New York).

Detroit directors insisted they wouldn't sell: "With such a strong team on his hands, it is not to be wondered at that Manager Watkins desired to maintain the organization. The Western League was rapidly disintegrating, there is no vacancy in the American Association, and his only hope was the National

League." Detroit directors were receptive to change, and talks continued for several days. The newspaper also liked the idea, noting that the Wolverines were full of holes that needed filling: "Something must done, and quickly to close that breach and all others, if the club is to win any games worth mentioning. The gain of players from Indianapolis seems to offer the means for climbing up higher. With the consolidation of the teams there will be a vigorous weeding out." Negotiations were completed when Detroit directors agreed to pay the Indianapolis club $5,000 for the right to sign its players. It was expected that many of the Hoosiers would displace the weak performers on Detroit and that only Weidman, Bennett, Wood and Hanlon would be retained.[10] Watkins was named the new manager and Morton was let go, his final record showing seven wins and 31 losses.

On June 15, Detroit directors Frederick Stearns and John B. Molony traveled to Indianapolis to finalize the deal. They discovered that nearly every member of the team had already received telegrams offering them positions with other clubs in the National League, American Association, and the Southern and Eastern Leagues. The players assured Stearns and Molony, however, that they would sign contracts with Detroit as soon as they were able to do so. But the Western League had not yet expired, and it was a party to the National Agreement, which stipulated that players had to wait 10 days after being released before signing with a new club. The problem would not exist if the Western League had simply expired, but it was hanging on. Despite the 10-day rule, Stearns and Molony discovered that managers from other teams were tempting the players with lucrative offers, and the Detroit directors feared they might lose some of the men. Two were said to be ready to jump to Cincinnati. On June 17, the *Free Press* described the scheme that was concocted by Stearns and Molony to protect their interests and to keep the new men away from temptation:

> It was deemed best to remove them from all outside influence, and the entire team came to this city yesterday morning with the Detroit directors. From Detroit they proceeded by rail to Toronto and will there take a steamer for a pleasure trip down the St. Lawrence to the Thousand Islands. They will join the Detroit club here the middle of next week.[11]

Some accounts of the cruise differed, although *Sporting Life* reported the same destination, which would have taken the men onto Lake Ontario. One recitation, attributed to Hoosiers catcher Deacon McGuire, had the players being sent by train to Cleveland, where they boarded a little steamer that set out on Lake Erie. The captain was ordered to stay out of sight for 10 days, then deliver his human cargo to Detroit.[12] An article in the weekly *Michigan Alumnus* in 1922 featured Stearns' reminiscences about his playing days at the

University of Michigan and his time with the Wolverines. It included the story about the lake cruise. In this version, Stearns and his manager hired a yacht and toured the Indianapolis players around Lake Michigan.[13] That excursion would have first required a long rail trip across the state to get there, which was not mentioned. Yet another account specified a third body of water. The undated and unsourced newspaper clipping from 1923, published when Stearns was retired in California, described the "kidnapping" and said the men cruised on Lake St. Clair, just northeast of Detroit. "The players were infuriated," Stearns was quoted as saying. "Some of them were far from being good sailors and were sea-sick most of the time. However, we kept them practically prisoners until the time limit had expired, when we brought them back to Detroit, where they all signed their contracts."[14] Still another version of the story put the ship in Lake Huron.[15]

One of the players held prisoner, Hoosiers outfielder Sam Thompson, recalled the experience for *Free Press* writer Maclean Kennedy, who highlighted Thompson's career in a lengthy 1913 article. Kennedy described the "cruise" in colorful detail, beginning with the arrival of the Hoosiers in Detroit:

Slugger Sam Thompson was acquired from Indianapolis in 1885, along with manager Bill Watkins and other players. Thompson became one of the National League's best hitters. In 1887, despite the addition of the Big Four hitters a year earlier, he led the Wolverines in most hitting categories (National Baseball Hall of Fame Library, Cooperstown, New York).

That evening the boys from Indiana were entertained right royally. Next day a fishing trip was on the program. The players were all strongly invited. They were delighted, never for a moment dreaming that it was all a scheme and they were innocent victims.

The steamer *Annette* was placed at their disposal, laden with everything possible to make life happy. The first day and night everything was lovely: lots of fish and fun. For three days the players remained unsuspicious. About the fourth day out they began to show signs of uneasiness and getting a little suspicious, asked the captain when they would land in Detroit. But the "Cap" laughed them off. The sixth day the players got desperate, making positive demands to return to Detroit. They threatened to hang "der captain" to the yardarm; but the brave commander told them only over his dead body could they get possession of the vessel, telling them his orders were to keep them out to sea for ten days.

In a consultation they came to the conclusion to submit, as none of them could navigate a sea-going craft. Many of the boys had never been on the water before, outside sailing a raft on the duck ponds, and as no land was in sight they made up their minds to abide by orders.... They landed in the city in the forenoon, hurried to the hotel, where regular contracts were awaiting their signatures.... When Sam got his mail that had accumulated during the trip, he found offers from every baseball club in the country and many of the other players were in receipt of scores of offers. So the Detroit magnates showed some inside baseball brains and great finessing in sending the players away from all tempters for that period when they belonged to no club.[16]

Thompson, personally thrilled to sign with Detroit, recalled his forced confinement for the *Washington Post* in 1906. He described the trip in his own words, which did not include "brainy" or "finessing":

We didn't touch land during the time and no boat was allowed to come near us. We were prisoners, but well cared-for prisoners. Anything in the line of creature comforts you could find packed away on ice. We lived on the best in the market, and spent the rest of the time in fishing and playing poker, chips having very thoughtfully been provided. On the night of the tenth day, at midnight, we were all taken ashore where Watkins met us and signed us to our contracts.[17]

The contracts were signed shortly after midnight June 23, bringing to 23 the number of players Detroit had under contract. One unexpected result of the "cruise" was that the newcomers developed "sea legs," which affected their equilibrium and made practice difficult at first. The wonder of the cruise scheme is that having confined the men without their consent, Stearns didn't face criminal charges of some sort. A man unafraid of bold or unconventional steps, Stearns had accomplished what he had set out to do. And he was just beginning.

To this day, confusion lingers about the body of water on which the players spent their 10 days. Lake St. Clair is too small to lose sight of land for any length of time. But after the players were safely ashore and signed, the *Free Press* said they had spent some of their time fishing at "the Flats," a low-lying, river-delta paradise for fishermen and hunters at the north end of Lake St. Clair.[18] The paper's original story, repeated in *Sporting Life*, about the trip down the St. Lawrence and through Thousand Islands may have been a ruse to throw competing managers off the trail of the prized players. After all, *Free Press* sports editor Charles Mathison had been the official team scorer in the past and may have been complicit in the deception. Conveniently, he was also *Sporting Life's*

Detroit correspondent. He may have also wanted to keep the rival *Detroit Post* in the dark. *Post* sportswriter William White had succeeded Mathison as official scorer, and newshound Mathison enjoyed embarrassing White with his more comprehensive coverage of the Wolverines in the pages of the *Free Press*. The true itinerary of the baseball sailors may never be known.

While the players cruised, Detroit continued to lose. From June 15, when word of the Indianapolis negotiations leaked out, until June 25, when the former Hoosiers first appeared on the field for Detroit, the Wolverines won two games and lost six. They were mired in last place with a record of seven wins and 31 losses. New manager Bill Watkins continued to scramble to complete the roster because Indianapolis pitcher Larry McKeon and his catcher, Jim Keenan, had refused to report to Detroit. Instead, as feared, the pair signed with Cincinnati of the American Association. The Hoosiers' backup pitcher, Dan Casey, 22, a lefty, was initially reluctant to join Detroit but eventually was persuaded to come around. Watkins signed Charles "Lady" Baldwin, another lefty, from the Milwaukee Brewers of the still-tottering Western League, to replace McKeon. Chicago's Al Spalding had been chasing Baldwin, but Watkins and Wolverines secretary Bob Leadley persuaded the southpaw that Detroit offered him a greater opportunity. Baldwin, 26, whose family had moved from New York state to Michigan when he was a boy, picked up his unlikely nickname from teammates because, unlike them, he refused to drink, smoke or swear. Baldwin had a terrific curve ball and developed an "in-shoot" and drop ball that made him effective against right-handed batters, with whom southpaws often struggled. He would soon make Watkins look good by posting a miserly earned run average of 1.86, while winning 11 games and losing nine during the balance of 1885. And far better days lay ahead for Baldwin in Detroit.

Pitchers Stump Weidman and Pretzels Getzien were kept, but infielders Scott, Quest, and Phillips, and outfielder Dorgan were released. Chub Collins, 27, from Dundas, Ontario, was signed to replace shortstop Phillips, who joined the Pittsburgh Alleghenys of the AA. Collins had played for Watkins in Indianapolis and appeared with Buffalo in 45 games in 1884. Watkins also found Mox McQuery to replace Scott at first base. A six-foot-one, 23-year-old Kentuckian, McQuery had played 35 games with the Cincinnati Outlaw Reds of the Union Association in 1884.

High hopes accompanied the signing of the former Indianapolis players. Sam Crane, 31, of Springfield, Massachusetts, would become the new second baseman. Like McQuery, he had played with Cincinnati of the UA (and before that, New York in the AA and the Buffalo Bisons) and was one of the few newcomers to continue with Detroit after the 1885 season. Deacon McGuire, 21, of Youngstown, Ohio, was in his second year of what would be a 26-year career for the durable catcher who also played first base. McGuire had played with Toledo in the AA before joining the Hoosiers. He had moved to Michigan, where he proved to be one of the very few receivers able to hold onto the delivery of Lady Baldwin.[19] Gene Moriarty, 22, of Holyoke, Massachusetts, was signed to play the outfield. A weak hitter, he was injured after 11 games when he slammed into a fence at Recreation Park, breaking a toe and badly scraping two knees. He was released soon afterward. Jim Donnelly, 19, of New Haven, Connecticut, became the new third baseman. He had played with Watkins on the feeble Indianapolis AA team of 1884.

By far the strongest of the former Hoosiers would prove to be Sam Thompson, 25, a native of Danville, Indiana. The six-foot-two right fielder, considered a huge man in that day, batted from the left side and had yet to make an appearance in a major league game. He would have to wait awhile longer. He and Moriarty had similar batting records, but Moriarty had been fielding better so Watkins decided to use Thompson as a backup. The team also had trouble finding a uniform large enough for the Indiana giant. To keep him sharp, Thompson was loaned to the Cass Club for a trip to Hamilton, Ontario, for a July 1 Dominion Day holiday game against the Clippers. Thompson went four-for-four against the strong local nine, picking up three home runs and a double. One of his homers

Charles "Lady" Baldwin, a lefty whose nickname came from his refusal to drink, smoke or swear, joined Detroit in 1885 and won 42 games for the Wolverines in 1886. That was good for a first-place tie in the National League with New York's Tim Keefe. Baldwin was never the same after that, however, as his heavy workload that year apparently overtaxed his arm. He won 13 games in 1887 and only three in 1888 (Library of Congress).

7. Retooling

sailed so far over the outfield fence that the ball was never found. Despite Thompson's major contributions and towering presence, Cass lost the game, 8–6.[20]

Thompson was itching to see his first action with Detroit, and it came sooner than he expected. The next day, back in Detroit and during a game against New York, right fielder Moriarty was injured chasing a foul ball in the fifth inning and Thompson replaced him. In his first at-bat, Thompson singled on a short hit to center field. Detroit blanked the Giants, 4–0. A story circulated for years that Thompson had been sitting in the stands when Moriarty was hurt and had to borrow the injured man's pants—which he split open while running to second, much to his own amusement and that of the crowd. But director Stearns witnessed the event and had another version. He confirmed that Thompson was called down from the grandstand to replace Moriarty. "Sam didn't have a uniform. The only thing he changed was his shoes, and he played in civilian clothes."[21] Regardless, the easy-going Thompson would become a crowd favorite during his four years in Detroit at the beginning of his 15-year major league career. "Big Sam" would play in 1,410 games and record a lifetime batting average of .331, with 1,306 runs batted in. He became baseball's greatest clutch hitter of his time and recorded a lifetime batting average of .331, earning him a place in the Hall of Fame. Thompson's bat and the strong, accurate arm he developed from the outfield materially helped the Wolverines.

Perhaps the key addition for the Wolverines was manager Bill Watkins, 27. He was still in the early days of what would become a long and successful career as a manager. Watkins was born in Brantford, Ontario, on May 5, 1858, the oldest surviving son of a successful dry goods merchant and his wife. Upon the death of his mother when he was 10, Watkins was sent to live with grandparents who educated him at local schools and then sent him for a year to the exclusive Upper Canada College in Toronto. During his school days, Watkins was introduced to baseball. He eventually moved to Port Huron, Michigan, just across the St. Clair River from Sarnia, Ontario, after playing a few years in his home province. He played for the semi-professional Maple Leafs of Guelph, which had historically been one of Canada's top baseball teams, then joined the Atlantics, another top-notch club, in St. Thomas. With both clubs, he was manager while playing the infield. In 1882 and 1883, he led his new club in Port Huron to the Michigan State championship. Watkins then joined Bay City of the Northwestern League, which was making a run for the pennant when it dissolved in July of 1884.

Later that same month, Watkins joined the weak Indianapolis Hoosiers of the American Association to play third base. On August 10, he was named playing manager and moved himself to second base. His fielding and batting were average, but improving nicely, when fate intervened. On August 26, fastballer Gus Shallix beaned him in the temple during the first inning of a game against Cincinnati. It was nearly fatal, with Watkins slipping in and out of consciousness for several days. He recovered, however, and returned to the lineup, where he struggled. He hit and fielded so poorly that he benched himself after his October 13 outing. Watkins never played again. Meanwhile, his Hoosiers finished the season second-last in the AA with a record of four wins and 18 losses. The team collapsed when the season ended. Early in 1885, Watkins was an organizer of the Western League, which fielded teams in six Midwestern cities. He managed a new Indianapolis entry, borrowing the Hoosiers name from his former AA club. Under Watkins's leadership this team proved to be the class of the new league. By the time he made his fateful trip to Detroit in June, however, the Hoosiers were faltering financially and the entire Western League seemed doomed.[22] The failure of Indianapolis proved to be the last straw, and on June 23 the Western League expired. In Detroit, the directors of the ball club, particularly Stearns, were impressed by Watkins and his knowledge of the game and its players. They decided to take a chance on him to pilot the revamped team. Their faith would be rewarded.

The new-look Wolverines took to the field for the first time on June 25 for the third and final tilt in a series with Providence, having split the two previous games. A crowd of 1,500 turned out to see the new men perform. They would be let down. Detroit's former pitcher, Dupee Shaw, was in fine form while Dan Casey didn't trouble the visiting hitters. The catching of McGuire and the sharp work of McQuery at first and Donnelly at third drew positive comments, however. Other newcomers to play that day were Collins at shortstop, Moriarty in right field and Crane at second. The only faces familiar to the crowd were Wood and Dorgan, in their usual places in left and center field. Detroit managed only three hits and was shut out, 7–0. It was an inauspicious start, but things quickly improved. Of the remaining 17 games in the Detroit home stand, the Wolverines won 13, defeating New York, Boston, Philadelphia and St. Louis. On July 2, the first game Sam Thompson played, Detroit handed New York its first shutout of the season, 4–0, with Getzien picking up the win.

Crowds improved with the success of the team. More than 2,500 cranks attended the Boston games, for instance. A 9–5 win on July 13 over St. Louis, with Baldwin pitching, lifted Detroit out of last place, edging past Buffalo, which that same day sold pitcher Pud Galvin to the Pittsburgh Alleghenys. The sale of their ace led to speculation the struggling Bisons were for sale or would simply disband. Crowds had been thin at its new field, Olympic Park, which cost $7,000 to acquire and upgrade. Buffalo was averaging 300 to 400 spectators per game when 800 were needed to break even. Aside from future Hall of

Famer Galvin, the Big Four batters of Dan Brouthers, Deacon White, Jack Rowe and Hardy Richardson were the team's greatest assets, and rumors began circulating that suitors, including Pittsburgh, had been calling. Meanwhile, the Wolverines' record had improved to 20 wins and 35 losses before they hit the road for a 16-game Eastern trip that began July 18 in Philadelphia. "Detroit is mowing down everything before them," *Sporting Life* noted, predicting that the infusion of new talent might make it a contender yet.[23]

The road trip through Philadelphia, New York, Boston and Providence was not particularly successful. Watkins introduced the first four-man pitching rotation in baseball: Weidman, Getzien, Casey and Baldwin.[24] But the Wolverines won only four of the 16 games, and Watkins dropped the rotation and went back to playing hunches on who would pitch on any given day. Meanwhile, the directors of the Indianapolis Club filed a lawsuit against Detroit, saying the Hoosiers were still owed $3,000 of the $5,000 in the deal to acquire the rights to its players. Detroit had not come up with the $2,000 cash or the $1,000 in stock promised as part of the deal, Indianapolis alleged. Detroit countered that it withheld the payment when the battery of McKeon and Keenan refused to join their teammates in Detroit.[25]

Much more was happening behind the scenes in late July while the Wolverines struggled along the East Coast. Detroit director Stearns spotted an opportunity. He and manager Watkins travelled to Buffalo to persuade the Bisons to sell the Big Four, hoping they'd finish the season in Detroit. The newspapers were saying, however, that the four were refusing to be sold off. They would demand their releases if Buffalo faltered and would then accept the best offers made to them.[26] Stearns soon discovered that he had an ace in the hole. Brouthers was friends with Detroit's center fielder, Ned Hanlon, and told Hanlon he'd be happy to jump to Detroit. But the Detroit directors were forbidden to speak to any player under contract with another team, pursuant to the National Agreement. A plan was hatched. The four were persuaded to sign contracts to play the 1886 season in Detroit, provided they won their releases from Buffalo. Talks continued with Buffalo president Josiah Jewett and other directors, who wanted to sell the entire team, not just their star players. And they wanted a large sum to pay off their debts and recover five years of investment made in the Bisons. Detroit offered $2,000 for the club, but Buffalo demanded $12,000. It was said that directors of the Pittsburgh Alleghenys and the Cincinnati Reds of the American Association were also talking to the Buffalo directors. Those clubs wanted to buy the entire team as a way of gaining entry into the National League.[27]

Stearns returned to Detroit in late July without the Big Four, but he was determined to keep trying. He stayed in touch with Buffalo, trying to engineer a deal, but remained vigilant for any players who might become available sooner. Upon learning that pitcher Hoss Radbourn had run afoul of directors in cash-strapped Providence who felt he was coasting, Stearns made some preliminary inquiries aimed at acquiring the hurler and center fielder Paul Hines.[28] Radbourn won a stellar 59 games in 1884, but his performance had tapered off and struggling Providence would disband at season end. Radbourn was remembered in Detroit for his 18th-inning heroics in 1882 when his walk-off home run gave the Grays a 1–0 victory over the Wolverines. He had become one of the top pitchers of his day, and Stearns wanted him. Radbourn was suspended for "indifferent work" in early September, a move which caught the interest of many teams, not just Detroit.[29]

In the midst of all the intrigue about Buffalo and Stearns' pursuit of talent, a long-simmering feud hit the law courts on August 1. The Detroit Base Ball Club, operating as the Wolverines, filed a lawsuit against a neighbor of Recreation Park who had been profiting from the Wolverines games. The club wanted John Deppert, Jr., to remove seats he had erected on a tall barn behind his home at 743 Beaubien Street, just beyond the right field fence. The harness-maker and carpenter was charging patrons 15 cents to watch baseball games, compared to the 50 cents charged at the park. Over the years, the Wolverines had tried to block the view by raising its fence, but Deppert replied by building his seats higher. In response, the club attached a canvas screen between telegraph poles, but Deppert went still higher. The team complained to city building inspectors in a bid to have the rooftop stand condemned, but Deppert merely strengthened it and carried on.

The Detroit directors felt that Deppert was depriving them of revenue. They decided to sue and won a preliminary injunction to shut him down until the case was tried. Deppert and his lawyer argued, however, that he had the right to enjoy the "fresh and cool air" above his barn. Deppert ignored the injunction and was brought before Judge J. Logan Chipman for contempt. On September 13, Chipman dismissed the injunction, ruling that Deppert was not being a nuisance. "It may be a meanness to make money at the expense of the exhibitions given by his neighbor; but I know of no power in a court of chancery to restrain every meanness." The judge said charging admission made no difference and saw the matter as one of morality rather than legality.[30] The trial itself was heard on February 17, 1886, when Chipman ruled against the baseball club, allowing Deppert to continue his freelance grandstand operation unimpeded. The judge said he found no evidence Deppert had enticed cranks arriving at Recreation Park onto his rooftop with the promise of a lower admission fee. As the ball club could prove no pecuniary loss, he dismissed the case. The club appealed the ruling to the Michigan Supreme Court, which on April 24 upheld the lower court decision. In so doing, the high court noted that Deppert had the right to do what he wanted with his own property.[31]

Detroit was not alone in facing the challenge of competition from rooftop viewing. Other cities had similar issues as baseball continued to grow in popularity. In Chicago, for instance, rooftop seating would become an accepted part of the baseball landscape outside Wrigley Field. In recent times, the Chicago Cubs tried to shut down its neighbors but failed, then took a cut of rooftop revenue, and finally opted to purchase most of the abutting properties when the stadium was upgraded.[32]

Detroit's losing streak continued when Chicago came to Detroit for a four-game series beginning August 12, and Baldwin, Getzien, Casey and Weidman each lost one of them. Casey was fined $100 for his poor play in a 9–4 loss to Chicago on August 14. An additional $50 was levied for insubordination when he refused to collect tickets in the ladies' grandstand four days later. Manager Watkins was proving to be a stern disciplinarian, quick to penalize his men for what he deemed sub-par performance or infractions. A five-game series with Buffalo followed, and Baldwin picked up the only win, 9–4, in the final game on August 22. Watkins was in no mood to deal with difficult players, and he clashed again with Casey when he refused to pitch against Buffalo on August 20. Watkins suspended Casey without pay and later released him. Casey had won four games for Detroit and lost eight. As Detroit prepared for its final Western swing, it had dropped to last place again, with a record of 25 wins and 55 losses. Buffalo had edged up to sixth.

Detroit kicked off a 12-game Western trip on August 25 with an 8–0 shutout at the hands of Chicago. It picked up only one win in the remaining three games in the Windy City before moving on to St. Louis for four games against the struggling Maroons. In the first game on September 1, Charlie Bennett belted a grand slam home run off St. Louis pitcher Henry Boyle in the first inning and Detroit romped to an 8–3 win. Bennett's bash was one of only three grand slams recorded the entire season. Detroit swept the following three games before finishing the trip with four games in Buffalo. Despite the loss of their ace, Galvin, the Bisons put up a good fight and won all four games, giving the ball to Pete Conway, Bill Serad and Pete Wood. At they headed home for their final home stand after a narrow, 6–5 loss on September 12, the Wolverines were in seventh place, 6½ games back of Buffalo and 1½ ahead of tail-ender St. Louis.

Events would were about to unfold that would distract attention from Detroit's disappointing on-field performance and shake the baseball establishment to its very roots.

8

A Big Deal

"Bought Another Club: The Detroit Management Purchase the Buffalo Franchise," screamed the headline in the September 16, 1885, morning edition of the *Detroit Free Press*. The newspaper's scoop even surprised a director of the Detroit club, who readily confessed to the reporter: "I haven't heard of it, but I shouldn't be surprised if the report is true, for although I am a stockholder, I never know what is going to be done until long after the bargain is consummated."[1] Such was the lot of shareholders when Frederick Stearns was on the move.

The brief but sensational report said the entire Buffalo operation had been acquired for $7,000. Manager Watkins, it said, had been scouring the East for the past couple of weeks looking for new players, and this was the result. The object of the deal was to secure the services of the Big Four hitters: Dan Brouthers, Jack Rowe, Hardy Richardson and Deacon White. The Bisons team would finish the season in Buffalo and the franchise would transfer to Detroit for 1886. The startling news was initially met by denials from directors and shareholders, who said they knew nothing or had been sworn to secrecy. The *Free Press* couldn't resist noting that those unhappy at being surprised included William White of the *Post*, "because as official scorer it mortified him to be scooped" by his journalistic rival. The *Free Press* followed its scoop the next day with evidence to back up its story. It carried a transcript of Stearns' telegraph from Buffalo seeking the $7,000 to consummate the deal and added that the Big Four were expected to join Detroit as early as Saturday, September 19, for a game against New York.

On September 17, Stearns confirmed the sale to a reporter from the newspaper while he and president Joseph Marsh tried in vain to learn from him who had leaked the information. Stearns said he was motivated to act when he became aware that Boston and other teams were trying to sign the Big Four, so he went to Buffalo "against the advice of his associates." Stearns said he spent three days haggling with the directors there. When he talked Buffalo down to $500 for each player from their initial demand of $3,000 apiece, he sent for fellow director John Molony to help him seal the deal. Stearns confessed: "We only need the 'big four,' but we may have to take the franchise. The 'big four' are anxious to come here and we've got 'em—contracts all signed. Hence I have no fear of losing them, unless the train runs off the track and breaks their necks." Asked whether Detroit now owned the franchise, Stearns replied: "We may have to take it—we don't need it.... If Cincinnati or Pittsburgh or any other city wants it we'll sell it to 'em."[2] The latter remark was a dig at the two clubs who in recent weeks had been rumored to be interested in buying the Detroit franchise to gain entry to the National League. They had been reportedly willing to pay as much as $10,000.[3]

Dan Brouthers, a giant of a man, patrolled first base and wielded a powerful bat. He was among the Big Four players who rose to fame in Buffalo and were acquired by Detroit in a controversial 1885 deal, the first sale of a franchise in National League history. Brouthers was always among the National League leaders in hitting (National Baseball Hall of Fame Library, Cooperstown, New York).

Within days, *Sporting Life* reported further details in its extensive "inside story" of Stearns' coup under the front-page headline, "A Stunner. Bisons Sell Out." It said that Stearns first went to Buffalo in late July in a bid to see whether Brouthers, Rowe, Richardson and White would sign with Detroit because Buffalo was "on the verge of dissolution." The players were receptive to joining Detroit, but not until the 1886 season. Talks continued, despite the League rule forbidding players from signing up while still under contract. Detroit center fielder Ned Hanlon was a friend of Brouthers and helped Stearns, Molony and secretary Bob Leadley as discussions continued for several weeks. During the Wolverines' series in Buffalo September 10–12, the four coveted players again met with Watkins and Leadley in a hotel room. There, the latter drew up contracts in which the four agreed to play for Detroit in 1886, *if* they were released by Buffalo. All four signed. *Sporting Life* said getting contracts with the four Bisons had further ramifications.

It was considered particularly fortunate, as the chances of securing two other crack players from another League club were materially strengthened. These two had said they would come to Detroit if the four Buffalo men came. The contract was virtually gold for six first-class players.[4]

The two unnamed others were likely Hoss Radbourn and Paul Hines, whose Providence team, like Buffalo, was in dire straits financially. Radbourn had clashed with its management and was looking at his options. As it turned out, when Providence disbanded at the end of the season, the League took all its players, and Radbourn and Hines were assigned to Boston and Washington, respectively.

Sporting Life noted that Detroit's next step was to obtain releases for the Big Four immediately. Detroit began negotiating with Buffalo's directors, who insisted that Detroit take the entire franchise, not just the foursome. Buffalo held firm. It wanted to retire all liabilities and provide a 20-percent dividend for its long-suffering shareholders. The Buffalo directors prevailed. The papers finalizing the deal, and the payment of $7,000 were executed on the night of September 17. Contracts were then signed with the players for the rest of the season and sent off to League president Nick Young. At midnight, Watkins boarded a train for home, accompanied by Brouthers, Rowe, Richardson and White, saying he planned to play them two days later against New York. Watkins pronounced himself a happy man as he boarded the train, despite a wire service report out of Buffalo revealing how much Detroit would pay the newcomers. He

Jack Rowe, a sharp-fielding shortstop, was another member of the Big Four that Detroit acquired from Buffalo at the end of the 1885 season. Rowe married a woman back in Buffalo, and he and teammate Deacon White also invested in a Buffalo team they hoped to return to the National League (Library of Congress).

wouldn't divulge the player salaries, but insisted the published accounts were "grossly exaggerated." The *Associated Press* said Brouthers and Richardson would receive $4,000 apiece, while Rowe and White would be paid $3,500. The foursome did receive that pay for 1886, making them among the best-paid players in baseball and raising concerns among team owners anxious to curb rising salaries. By comparison, the average industrial wage during the 1880s in the United States ranged from $350 to $400 for an entire year, so they were doing very well.

Reaction to the blockbuster deal was swift. And negative. *Sporting Life*, whose Detroit correspondent was *Free Press* sports editor Charles Mathison, devoted many columns to it, noting that nearly every club in the League and Association had been hoping to land the big fish from Buffalo. "The disappointment over the scoop is naturally great; so much so, in fact, that already a movement is apparent to break the deal and deprive Detroit of the fruits of her cunning manoeuvre [sic] on the ground of illegality." Also unhappy was League president Young, whose assessment was blunt:

> I received a despatch [sic] from Buffalo stating that the Buffalos had released certain players and that the Detroits had engaged them. I immediately telegraphed to the officers of both organizations that their action was contrary to the Saratoga agreement, which was to the effect that both the American and League clubs should not negotiate with any player now under engagement with any League or American club prior to Oct. 20, 1885. Such an agreement certainly stands in the way of any such transfer as has been stated, and if the officers of these two clubs have violated the agreement they must answer for it.[5]

Young's comments prompted George Hughson, secretary of the Buffalo club, to deny there was anything improper about the transfer. Hughson told *Sporting Life*:

> The Detroit management obtained control of the Buffalo club by the purchase of a majority of its stock. This was certainly legal. As to the transfer of the players after the purchase, the former Buffalo management could not control it and we can see nothing illegal in it. The Buffalo club still exists under the new [Detroit] management and is bound to play out the schedule. The new directors have personally bound themselves to do this.[6]

Club owners in both the National League and American Association were reported to be incensed at Detroit's move, not only because they had been eyeing some members of the Big Four themselves, but because they had been outwitted by Frederick Stearns, a newcomer. The transfer of a franchise and its roster had never occurred before, and they denounced it vehemently. Like League president Young, they relied on a just-devised, but not yet ratified, update of the National Agreement reached August 24 at Saratoga, New York, to argue that it was illegal. Notice of that agreement, reached by both leagues, was sent to all club owners just about the same time as the Detroit-Buffalo deal was signed. Squabbling over the agreement, its intent, its contents and its timing would be protracted. According to a *Sporting Life* correspondent, the reaction out of New York City and Boston was particularly strident:

> NEW YORK, Sept. 19.—Editor Sporting Life:—The news referring to the Buffalo-Detroit deal occasions great excitement in New York and Brooklyn base ball circles. The Saratoga conference committee issued a pledge signed by Messrs [Art] Soden [of Boston], [Al] Spalding [of Chicago] and [John] Day [of New York] on account of the League and Messrs [Charlie] Byrne [of Brooklyn], [Chris] Von der Ahe [of St. Louis] and [Lew] Simmons [of Philadelphia] on account of the American Association, asking all clubs to refuse to negotiate or contract with any player at that time under contract with any League or American club, and Secretaries [Wheeler] Wykoff and [Nick] Young have issued notices publishing the fact. The action of Detroit and Buffalo, if true as reported, is a flagrant violation of the solemn pledge signed voluntarily by each. Mr. Day of this city, and Mr. Soden, of Boston, are indignant over this breach of good faith, and will circumvent it at all hazards. Mr. Spalding, of Chicago, an original party to the pledge will, as an honorable gentleman, stand by them. Mr. Day has instructed Manager [Jim] Mutrie to play no games with Detroit in which any Buffalo player is named, and he will see that his orders are obeyed. No doubt other League clubs will do likewise. It is safe to assume that Secretary Young will issue no notice of the release of the Buffalo players, nor will he approve any contract made by any club with said players.... The action of the Saratoga conference committee will be ratified, and if Detroit or Buffalo think that by deception and chicanery they can upset the work of the level-headed men that composed that committee they will soon learn that they have made a mistake.[7]

The so-called Saratoga Agreement was intended to keep the peace between the National League and the American Association and prevent them from poaching each other's players. A key part of the pact prohibited clubs from negotiating with players for the 1886 season until October 20, 1885. Other provisions capped player salaries at $2,000 and prevented the payment of advances on those salaries. Another part of the agreement was kept secret and not revealed until both leagues ratified the entire package of reforms on October 17. It was a provision that saw the birth of the modern waiver rule. The new rule provided that in the 10 days after a player was released, only clubs from the same league could negotiate with him. After that, the other league was free to pursue him. This was intended to slow the movement of players from one loop to another to keep the League and Association out of bidding wars and driving up player pay.

As the firestorm of controversy raged, and in the midst of its four-game series against the New York Giants, the Wolverines boarded an eastbound train for a previously arranged September 18 exhibition game in London, Ontario, against the Cockneys of the Canadian League. There they faced a strong team that included former Wolverine Joe Quest at second base. Appearing in his first game with London was Lou Bierbauer, a native of Erie, Pennsylvania, who had played with Erie, as well as Hamilton and Guelph in the Canadian League. Bierbauer, a shortstop, was about to begin a major league career and achieve baseball immortality as the centerpiece in a clever deal pulled off by Pittsburgh after the 1890 season that would be criticized as "piratical," giving birth to a new identity for the club as the Pirates. In Canada, Bierbauer was already embroiled in controversy. His signing by second-place London while still under contract to fourth-place Guelph prompted the latter club to blacklist him, leaving the two clubs at war. London gave a good account of itself against Detroit and was ahead, 9–8, after seven innings when the game was called because the visitors had to catch their train for home.

As the team rolled westward for the next day's concluding game with New York, the Wolverines had plenty to think about. Would the Big Four actually play in the game, and who from the existing roster would soon be looking for work? Within hours, Watkins advised McQuery, Crane, Donnelly and just-acquired shortstop Jim Manning that they would be sent to Buffalo to help fill the sudden holes in the Bisons' roster. That same evening, at the Russell House Hotel, "an animated session" took place between New York manager Jim Mutrie and directors of the Detroit club. Mutrie insisted he would not play Detroit the following day if the Big Four appeared in its lineup. He had clear instructions from his directors, who felt the transfer was illegal. But the Detroit directors wouldn't back down. They insisted the deal was fine and that the Big Four would take to the field. Mean-

Hardy Richardson, a heavy-hitting left fielder, was another member of the Big Four that Detroit acquired from Buffalo late in 1885. A versatile player, he also performed well in the infield, mainly at second base (Library of Congress).

while in Buffalo, the *Express* headlined a rather funereal story about the sale of the club and its players thusly: "The Glory has Departed."[8]

The Big Four were among the players Detroit brought to Recreation Park on September 19 for the fourth and final game of its series with New York. The Giants, who were three games behind Chicago in a tight pennant race, had won two of the previous three games from the Wolverines. Its directors instructed Mutrie to take his players home if the foursome from Buffalo showed up. New York had a powerful ally in National League president Nick Young, who telegraphed game umpire Bob Ferguson in anticipation that Detroit would field Brouthers, Rowe, Richardson and White. Young declared the deal invalid and ordered Ferguson to award the game to New York by default if Detroit had the men on its game-day roster. Upon learning of Young's decree, the Detroit directors reluctantly relented, and manager Watson persuaded McQuery, Crane, Manning and Donnelly to return to their familiar positions.[9] New York got off to a strong start, putting four runs across the plate in the first inning before Lady Baldwin was able to settle down to business. Detroit came back with two runs in the third inning and tied the game when Sam Thompson homered in the fifth with a runner on base. The Wolverines went ahead with a single run in the seventh, but New York plated two runs in the ninth to eke out a 6–5 win.

Manager Watkins and the four newcomers were found at the Brunswick Hotel the following day, where the manager complained bitterly that clubs who wanted the Buffalo players were trying to "twist" the Saratoga Agreement to deny them to Detroit. The men all said they wanted to play for Detroit, and White said it was clear to him that the Saratoga deal was only intended to deal with contracts for 1886, not for the current season. Stearns weighed in on the controversy to say that none of the Buffalo players acquired by Detroit would return to their former team, adding, "any effort to persuade them to do so will be less than worthless." He said that if they couldn't play for Detroit, they would have to sit for the remainder of the season. Stearns said the other clubs in the National League were simply upset at being outwitted by a tail-end team. He had heard a rumor that his team would be expelled, but he doubted that the six votes necessary could be found among the eight team owners. Meantime, he said the Big Four would remain in the city "for a few days only."[10]

Brouthers, Rowe, Richardson and White didn't stay around as long as predicted. On the evening of September 21, they left Detroit for an unknown destination, or destinations. The *Free Press* lamented that "one of the greatest strokes of managerial enterprise in the annals of base ball has apparently come to naught," doomed by the powers in the League who wielded the Saratoga Agreement as a weapon to keep Detroit from improving its prospects. The newspaper wondered aloud where the Big Four would be permitted to play the following season.¹¹

Philadelphia began a series in Detroit on September 22, when only 300 chilly fans, as they were becoming known, saw the Wolverines down the Phillies, 4–1. McQuery, Crane, Donnelly and Manning were still in the lineup. The same day, it was reported in Boston that Art Soden, the notoriously tight-fisted owner of the Beaneaters, wanted the Big Four and would pay more for them "than any other club in the country."¹² The uncharacteristic assertion turned heads in the baseball community, but underlined how much Soden was determined to improve his franchise's sagging fortunes. His Beaneaters would finish the season in fifth place, 41 games behind Chicago. Detroit lost, 12–5, to the Phillies the next day, but bounced back with wins of 6–3 and 10–6 to complete the series. It was reported from Buffalo that the Big Four had appeared in that city briefly, and on September 23 they scattered; Brouthers to Chicago, White to his farm in Corning, New York, Rowe to Colorado and Richardson on a hunting excursion.¹³ They would forego any salary until their deal with Detroit was recognized.

Meanwhile Buffalo, which scrambled to fill the sudden holes in its lineup, played miserably with inexperienced and inexpensive players. New York easily swept five games from them, between September 21

James "Deacon" White, third baseman, was the fourth member of the Big Four to join Detroit in late 1885. A veteran whose professional career dated back to 1871 in Cleveland, White was in the twilight of his career but still performed admirably in Detroit. His nickname came from his gentlemanly deportment at a time when many players drank too much, partied too hard and consorted with ladies of questionable background (Library of Congress).

and 26, by scores of 10–0, 17–2, 11–3, 15–1, and 4–1. Supporters of the club were as dispirited as the players. Only 100 spectators turned out to Olympic Park when Buffalo played host to Boston on September 29 and was pounded, 12–3. The Bisons lost the remaining games in the series by scores of 5–3, 7–3, and an embarrassing 18–0 shutout on October 3. Buffalo pitcher Pete Conway surrendered 18 hits in the latter six-inning game, called on account of darkness. He was not relieved by manager Jack Chapman, whose cupboard was bare. During September, Buffalo had won five games while losing 15. The Bisons' last games in Olympic Park were both played on October 7, when they lost to Providence, 4–0 and 6–1. The games were called after five innings to make them official. Attendance amounted to 12 souls that chilly day, and gate receipts totaled a mere three dollars.[14] To salvage some gate money from the series, Buffalo's final two season games were shifted south to Elmira, New York, for a doubleheader of five-inning games. Providence won both ends of it, 3–0 and 7–3. After 16 straight defeats, Buffalo's record for the season came to 38 wins with 74 losses, two games ahead of the last-place St. Louis Maroons. After seven seasons in which Buffalo had placed as high as third on four occasions, the city's run in the National League was over.

In Detroit, the Wolverines easily swept four games from Providence, then lost only one of four against Boston, to wind up their final home stand with 11 wins and five losses. The team had been able to focus on its game despite the storm of controversy and the uncertainty surrounding the club and its lineup. Overall, Detroit finished sixth, three games behind Boston and 44 games behind pennant-winner Chicago. Its final record was 41 wins and 67 losses. The innovative deal to acquire the Indianapolis players had paid off and produced what amounted to two distinct seasons for the Wolverines. Before the deal, Detroit had won seven games and lost 31. With the influx of new talent and Bill Watkins as new manager, the record was 34 wins and 36 losses. In the second "world's series," Chicago played the AA champion St. Louis Browns of Chris Von der Ahe. It was arranged as a best-of-seven series, but after it was knotted 3–3 with one tie, the interleague championship was declared a draw.

In late September, Detroit president Joseph Marsh and director John B. Molony, a brick manufacturer and collector for Internal Revenue, met with Chicago president Al Spalding in the Windy City. The Detroit men wanted to make the case that their deal with Buffalo was legal and to enlist Spalding's support. Harsh words were apparently exchanged in private, but afterward the trio told reporters they were in accord. Buffalo would continue on, and the Big Four would not play for Detroit in the current season. In fact, Marsh admitted a "blunder" in overlooking provisions of the Saratoga Agreement, notice of which had arrived at his club in the form of a letter, adding "so little consequence had we attached to it that that we did not even keep a copy of it on file." Marsh promised to "make things right with the League management." Appeased, Spalding withdrew his objection to a plan under which Buffalo would play its final home games against New York in New York.[15] That notion, to make some gate money for the desperate Bisons, was originally opposed by Chicago as providing an unfair advantage to New York in its tight pennant race with the White Stockings. As it turned out, the only home games Buffalo switched were the two it played in Elmira against Providence. The visit to Spalding by Marsh and Molony was a wise move and would pay off when the National League later considered Detroit's deal amid calls from some quarters for its ouster. Spalding would play a key role in subsequent events, siding with Detroit and declining to join the war hawks in clubs like Boston.

Controversy continued to swirl about the Detroit-Buffalo deal despite Marsh's newfound admission that Detroit's deal had not been consummated before Saratoga had been "promulgated."[16] Directors felt confident in the assurances from the players that they would play for Detroit next year because of the contracts they had signed that the club insisted were legal. For its part, *Sporting Life* said Brouthers, Rowe, Richardson and White were looking forward to Detroit, where they had several "close friends."[17] Despite that, the "What Will the 'Big Four' Do?" headline on the front page of its October 7 edition reflected the question that continued to preoccupy the wider baseball community. The foursome could not be approached by teams until October 20, and aside from Boston's "will-pay-more-than-anyone" stance, several teams clearly still wanted them. "But will Detroit get them?" *Sporting Life* asked. "Time will tell. The Detroit people say little, but express themselves as satisfied with the turn affairs have taken, and give assurance that they will certainly have the men, provided nothing is done at the next League meeting to euchre them."[18]

A special joint meeting of the National League and American Association convened in New York October 17 and 18 to formally ratify the Saratoga Agreement. Representing Detroit were president Marsh and director Molony, while appearing for Buffalo were former director J. B. Sage and new director Frederick K. Stearns. There was much business to transact, with far-reaching consequences. The maximum salary to be paid any player was set at $2,000, despite grumbling from some team owners. Advances on player salaries were banned. October 20 was set as the date before which no team could contract a player for the following season, and the reserve rule was extended to 12 players. The formerly secret provision that a same-league club could approach a player within 10 days of his release, after which other leagues could contact him, was disclosed and approved. A board of arbitration to solve disputes between the two leagues was established. National League representatives decided to leave the knotty questions surrounding Detroit and the future of the Buffalo and Providence franchises to the annual meeting the following month.

While baseball's magnates discussed business in New York, the Big Four were hunting and fishing. Brouthers, Richardson, Rowe and White reported to Detroit on Friday, October 16, four days before it would be open season for *them*. They promptly departed for the St. Clair Flats, the marshy hunting and fishing grounds at the north end of Lake St. Clair, about 30 miles northeast of Detroit. The area was dotted with hotels favored by outdoorsmen, although they may have stayed at a lodge owned by one of Detroit's wealthy directors. By now, even the *Free Press* was doubting the legality of the contracts the players had signed for next season, but expressed confidence they would sign new ones.

> The "Big Four" have been up the Flats for several days, but it was not because of any fear on the part of the Detroit club. It was a move at the suggestion of the players who desired to escape the annoyance of telegraphs, letters, and delegations from places where they do not wish or expect to play next season.[19]

The newspaper predicted that Hoss Radbourn, the Providence hurler, would also be signing a contract with Detroit, along with center fielder George Gore of Chicago and a promising new pitcher. During a post-season exhibition game against Zanesville, Wisconsin, Watkins had been impressed with Cleveland native Larry Twitchell. The young hurler had held Detroit to four scattered hits, using an effective curve. Watkins offered him a contract for the coming year.

Upon returning to Detroit from the deliberations in New York, director Stearns said a final decision on the Big Four would be made at the League's annual meeting on November 17. He said the Chicago and New York clubs had agreed to keep their hands off the players, although they were wanted by Boston and Philadelphia. There was no doubt in his mind that Detroit would prevail and sign all four.[20] As Stearns spoke, the foursome returned from the Flats and booked into the Brunswick Hotel, where they showed off "a couple dozen ducks they had bagged." All seemed to be in a positive frame of mind, and new contracts were apparently signed. Deacon White confided to a reporter: "You may say the four will play together, and they'll play in Detroit if they play anywhere."[21] With that, the coveted men left Detroit by train late on October 21 to return to their homes; Brouthers to Wappingers Falls, New York, White to Corning, and Rowe and Richardson to Buffalo. The fates of all would remain in limbo until the League's tenth annual meeting nearly four weeks later.

The Saratoga Agreement had fueled growing resentment within the ranks of professional ball players, already chafing at their diminished status in their own game. Blacklists, reserve clauses, the increasing use of arbitrary fines, and forcing players to do menial jobs around the ballpark when not playing, such as collecting tickets, were bad enough. The latter requirement had seen Detroit pitcher Casey clash with manager Watkins, who fined him for his refusal to take the assigned ticket-taking task. But limiting player pay to $2,000 and banning the payment of advances alarmed most players, who resented their treatment at the hands of owners who profited from their play. The seeds of discontent were spreading. In 1885, Philadelphia sportswriter William Voltz, who had managed ball clubs in Chattanooga and Toledo, came up with the notion of a benevolent association for players. It was intended to create a fund for sick and needy players. By some accounts, Voltz attracted 200 members who paid $5 in monthly dues. Organizing this way was becoming commonplace in other workplaces. In industrial America, unions had been established to defend the rights of workers from the abuses of capitalist owners. Labor was developing a voice.

Once baseball players learned that the owners planned to limit their salaries, the notion of organizing began to resonate. The most militant were nine members of the New York Giants, including shortstop John Ward along with Joe Gerhardt and Mike Dorgan, members of the Detroit Wolverines in 1881. On October 22, the New York players established a chapter of the Brotherhood of Professional Base Ball Players to protect and promote their interests individually and collectively and to promote a high standard of player conduct. Former pitcher Ward, a law school graduate, became president of what began as a secret organization.[22] Had League and Association owners been able to police themselves on the new $2,000 limit they instituted for the 1886 season, the Brotherhood might have grown more quickly. As it was, the limit was largely ignored, with personal service contracts growing in popularity. Consequently, the organization took a year to reach a membership of about 100. By 1888, however, when player pay cuts and salary limitations again surfaced, the Brotherhood was prepared to act. It rebelled and founded the Players' League to challenge the League and Association for the 1890 season.

The much-anticipated annual meeting of the National League was held at New York's Fifth Avenue Hotel, in November of 1885. Directors, including Detroit's John B. Molony, faced a meaty agenda. Upon their arrival, rumors filled the corridors and parlors that Detroit would be ousted or perhaps would secede from the League if it could not retain the Big Four. Detroit would then join new clubs to be formed in New York, Brooklyn, Washington, Boston, Cincinnati and St. Louis in a league without salary limits or mandatory admission fees.[23] There was plenty of intrigue to go around at the gathering of such great importance to the League and to Detroit. Molony and president Marsh again represented Detroit, while Frederick K. Stearns appeared as a representative of both Detroit and Buffalo. After preliminary business and decisions about rule changes, the matter of the Big Four was brought forward. Detroit found supporters in Buffalo (naturally) and Providence. Boston and Philadelphia, who had coveted some or all of the four players, proved antagonistic and found some support from New York. Chicago had already obtained all the players it wanted for the following season, and Al Spalding remained neutral. St. Louis felt Detroit was entitled to the men it had purchased. After an hour of arguing, the matter was turned over to special committee consisting of Chicago's Al Spalding, New York's John Day and League president Nick Young.

The next day, after six hours of deliberation, the special committee recommended that Detroit be allowed to keep the Big Four. The committee noted that the four players wished to play for Detroit and to their credit had maintained that position despite the furor and competition for their services. The convention adopted the decision by majority vote.[24] This prompted the *Detroit Free Press* to gloat: "No concessions were made by Detroit and the victory was most complete."[25] It was learned only later that Detroit voluntarily surrendered the Buffalo franchise to the League as part of the settlement.[26] As expected, provisions of the Saratoga Agreement were adopted and became part of an updated National Agreement. But the knotty question of what to do with the Buffalo and Providence franchises was not resolved. A place in the League was offered to Brooklyn, but it opted to stay in the American Association. Washington was interested, but before adjourning, delegates deferred the matter of Buffalo and Providence and whether they would be replaced to a special committee given permission to act. In the meantime, Providence and Buffalo would remain as members of the League until the spring meeting. Nick Young was returned as League president, and Detroit's John B. Molony was among those drawn by lot to continue as a director.

The reaction in Detroit was one of joy, with praise heaped upon Stearns and Watkins. *Sporting Life's* Detroit correspondent, Charles Mathison, could barely contain himself:

> Rah! The "big four" are ours at last. One of the finest strokes of managerial enterprise ever known in the base ball world has taken root, and the next season "four daisies" will bloom in Recreation Park, to the unbounded delight of Detroiters and the edification of visiting clubs. And what a reception we will give the Gotham Giants and Anson's infants.[27]

The roster for 1886 would be a strong one. First-rate pitchers Baldwin, Getzien, Weidman, Casey and newcomer Twitchell would be supported by the bats of Bennett, McGuire, Rowe, Brouthers, Richardson, White, Thompson, Hanlon, Wood, and Manning. The hitters, the report said, "will be a terror to pitchers." It dismissed the notion that Detroit wasn't able to support a "first-class nine....

The truth is that this is one of the best ball towns in the country, and will come to the front next season in a manner to take away the breath of carping critics."

About the same time Detroit was rejoicing, its new shortstop, Jack Rowe, also had his own reasons to smile. Aside from a new contract as a Wolverine, he had something else to celebrate as reported by the *New York Clipper*: "John C. Rowe, well-known as one of the 'Big Four' was recently married to a rich and beautiful widow of Buffalo."[28] She was Louisa Schachtel, whose husband, successful fresco artist Ernst Schachtel, had died in early 1884. Rowe moved into her large house two blocks from Olympic Park. Another new member of the Wolverines had also left his heart in upstate New York. Two months after Rowe's nuptials, left fielder Hardy Richardson married Lily M. Davis in Utica.[29]

The optimism surrounding Detroit and its chances for 1886 was contagious. In early December, manager Watkins reported that he had received more than 100 applications from ballplayers anxious to join the club. He said they were not just "fresh aspirants," but included some with plenty of experience. The club already had an oversized roster for its next campaign, however, and was more likely to shed players than hire new ones. Outfielder George Wood, who had been with Detroit since its inaugural season, was released to Philadelphia, in recognition of support Detroit received from the Phillies during the League's annual meeting.[30] Casey and McGuire were expected to join him there.

Club secretary Bob Leadley reported that average attendance at Recreation Park had been 700 during the 1885 season. Given former president William Thompson's assertion that Detroit needed 1,000 paying spectators at each game just to break even, it was clear that because of its free-spending ways, the club had lost money. But Leadley predicted the situation would soon change with a winning nine. "With one of the best—if not the best—clubs in the country representing Detroit, I expect we will have to enlarge the entrance and put in another turnstile."[31] It didn't stop there. A new, 100-foot-long grandstand was erected in right field, reaching a height of 70 feet "for the express view of shutting out the view from Deppert's ten cent [sic] roost."[32] The existing stand reserved for ladies was extended by 80 feet. New clay and cinders were placed along the base paths, and the entire park was "generally brightened up" for the next season.[33] Shortly before Detroit's first home game of 1886, club president Marsh finally persuaded the Brush estate to remove a large tree standing in center field, "and nothing now stands in the way of the sluggers."[34]

Wolverines salaries for 1886 were expected to top $36,000, including $5,350 for the managers.[35] The latter figure included pay for manager Watkins and secretary Leadley, but was not broken down. To finance the club, a new stock offering to Detroiters was said to be "going off like hotcakes." By early December, $15,000 in stock was issued with predictions that another $5,000 "will be gobbled up in short order."[36] Meanwhile, a local entrepreneur decided to cash in on the return of ball fever in Detroit generated by the new men from Buffalo, by announcing he was now carrying "Big Four" brand cigars.

The next season was anticipated eagerly, with much speculation about Detroit's chances and the shape of the League. With the corpses of Buffalo and Providence still counted as members and no replacements yet named, rumors surfaced that the loop might retract to six teams. Detroit directors were opposed to a six-team circuit and insisted that eight strong teams were possible, suggesting that Pittsburgh could easily replace Buffalo and another team found. Manager Watkins came up with his own plan, described to the *Free Press*:

> I have got an amendment to offer to this six-club scheme. My idea is to amalgamate the National League and American Association. Organize a league of twelve clubs, New York, Brooklyn, Boston, Philadelphia, Baltimore and Washington in the East and Chicago, Detroit, Cincinnati, Louisville, St. Louis, and Pittsburgh in the West. Play a schedule of 132 games, twelve with each club. Have a general admission of fifty cents. Allow Cincinnati, Louisville and St. Louis to play exhibition games on Sunday, but no championship games. This league would then be so strong that no league or association could be organized to compete with it. Having the principal cities in the country as members, it would have a monopoly.... It would be a financial success.[37]

Watkins sounded like the league magnates who fancied monopolies and financial success, likely because he had lived the business end of the game as an owner in Indianapolis. But he proved to be a voice in the wilderness. Amalgamation was a non-starter. The American Association was just hitting its stride, although League magnates still considered it an inferior organization. Another two months would elapse before the National League found replacements for Buffalo and Providence. On January 16, it was announced that Washington was admitted to membership, taking the place of Providence, whose affairs had been concluded just before Christmas. Washington was willing to post a $5,000 bond after Indianapolis had balked at the same requirement. Yet another committee was established to name a replacement for Buffalo, chaired by Al Spalding and consisting of Joseph Marsh from Detroit and Henry V. Lucas from St. Louis.[38] On February 9, Kansas City was accepted on a one-year trial basis, after posting a similar bond and promising to compensate visiting clubs for the extra expense to travel so far to the west. Milwaukee and Indianapolis had also applied, but came up short. A clandestine effort by the League to pilfer another AA team, Cincinnati, had failed, and Kansas was accepted as a compromise.[39] The Kansas Cowboys would be allowed to build their roster from the pool of players left without contracts by Providence and Buffalo, as well as Donnelly and McQuery, who had been released by Detroit.[40] The Cowboys would sign both McQuery and Donnelly, along with Stump

Weidman and former Wolverine Frank Ringo. But the new club would founder toward the end of the year, to be replaced by the AA Pittsburgh Alleghenys in 1887.

After a season in which it bolstered its lineup with two blockbuster deals engineered primarily by Frederick K. Stearns and Bill Watkins, all that was left for the Wolverines to do in 1886 was to rely on their blue-chip talent to start winning games.

Expectations were sky-high.

9

Going for It

For William G. Thompson, founder of the Wolverines and the club's first president, 1886 got off to a poor start. On January 1, the six-year-old Detroit Music Hall, a downtown attraction located on Brush Estate property on Randolph Street, burned down. Thompson, Alfred E. Brush and other trustees overseeing the estate were faced with a difficult decision about the property. By late February, they decided to rebuild the theater as a modern, steam-heated facility with 2,500 seats at a cost of about $100,000. The entire block around it would be rebuilt with another $200,000, to honor the memory of Edmund A. Brush, Thompson's former father-in-law, the developer and wealthy landowner who was the estate's namesake.[1] Thompson took an active role in planning the new facility and travelled far afield to study the latest in heating and lighting systems with which to equip it. The theater opened in September, about $25,000 over budget, and renamed the Grand Opera House.

At the beginning of February, Thompson's mother-in-law, Mary Campau, widow of wealthy real estate mogul Daniel J. Campau, died. It wasn't so much her death at age 69, but events following it that produced significant grief for the former mayor—and much amusement for both his friends and enemies. Thompson was among the mourners at her well-attended funeral mass on the morning of February 3 and later burial at Mt. Elliott Cemetery. That night, he was with friends, including Wayne County auditor William Mahoney, at Tom Swan's saloon on Woodward Avenue. About 1 a.m., Edward Bagard, a former saloon-keeper and more recently a dealer in beer, wine and spirits, walked in and made a beeline for Thompson. Bagard, a well-educated man with whom Thompson had feuded in the past, had fled France, where he'd been a member of the republican Girondist movement opposed to the monarchy. What followed at Swan's that night was witnessed by several patrons, and their accounts differed wildly. In one telling, Bagard struck Thompson several times in the head with his cane, drawing a large amount of blood and prompting Thompson to collapse into the arms of a companion. Because of the severity of the blows, some bystanders thought Thompson's skull had been crushed. The injured man was rushed to his home and a doctor summoned. It was feared Thompson might not recover, according to some accounts.[2] The altercation between the burly Bagard and the dapper but slight Thompson was based on some sort of political disagreement. Thompson, a longtime Republican, became what was known as a "mugwump" by converting to the Democrats to help elect Grover Cleveland as president in 1884. In so doing, the former mayor disappointed many of his longstanding Republican friends in Detroit and Michigan, while becoming a leading Democrat in a state which traditionally favored the Republicans. It is not clear, however, how Bagard and Thompson became antagonists and whether the former mayor's party-jumping had anything to do with it. Another account of their fateful barroom encounter soon emerged to suggest it had been far less serious, if not farcical. In fact, a newspaper in Chicago described it as "a funny fracas."

> It turns out that Thompson was not much hurt. The blood that messed up the tiling [floor tiles] in Swan's was principally from the ex–Mayor's nose, which was tapped by Bagard in an unscientific but effectual fashion. His wounds on the head were inconsequential, and he came down-town today [February 4] not looking much the worse for his thumping.[3]

One of Thompson's friends was quoted as calling it "one of the funniest fights I ever saw. The minute Thompson was hit he clasped his hands to his lip and bawled out: 'O my, don't let this get into the papers!' He danced around the saloon like a decapitated bantam rooster, crying, 'O, keep it out of the papers!'" Thompson didn't want the public to learn about the incident, mere hours after the interment of his revered mother–in–law. His marriage to Adele was proving difficult, and he was anxious to avoid more problems on the home front, where she complained bitterly about his drinking. Besides, it was also unseemly conduct for a trustee of the Brush Estate. Bleeding profusely, Thompson climbed into a carriage for home, pleading with his friends gathered on the sidewalk: "For God's sake, boys, go and get this suppressed." Bagard never faced any charges, likely because Thompson was determined to play down the incident. Thompson's friends had some clout with the newspapers. Detroit journals, including the *Free Press,* carried nothing about it. Word did reach the *Chicago Tribune* and some sporting publications, however.

On March 11, five Wolverines and manager Watkins boarded an early morning train for Savannah, Georgia, where they were to meet the remaining members of the team and begin spring training. Six weeks of work and practice games were intended to get the club in shape for the season opener on April

29 in St. Louis. Games were played in Savannah, Macon, Atlanta, Charleston, and Chattanooga. As the weather warmed up, the Wolverines migrated north for contests in Cincinnati, Pittsburgh, Baltimore, Hartford, Jersey City, Newark and Rochester. During their Southern travels, the Big Four pounded pitchers hard once they shook off their rust, while newly signed pitcher Larry Twitchell delivered some strong performances and showed an unexpectedly good bat. Cincinnati, expected to be one of the stronger American Association teams, was defeated three times in a row. Watkins said the performance of the club exceeded his highest expectations, and he was particularly impressed with the work of Twitchell.[4] The players appeared briefly in Detroit to have their team and individual photographs taken before departing for St. Louis and their first League game.

Nearly 5,000 spectators crammed into Union Park on April 29 for the Maroons' home opener against the significantly upgraded Detroit club about which so much had been written. The Big Four didn't disappoint as they collected six of the 14 hits off St. Louis hurler Charlie Sweeney. He struggled with the Detroit batters, seven of whom hit from the left side of the plate. Lady Baldwin had a devastating curve and allowed only three hits in the 9–2 win. The Maroons, nicknamed the "Black Diamonds" because of the large number of one-time blacklisted players on their roster, bounced back the following day to win, 8–6. Twitchell, obviously nervous, took the loss in a slugfest in which the Maroons outhit the visitors, 13–11. He walked five batters and gave up a ninth-inning home run. Detroit took the third game of the series, 9–6, on May 1, before heading west to Kansas City, where they picked up wins on May 3 and 5.

While in St. Louis and Kansas City, the team couldn't miss seeing disturbing news reports, particularly those emanating from Chicago, their next destination. The labor movement was agitating for an eight-hour workday, and while some employers had granted that demand, others stood firmly against it. Worker protests were particularly strong in Kansas City and Chicago. Nationally, it was estimated that 50,000 workers were on strike at the end of April and another 105,000 were threatening to walk off their jobs.[5] Unrest spread quickly. Within a couple of days, an estimated 35,000 men were on strike in Chicago alone, and tens of thousands more joined them by May 4, shutting down all but one of the railroads serving the transportation hub. In New York, 15,000 workers took to the streets in protest, with another 8,000 marching in St. Louis.

Chicago was a flashpoint for violence. On May 3, a long-simmering strike at the McCormick reaper plant erupted in violence, and police fired into a crowd of strikers, killing two. In response, agitators, among them anarchists, called for a "revenge" protest on the evening of May 4 at the West Randolph Street Haymarket. The gathering was peaceful, and Mayor Carter H. Harrison, who was present, urged police to stand back. But as the crowd began to shrink, one speaker demanded that demonstrators "throttle" the law. This prompted police Inspector John Bonfield to move in with the 176 officers under his command and order those still present to disperse. At this point, someone tossed a bomb into the ranks of police, killing one officer instantly. Police replied by firing their guns into the crowd. An unknown number of protestors was killed or wounded, while eight officers died and 60 were hurt. The Haymarket violence shocked the strikers, and demonstrations subsided after the bloodbath. Business and political leaders, along with newspapers, blamed foreign agitators and anarchists for the newfound militancy of industrial workers. For his part, Mayor Harrison banned further meetings and marches in the city. Police arrested hundreds of people, and eight anarchists were put on trial for murder. An inflamed judge and jury ruled that the accused men were part of a conspiracy, and seven were sentenced to death after a trial now considered one of the worst miscarriages of justice in American history.[6] The identity of the bomb thrower was never determined.

    Luckily, the White Stockings were miles away and avoided the turmoil at home. They began their season in Kansas City, with defeats of the Cowboys on April 30 and May 1. Then it was off to St. Louis, where they won two out of three games in a series ending May 5. Chicago's home-opening game at West Side Park was May 6 for a series with Detroit, and by then life in the Windy City was returning to normal. A crowd estimated at 6,000 turned out on a fine summer-like day to see the reigning League champions clash with the much-ballyhooed nine from the City of the Straits. For many fans drawn to the game, baseball was a reminder of happier and simpler times, a couple of hours' respite from a world gone mad. Owners of the club quickly tapped into that sentiment. As the home club awaited the arrival of the Wolverines, a pennant proclaiming "Champions of the United States, 1885" was unfurled and run up a flagpole, where it snapped smartly in the breeze. In so doing, the team conveniently overlooked the non-decision in the previous fall's "world's series" with St. Louis.

    The Wolverines were delayed and didn't arrive at the park until the appointed time for the game, by which time the skies had grown dark and the temperature had plummeted. Chicago put John Clarkson in the pitching box, and he easily muted the visiting bats except for catcher Charlie Bennett, who homered in the third inning. Lady Baldwin was tagged with the loss, and the White Stockings warmed the hearts of their shivering fans with a 5–1 win. The following day, before a crowd of 2,500 in warmer conditions, Chicago's Jim McCormick kept the Detroit sluggers in check as the home team again downed the Wolverines, this time 6–2. On May 8, however, Pretzels Getzien was sharp and Detroit played error-free ball, relying on lively bats for a come-from-behind 5–4 win to disappoint the 3,500 spectators hoping for a Chicago sweep. The series with Chicago would be a precursor for Detroit's season. Cap Anson and his White Stockings would be Detroit's most difficult opponent during the 1886 campaign when both clubs vied for League supremacy.

Detroit opened at home on May 10 before 3,500 spectators under threatening skies. Sporting smart new white uniforms, the Wolverines were cheered almost continuously as they downed the New York Giants, 9–2, in a seven-inning game called on account of darkness. Lady Baldwin allowed seven hits while Tim Keefe of the Giants struggled, giving up 14 hits in the lopsided affair. The following day, before a crowd of 3,200, Getzien pitched a four-hitter to lead the Wolverines to a 10–0 blanking of the Giants. New York pitcher Mickey Welch allowed 13 base hits, including fifth-inning doubles to Hardy Richardson, Deacon White and Jim Manning. The win put Detroit in a first-place tie with Chicago, both clubs sporting records of seven wins and three losses. On May 12, Detroit completed its sweep of New York with a 9–5 win to take first place on its own while Chicago sat idle. It marked the first time Detroit had been first since brief stints during their 1881, 1882 and 1883 campaigns. During the New York series, the Big Four belted 24 hits to produce 12 runs. With 116 hits to date, Detroit easily led the League. New York was second with 104 while Chicago had 87.[7] The Wolverines' lumber company was performing as expected.

The Boston Beaneaters were the next guests at Recreation Park, and Detroit swept the three-game series in which Sam Thompson hit the first home run of the season on May 13 in a 4–3 win. His blast sailed over the right field fence beyond which sat Deppert's cut-rate customers. In that same game, Thompson batted in three runs, made several terrific catches and turned one of them into a double play. Detroit swept a three-game series from Philadelphia and then three more from Washington to complete its first home stand. During a 13–3 shellacking of pitcher "One Arm" Daily and Washington on May 22, Detroit had 15 hits, including two triples by Thompson, who was reportedly suffering from malaria.[8] Two days later, the Wolverines had a satisfying 7–4 win over their former hurler, Dupee Shaw, while the Nationals committed 10 errors. It marked Detroit's 13th win in a row for a League-leading 17–3 record. The games averaged about 3,000 fans, putting smiles on the faces of directors, including the hard-driving Frederick K. Stearns, who had become second vice-president. Even former club president and ex-mayor Thompson pronounced himself well pleased at the improved fortunes of the club, saying at one point: "Seeing the Detroit Club win a game is such an unusual luxury and an event so inconceivable in the past that it gives profound joy."[9]

9. Going for It

The 1886 Wolverines made a strong showing and placed second behind Chicago in the race for the National League pennant. Back row, from left: Larry Twitchell, Charlie Bennett, manager Bill Watkins, Lady Baldwin, and a catcher identified as C.L. Hall who did not appear on the official roster. Middle row: Pretzels Getzien, Dan Brouthers, Jim Manning, Ned Hanlon, Deacon White, Sam Thompson. Front row: Jack Rowe, Sam Crane, Hardy Richardson (National Baseball Hall of Fame Library, Cooperstown, New York).

Detroit continued its winning ways in Boston on May 28–29 with victories of 7–3 and 9–4. A doubleheader on Decoration Day, May 31, in New York brought Detroit's 15-game winning streak to an end. In the morning game, the Giants edged the visitors in dramatic fashion, 6–5, in 10 innings before 7,000 fans. Worse than the defeat, however, was the loss of a key player. In the bottom of the tenth, the leadoff batter for the Giants, first baseman Roger Connor, popped out to Richardson at second. New York shortstop John Ward then connected with a Getzien pitch, sending it high into the air over shortstop Jack Rowe into shallow left field. Rowe back-pedaled as left fielder Jim Manning raced in amid the cheers of the large crowd that made communication between the men impossible. Rowe and Manning collided heavily, Rowe turning a somersault as Manning dived for the ball with both hands under it. Ward had reached second when time was called to check the downed men. Rowe was fine, but Manning, thinking his left arm was dislocated, walked to the bench and had some players pull on it. The next Giants batter, left fielder Pete Gillespie, singled to bring home Ward, and the fans were delirious at snapping Detroit's winning streak. A doctor examined Manning and found a broken bone in his forearm and a sprained wrist. His arm was set and he was sent home to Fall River, Massachusetts, to recover. He continued to receive $75 a week under an accident insurance policy taken out by Detroit directors.[10]

The afternoon game drew an astonishing 20,632 paid customers to the Polo Grounds, the largest ever crowd to attend a baseball game to that date. Police had trouble controlling the fans who spilled onto the field and gatecrashers who jumped the fences. Some estimates put the actual crowd count as high as 35,000.[11] After a delay while police reinforcements arrived, both teams agreed that any ball hit into spectators gathered in the outfield would be ruled a single. New York tallied a run in the bottom of the first inning, and Detroit replied with a single run in the fourth. Baldwin outperformed Welch this day, the former allowing six hits, the latter 15. Richardson and Rowe each sent Welch offerings into the crowd and were credited with singles. Detroit added another run in the seventh inning and two in the ninth to take the game, 4–1, sending the masses home unhappy. They were particularly upset at umpire John Eagan, who was escorted from the field by two mounted policemen and eight more on foot. In the midst of the frenzy that day were manager Watkins and Getzien, who were stationed at the turnstiles, as was visiting club practice. Getzien was manning the entrance for carriages, and "numbers of men jumped from vehicles over his head into the grounds" and thus were not part of the crowd count or gate receipts.[12] Still, Detroit's share of the day's proceeds amounted to a lofty $4,200.[13] The club, with its star-studded roster, was becoming a great draw in League parks, even better than at its own. In the first five weeks of the season, Detroit's income was double what it had been at that point in the past, prompting the *Free Press* to observe: "a winning team is a money-making team, however large the salary list."[14] At the end of May, Detroit sat atop the League with a record of 20 wins and four losses, one game ahead of Chicago and 4½ better than New York.

After losing its final game in New York, 8–4, with a shaky performance from Baldwin, Detroit made its way to the Swampoodle Grounds in Washington for what would be a memorable three-game series. Pretzels Getzien took the ball for the first game on June 2 and, helped by a Hardy Richardson homer, came away with a 6–4 win. Manager Watkins turned to Getzien again the following day, knowing his hurler thrived on back-to-back outings. The Nationals tied the game at 2–2 in the bottom of the ninth, and it wasn't until Dan Brouthers singled to left field, bringing in Sam Crane, that Detroit went ahead again in the top of the 11th. Getzien retired three Washington batters on fly balls and Detroit earned a hard-fought, 3–2 victory. Watkins gave the ball to Getzien for a third straight game on June 4 that would last 14 innings. Pretzels seemed as fresh at the end of the game as at the start, and "pitched one of the greatest games of his life."[15] But he received little support from Wolverines batters, who were troubled by the delivery of Bob Barr. And the Big Four and Thompson may have been tired from their tour of Washington, which had included climbing to the top of the new Washington Monument. The game was tied, 1–1, after 14 innings, when it was called because of darkness. Getzien had shown what a durable performer he could be, pitching 34 innings on three consecutive days, surrendering 22 hits while picking up two wins and a tie.

Baldwin benefitted from his days off and took the ball on June 5 to start a series in Philadelphia before a crowd of 8,700. The lefty shut out the Phillies 3–0, but needed 14 innings and an error made by opposing pitcher Dan Casey to pull it off. Casey, the former Detroit hurler, muffed a pop-up by Deacon White with two out in the 14th, allowing Thompson to score. White and Bennett also crossed the plate, and the Phillies were retired in order to end the game. Baldwin gave up seven hits to 12 for Casey. After a 5–1 loss to Philadelphia on June 7, with Getzien pitching, the Wolverines slipped to second place, but were soon back on top. They would not relinquish the League lead again

An 1886 game at Recreation Park, likely against arch-rival Chicago, which invariably drew large crowds. Note the fans and their carriages on the playing surface in the outfield. To the left of the grandstand can be seen rooftop stands erected by neighbors of the park who charged a reduced rate and incurred the wrath of directors of the Detroit club. The newly strengthened team made a concerted bid for the League championship, but was edged out by Chicago (Burton Historical Collection, Detroit Public Library).

until August 26. Baldwin picked up the 8–4 win in the final game of the Philadelphia series on June 8. Soon after leaving Philadelphia, manager Watkins signed Phillies catcher Charlie Ganzel to provide some relief for his rugged receiver Charlie Bennett, one of the top catchers in the League.

On June 11, Detroit began a successful home stand during which it won 16 of 20 games, with single losses to Chicago, Boston, Washington and New York. Noteworthy games included a June 12 win over the St. Louis Maroons, when Detroit set a major league record with seven home runs in a single game, a mark that would last until 1939. Jack Rowe and Sam Thompson each homered twice, while single blasts were launched by Charlie Bennett, Dan Brouthers, and Sam Crane. All came off the pitching of Charlie Sweeney, who could not be pulled because the Maroons had no backup. In all, Sweeney gave up 21 hits to the Wolverines. In the sixth inning, Sweeney beaned Brouthers, but after a gash behind his left ear was patched, Big Dan was able to continue. Getzien had a poor outing, giving up 11 hits, but it didn't matter with the big guns blasting away in a slugfest that Detroit won, 14–7.

The troublesome White Stockings arrived for a three-game series beginning June 19, and additional seats were installed at Recreation Park in anticipation of large crowds. Looking to sweep the Wolverines, about 200 Chicago supporters carried brooms and blared away on noisy tin horns. Lake steamers and trains brought hundreds more to the game from places like Cleveland and Toronto. In all, the crowd reached 12,000 for the first game and spilled onto the outfield grass. The teams agreed that fly balls hit into the crowd would be doubles. Baldwin pitched well and Thompson, still suffering from malaria, had three hits. The visitors edged Detroit, 5–4, picking up the winning run in the ninth inning on a wild pitch by Baldwin. It was the first home-field loss for the Wolverines in 1886, after 18 wins. Two days later, Getzien took the ball for the Wolverines in the second game of the series and came within a whisker of pitching a no-hitter before 6,000 fans. He was ably assisted by Ganzel behind the plate. It wasn't until the ninth inning that the visitors managed a hit, recording two and putting one run across the plate. But it was too little, too late, and Detroit took the game, 4–1, having pounded John Clarkson for eight hits. The rubber match was on June 22 and drew 7,000 fans to the park. Getzien was again called upon to pitch, and his curves were devastating. He allowed only six hits while Detroit batters had nine off rookie sensation Jocko Flynn. In the fifth inning, when his team was down, 4–0, Chicago captain Cap Anson disputed a base-running call made by umpire Jim Gaffney. Gaffney fined him $10, prompting the fiery competitor to hurl a string of epithets at an umpire unwilling to be cowed by the famous "kicker." He fined Anson a further $50 when the captain continued to hurl abuse, and added another $50 before Anson backed off to sulk. The $110 in fines set a major league record for one game.[16] And worst of all for Anson, his White Stockings lost the game, 5–4, when their late rally fell short. Aside from winning two out of three games and pulling five games clear of Chicago, Detroit had fattened their treasury even further from the 25,000 fans who attended the series.

Toward the end of the home stand, Detroit was pummeled, 11–2, on July 1 by Boston, with Getzien allowing 15 hits. About the same time, pitcher Larry Twitchell was sent home with a lame arm. He would make two attempts to return, neither of which went well. Boston was 18 games back of Detroit in fifth place.

A three-game series with Chicago kicked off the next road trip for the Wolverines, beginning July 8. About 400 Detroiters took trains to Chicago, mimicking Windy City supporters by sporting small brooms and hoping for a sweep. Detroit president Joseph Marsh and vice-president Frederick K. Stearns happily mingled with the hometown supporters, who were becoming known as "fans," the term "cranks" falling out of favor. Unfortunately, the series at West Side Park was indeed a sweep—for Chicago. Getzien struggled mightily in the first game as Chicago won, 9–4, while Detroit made nine fielding errors. The result pleased the 12,000 spectators who filled the park to overflowing. The following day, Baldwin was ineffective and Detroit was held to seven scattered hits for an 8–2 White Stockings victory before 5,000 fans. Big Dan Brouthers was out of the lineup with a bad cold, described by some sources as malarial fever. Marsh and Stearns took the train home that night, while the Detroit supporters who remained were demoralized and quietly tucked away their brooms. The final game drew 15,000 in a 3–1 Detroit loss, Getzien again struggling with his control. Anson homered off him, while Richardson took Clarkson out of the park for Detroit's only run. Despite the three losses, Detroit remained 1½ games ahead of Chicago. Having attracted 32,000 fans, the series was a significant boost for the coffers of both teams. The 27,000 drawn to the Decoration Day games in New York had generated $4,200 as the 30 percent share for the visitors. But while that was easily exceeded in the Windy City, the amount was not released publicly.

The Wolverines won eight games in a row after leaving Chicago, easily downing Kansas City and St. Louis three times apiece. Returning home, Detroit won its first two games against the Cowboys before losing an ugly one on July 21 when Getzien fell to pieces late in the game. He surrendered 19 hits to the seventh-place visitors, allowing Kansas City to cross the plate 10 times in the eleventh inning alone in a 12–2 victory. Detroit committed nine errors, three of them Getzien's. Manager Watkins was unhappy at the work of his pitcher and fined Getzien $10 for each of those ten runs for a total of $100. He also fined his captain and center fielder, Ned Hanlon, $25 for poor play. As had become his habit, Watkins was quick to express displeasure by levying financial penalties, and players began to grumble that he was inconsistent and seldom went after the big guns like Bennett, Thompson or the Big Four.

The Wolverines regrouped by winning three games against St. Louis before hitting the road for another Eastern swing. They easily downed Washington three times and Philadelphia once, with Getzien and Baldwin alternating appearances. A winning streak of seven games ended in Philadelphia on August 2, when the Phillies victimized Baldwin for a 6–4 win. Newcomer Billy Smith took the ball the next day and did no better in an 8–7 loss. Acquired from Macon in the Southern League early in July when Twitchell was sent home, this was Smith's second loss in three appearances. Baldwin was outpitched by Hoss Radbourn the following day in Boston when Detroit lost, 6–4. Twitchell returned on August 5 but had to retire after four innings when his arm again gave out. He would not pitch again until September 22. Richardson came in to finish the game, which Detroit won, 9–8, to snap a three-game losing streak. It was reported that Getzien was ailing from heatstroke that felled him during the series in Washington. Detroit continued to cling to first place because Chicago was in a bit of a slump.

Away from the field, directors of Detroit were forced to deny rumors rampant in New York that Al Spalding and his captain, Cap Anson, had become shareholders of the Detroit Base Ball Club. President Joseph Marsh and director Frederick K. Stearns called the story nonsensical. "That story is the silliest sort of rot," Stearns said. "The position of the Detroit club should not be misunderstood. It wants the championship and intends to get it if hard conscientious play will do it. The fine work so far done by the team should be sufficient answer to the malicious invention of enemies of the club."[17]

In case "conscientious play" wasn't enough, Marsh and Stearns were willing to further upgrade the Wolverines to get the championship they coveted. They approached St. Louis Maroons owner Henry V. Lucas, whose team was awash in red ink, and persuaded him to release feared slugger Fred Dunlap. The $4,700 paid to obtain Dunlap's services was the highest sum yet paid for a player.[18] His salary would be $4,500 under a personal-service contract, the same sort of deal signed with Detroit's other stars. Increasingly, clubs were using such personal-service contracts instead of traditional team contracts in a bid to circumvent the limits the League set for player pay. Detroit, flush with cash, was in the vanguard. Meanwhile, the departure of their second baseman, Fred Dunlap, prompted rumors that the sixth-place Maroons were about to disband. When Lucas sold Dunlap on August 6, the club owner was nearly broke and had been forced to sell off nearly $500,000 in real estate for

$285,000.[19] He had lost tens of thousands of dollars on the Maroons, it was said.

Dunlap's acquisition by the well-heeled Detroit club was a sensation. He was expected to further boost the hitting power of the already potent offense and shore up an infield whose only weakness was at second base. The 27-year-old Philadelphian was in the seventh year of a career in which he had posted impressive numbers with Cleveland and St. Louis. In 1884, for instance, Dunlap led the Union Association with a .412 batting average, 160 runs, 185 hits and a .621 slugging percentage. His numbers were still impressive two years later and would improve with a better team. To make room for him, light-hitting Sam Crane was released by Detroit and picked up by St. Louis.

Detroit directors had few qualms about spending money, it being noted that as of the first week of August home attendance at Recreation Park had reached 73,000, about 30,000 more than during the entire 1885 season. The free-spending ways of Marsh, Stearns and company to achieve on-field success had become the talk of the baseball world. "Detroit is not a very large city," observed *Sporting Life*, "but it is creating a great deal of commotion throughout the land." Newspapers, it said, were full of stories "of Detroit victories, Detroit defeats, Detroit deals, Detroit stock, and so on *ad infinitum*. Verily base ball is making the City of the Straits famous."[20] The latest transaction did not go over well in St. Louis or with some of the Eastern clubs in the League, who resented the amount of money Detroit was prepared to spend. Boston's tight-fisted Art Soden, in particular, was determined to keep a lid on player

Detroit paid the struggling St. Louis Maroons a record $4,700 to acquire second baseman Fred Dunlap in 1886 and then granted him a princely salary of $4,500 when the club opened its coffers to pursue the National League pennant. Dunlap had a falling-out with manager Bill Watkins after the successful 1887 campaign and was sold to the League's Pittsburgh Alleghenys (Library of Congress).

pay. Just as Detroit directors were adding firepower, however, they were losing arm power. Baldwin's arm was weakening, Getzien's appeared to be gone, and Billy Smith had yet to prove himself. And Twitchell was unable to return to the rotation. Pitcher Pete Conway was acquired from the Kansas City Cowboys and made his first appearance in an August 24 loss.

The month of August would be difficult for Detroit, winning just 10 of its 23 games. Getzien made five appearances and lost twice, and Baldwin lost six of 10 starts. One bright spot came when Detroit took two out of three games in its fourth series of the season with Chicago, whose fortunes were improving. The White Stockings won 17 of its 23 games in August. On August 20, Baldwin had a strong outing and Detroit defeated Chicago, 6–4, before 10,000 supporters at Recreation Park. Manager Watkins, however, was in St. Louis, trying to acquire Maroons shortstop Jack Glasscock and pitcher Henry Boyle. They agreed to join the Wolverines if the St. Louis club disbanded. (It didn't and they didn't.) Just a few days beforehand, Maroons owner Lucas had quit the club, saying he had lost $70,000 in three years.[21] Watkins was among several managers looking to scoop up St. Louis talent, while various groups talked about acquiring the entire club. Despite the widespread fears it would disband, the Maroons managed to finish the season. On August 21, the second game in the Chicago series, Getzien handed the Whites one of their worst defeats of the season, 12–5, before 5,000 happy Detroit fans. Getzien allowed 15 hits, but the White Stockings were undone by an uncharacteristic 10 errors, while the Wolverines were particularly sharp in the field. Richardson had two home runs, while Rowe was four-for-four at the plate. Chicago took the third game, 4–0, in front of another 5,000 fans, handing Detroit its only shutout of the year. John Clarkson was hard on the hometown hitters, keeping them hitless until the eighth inning, when Deacon White managed a single. At the end of the series Detroit remained in first place, 1½ games ahead of the White Stockings.

The Phillies were next to appear at Recreation Park, and Detroit dropped two out of three games. On August 26, the third game, Getzien gave up 14 hits to the light-hitting club and Detroit lost, 11–10, in a 10-inning game. The loss, combined with Chicago's 10–4 win over Boston, put Chicago in first place in the League standings. With Bennett injured and Getzien pitching poorly, the defeat weighed heavily on the players and directors. After the game, the Wolverines were summoned to the director' box "and the riot act was read to them in seven different languages." The players were reminded that they were drawing large salaries and were expected to play hard every minute they were on the field. Soon afterward, a commotion erupted in the team's dressing room when captain Ned Hanlon complained to Getzien about his play. The pitcher replied that Hanlon could go someplace very warm, prompting Hanlon to fine the pitcher $25 for insubordination. "Getz then launched into a string of epithets at Ned, who assessed him $25 per epithet." The total came to $200 before Getzien exhausted his vocabulary.[22] Manager Watkins upheld the fines at the insistence of his captain.

Dissension was not limited to the Detroit dressing room. Earlier that same day, president Joseph Marsh announced that he was stepping down from the club, citing increased duties at his firm. It was later revealed by *Free Press* sports editor Charles Mathison that Marsh had been caught between two factions in the club who were at odds about the direction of the newly profitable operation with $40,000 in the bank.[23] First vice-president John Molony led a group on the nine-member board that wanted to oust manager Watkins, replace him with club secretary Bob Leadley, and gain control of the club. On the board, he was supported by banker Frank B. Preston, Judge E. O. Durfee, and lawyer Joe Weiss, but opposed by Stearns, merchant James L. Edson and retiree Charles H. Smith. The 400 shares in the club were divided between the two factions. Marsh found the situation untenable and opted to resign. When the Molony-led directors realized they couldn't buy out the others, Preston sold his 100 shares to cracker maker George M. Vail for $7,500. Vail then cast his lot with Stearns and company, and the Molony foursome quit, selling their total of 40 shares to Stearns and Edson. Another 12 shares were also picked up by Stearns.[24] The board was reduced to five members, and Stearns was named interim president until the annual meeting slated for October. His elevation was rather symbolic because he had been the driving force on the board since joining it months earlier.

The second-place Wolverines picked up their pace, winning seven of the nine remaining games in their home stand before embarking on a short Western tour beginning with a September 9 stop in Chicago for their fifth series of the season. The White Stockings held a three-game lead and were riding a 14-game winning streak. New York had tailed off and was 10 games behind Detroit. The question was whether Detroit could regain its form and challenge Chicago. With its pitching woes, that would be a tall order. In hitting the team was solid, and Hardy Richardson was the League-leader in homers with nine. He led his team to an 8–3 win in the first game of the series, with three triples, while Bennett, newly back in the lineup from his injury, homered. In all, Chicago's Clarkson surrendered 14 hits, while Lady Baldwin allowed only five. The next day, it was Dan Brouthers' turn to shine. He drove three home runs off Jim McCormick and added a single and double. His 15 total bases set a National League record. But Pete Conway allowed 15 hits and Detroit made 10 errors, letting Chicago win, 14–8. The rubber match attracted 15,000 fans, who went home happy when the White Stockings won, 14–4, to extend their lead over Detroit to four games. Baldwin was rocked for 19 hits. The hunt for pitching help continued, and it was said that Detroit had set aside $5,000 "for any good pitcher who might be placed on the market."[25] It sounded like desperation from a club whose pennant hopes were slipping away.

Three games against Chicago on September 20, 22 and 23 were Detroit's final home appearances of the season. Detroit fans were praying for a Wolverines sweep, combined with an improbable string of victories and a Chicago collapse, to reclaim first place. Through September 19, Chicago had 82 wins with 26 losses, while Detroit had 77 wins and 30 defeats. With 17 games left to play, the Wolverines needed everything to break their way. Some fans had already given up hope, and attendance at home games had slipped to as few as 1,500 fans. But Chicago was always a good draw. The first game attendance was 4,000. Getzien pitched poorly while Clarkson was in good form. The home club and its supporters were critical of umpire Phil Powers, whose calls seemed to favor the visitors at every turn. Powers seemed easily intimidated by Chicago captain Cap Anson, notorious as a loud "kicker" when things didn't go his way. The White Stockings took the opener, 7–3.

Suspicion about Powers was underlined when the *Free Press* reported that after the game Powers was seen drinking and socializing with the Chicago players at a well-known local watering hole. "This has a bad look," the paper said.[26] Powers drew the ire of 2,000 fans and the Wolverines again the following day. Chicago was leading, 4–2, after four innings played in a steady drizzle, and Detroit bats were just beginning to solve Jocko Flynn. It began to rain quite hard but Powers let the fifth inning begin. Faced with a protest, he halted the game and after 30 minutes declared only four innings had been played, so the game did not count and would be played in its entirety two days later.

Threatening skies hung over the September 22 game, keeping the crowd to about 1,500. Larry Twitchell returned to the pitching box after weeks of nursing his lame arm back to health. Chicago was leading, 6–3, after six innings, and Powers again seemed to favor the visitors. In the seventh inning, Dan Brouthers pounded Flynn for a home run. About 20 minutes before five o'clock, Powers suddenly announced that the game was over and the score would reflect only six innings of play. He gave no reason, although it appeared to relate to darkness, prompting a reporter to insist there was plenty of light to continue play and it wasn't raining. Powers, it appeared to those present, wanted to snuff out any Detroit rally and give the game to Chicago. Enraged fans chased the umpire into the dressing room, where he hid until friends were able to spirit him away to safety. A young boy saw Chicago right fielder King Kelly in a carriage on nearby Brady Street and struck him with a stone. A melee ensued between fans and Kelly and his teammates when he tried to throttle the lad, but injuries were minor. Feelings ran high among local reporters. The *Free Press* said Powers had stolen the game for the visitors and warned him not to show his face again in Recreation Park. It added: "The spectacle of that piratical umpire brazenly filching a game from Detroit in order to gratify personal malice was one that incensed Detroiters as nothing in the history of the game here ever has before."[27]

Detroit filed a protest about Powers with National League president Nick Young. The very next day, Powers was back at the park to umpire the rained-out game from two days earlier. He gave the Wolverines and their 2,000 supporters little to complain about this time, however, and the home team won, 6–2, salvaging a single win in the series and finishing its season at home on a positive note. Baldwin was sharp, holding Chicago to four hits, while Clarkson was hit hard. Still, Chicago had a lead of 5½ games with 14 to play, clouding Detroit's championship hopes.

During the last road trip with stops in Boston, New York, Washington and Philadelphia, manager Watkins signed pitcher John "Phenomenal" Smith of the Newark club. Smith, a 21-year-old lefty, repudiated a contract he had already signed with the League club in New York, saying he had been plied with alcohol by the Giants and induced to sign. Smith agreed to accept $500 to play for Detroit for the final two weeks of the season, but promised to play for New York in 1887. New York obtained an injunction to stop Smith from playing in Detroit, but it was dissolved October 2 and Smith pitched his first game for the Wolverines two days later, a 4–3 win over Washington. He pitched in a 1–1 tie with Philadelphia on October 7 and lost 5–1 to the Phillies in his final appearance on October 9, the last day of the season. Smith hadn't been nearly as phenomenal as his nickname suggested, while picking up $500 for three games. Rather than New York, in 1887 Smith signed with Baltimore of the American Association, where he won 25 games and lost 30. Meanwhile, Watkins was pilloried in the St. Louis-based *Sporting News* for signing Smith, a player already under contract. Still smarting from the loss of Fred Dunlap and Watkins' effort to pick up other Maroons, *Sporting News* editor and unapologetic Maroons booster Alfred Spink opined: "there is less honor among the leaders of the game than there used to be." He was just getting started, and Watkins would become a favorite target.

On October 8, Lady Baldwin blanked the Phillies, 11–0, picking up win number 42 (with 13 losses), setting an all-time season record for wins by a lefty. Baldwin had seven shutouts, also a record. Interestingly, he was the only National League pitcher able to shut out the Phillies, doing so five times. His win total tied him for first place in the League with New York's Tim Keefe.

Baldwin amassed a League-leading 323 strikeouts and held batters to a .243 on-base percentage. He also had the third-best earned run average at 2.24, and the third-best winning percentage at .764. Getzien, meanwhile, was fifth with a .732 winning percentage, the only pitching category in which he was among the top five. Getzien had won 30 games and lost 11.

Chicago's final season record was 90–34, while Detroit's was 87–36, 2½ games back. The winning percentages of both teams were outstanding, at .726 and .707, respectively. Chicago's pennant was its second in a row and sixth since the League was established in 1876.

Chicago and Detroit had been very similar ball teams, but the former was even stronger offensively than the slugger-heavy Wolverines. Chicago led the League in runs, doubles, triples, RBI, walks, and on-base percentage. Cap Anson, who was inducted into the Hall of Fame in 1939, and King Kelly, added six years later, had been particularly effective. The pitching staffs had recorded very similar numbers, with Chicago having a slight edge in ERA, 2.54 to 2.85.

Detroit batters owned first place in four hitting categories. Hardy Richardson and Dan Brouthers led the League with 11 home runs apiece, and Richardson was first in hits with 189. Brouthers recorded the top slugging average of .581, while Richardson was fifth at .504. Brouthers was tops in total bases with 284 and was third with a .370 batting average, 181 hits, and 139 runs, one spot ahead of Richardson's 125. Sam Thompson had the third-most runs batted in with 89, one spot ahead of Jack Rowe with 87. Overall, Detroit had three of the League's top 10 hitters, Brouthers third, Richardson fifth and Thompson eighth, with batting averages of .370, .351 and .301 respectively.

The St. Louis Browns won the American Association championship and challenged Chicago to a second "world's series" in a row. St. Louis took the best-of-seven national championship four games to two, taking advantage of the White Stockings' late-series pitching woes. Gate receipts from the winner-take-all series totaled $13,920. Browns owner Chris Von der Ahe, generally credited with coming up with the term "fan," short for "fanatics," to replace "crank," was delighted at the number of them who had attended the series—whatever they were called. He distributed half of the proceeds to his 12 players, or $580 apiece, and kept the balance for expenses, umpire salaries and profit.[28]

The season had been financially successful for most League teams. Detroit cleared about $40,000, while New York earned $100,000, Chicago, $60,000, and Boston $50,000.[29] The money-losing St. Louis Maroons franchise was dissolved.

In Detroit, hopes were high for 1887, having come so close to capturing the pennant in 1886. But the club would soon learn that its free-spending ways and aggressive tactics had alienated League magnates, who were determined to curb player salaries and keep teams from buying the championship. Several owners didn't care for the way Stearns and his Detroit directors conducted themselves. Within weeks of the season ending, a dark cloud appeared that threatened not only Detroit's dream of baseball glory, but the future of the franchise itself.

10
Getting There

Detroit manager Bill Watkins was in a confident frame of mind when a correspondent for *The Sporting News* found him in the lobby of a local hotel at the end of the 1886 season. "Next year we intend to go after the pennant," Watkins said. "Our team will be somewhat strengthened next year, if the expenditure of money will do it, because we want the pennant, and it must wave in the City of the Straits in 1888."[1]

His comments earned him a brickbat from *Sporting News* editor Alfred Spink, who observed: "Watkins modestly takes all the credit for the success of the Detroit Club. There is nothing like a swelled head."[2] Spink was still angry at Watkins for snapping up Fred Dunlap from Spink's beloved Maroons and for pursuing other players from the financially tottering St. Louis franchise. It was well known that Watkins and president Frederick Stearns were prepared to spend freely to bring the National League championship home. On the eve of the annual meeting of the National League, it was apparent that a major topic for discussion would be the personal contracts some teams like Detroit offered to get around salary limits sought by the League. Stearns acknowledged it was an important issue, and Chicago's president Al Spalding agreed.[3]

Shortly before the annual meeting on November 17, a joint committee of the League and American Association made several sweeping changes to the rules for the upcoming season. Four strikes would be necessary to record an out, five balls would constitute a walk, and batters could no longer call for "high" or "low" deliveries. The strike zone was set between the knees and shoulders, and pitchers had to start their delivery with one foot on the back line of a slightly shrunken box, thereby establishing a pitching distance of 55 feet, six inches, an increase from 50 feet where it had been since 1881. In addition, walks would be scored as hits, a move that inflated batting averages for the 1887 season and drew widespread criticism. It would be abandoned after a single season.

League magnates gathered in Chicago, and it soon became apparent that an agenda was afoot to thwart Detroit ambitions to buy its way to a pennant, completely aside from the personal contract issue. First, Nick Young was returned as president, the Allegheny Club from Pittsburgh was approved to replace Kansas City, and exhibition games were allowed on Sundays.

Then came the bombshell that targeted free-spending Detroit. It wasn't a ban on personal contracts, as had been expected, because such a move would have affected other League clubs like New York. Instead, Boston's Arthur Soden came up with a plan to clip the wings of the high-flying Wolverines and simultaneously fatten the coffers of most League teams. Under existing practice, visiting clubs received 30 percent of the gate and Detroit, with its Big Four sluggers, had been a strong draw on the road, often attracting larger crowds than to its home games. Detroit, it was calculated, was walking off with at least $500 for each game on the road.[4] Soden proposed that all visiting teams should receive a "guarantee" of $100 a game. Boston, New York, Philadelphia and Washington supported the change, while opposition came from Detroit, Chicago, St. Louis and Kansas City (the latter club not yet formally ejected). Soden said he viewed the matter as so serious that he would form an Eastern League if his scheme was not adopted. Detroit's Frederick Stearns took dead aim at Soden, saying: "You have hit the mark. You ought to form an Eastern League, and I hope you will. We will be glad to get rid of you. When you go we can form a Western League from the Detroit, Pittsburgh, Cincinnati, Louisville, St. Louis, Kansas City and Chicago clubs that will be more profitable than any base ball organization ever has been."[5] The guarantee question pitted the more populous Eastern cities (Boston, 400,000; New York, 1.6 million; and Philadelphia, nearly 1 million) against the Western ones. Soden upped the guarantee to $125 for visiting teams and added a sweetener that gate receipts be split 50–50 for games played on national or state holidays. Chicago and St. Louis then supported the Eastern clubs, and the change was made. Reaction in Detroit was swift and negative. The *Detroit Free Press* was particularly incensed:

> The action of the league in forcing the guarantee system has thrown the base ball world into a high state of excitement. Detroiters are particularly worked up over the matter, as it was a blow aimed directly at the splendid club that now represents the City of the Straits. There is every prospect that the Detroit Club will drop out of the league and join the American Association. The management of the Detroits is very indignant at the action of the league and served to put the most money into the coffers of the very men who have connived at the burning injustice. President Stearns has received telegrams from all the Association Clubs urging him to bring the Wolverines into that organization and promising the very fairest treatment. At a meeting of the Detroit Board of Directors in the Russell House Saturday afternoon

it was decided to send manager Watkins to Cincinnati to attend the meeting of the American Association, which occurs Monday might. He is authorized to receive any proposition the association may make. The management of the Detroits do not propose to quietly submit to the imposition. President Stearns, Directors Vail and Edson and Manager Watkins all emphatically assert that they have helped these Eastern clubs to make their money and do not now propose to be pushed to the wall. Detroit will fight.[6]

Stearns and company calculated that their threat to bolt to the AA would get the attention of the League magnates. "Let no one delude himself with the idea that Detroit is making a bluff in this matter," Stearns said. "If the league doesn't do what is right with us, and do it quickly, we shall go into the American Association, which will treat us fairly."[7]

Chicago's Al Spalding said he believed Stearns was bluffing. He said that League clubs were determined to curb Detroit's spending, which far exceeded a sustainable level for a city its size, with "a salary list far beyond what good business judgment and common sense would justify." He understood what motivated Soden and his fellow magnates. Spalding said Detroit deserved no special treatment because it had acted selfishly in breaking up the Buffalo club, then by buying Dunlap, a move which hurt St. Louis, while Detroit relied on League teams to help fund its predations and extravagances.[8]

Having lost Pittsburgh to the League, the American Association was willing to consider Detroit for membership. Watkins, who said he preferred the Association to the League, was dispatched to the AA's special meeting on November 22 in Cincinnati, convened to find a replacement for Pittsburgh. Watkins joined representatives from Cleveland and Kansas City, both of whom were submitting formal applications for membership. Watkins and Detroit had made no formal bid, but he stayed in touch with club directors by telegraph while he monitored proceedings. Association magnates knew of Detroit's interest and dispatched three delegates from the meeting to consult Watkins.

> They returned with a report that the Detroit club, through its representative, would like to hear a proposal from the Association in reference to what inducements would be offered to the Detroit club to come over to the Association. After considerable discussion it was decided that such action would not be business-like, and that if the Detroit club was in really good faith it would have to apply for admission and state just what concessions in reference to the division of gate receipts they would expect. If the Association was not willing to give them what they requested they would then retire, and the matter would remain right where it had been in the first place.
>
> Manager Watkins at once telegraphed President Stearns a lengthy message, in which he asked him to either come to Cincinnati in person or vest him with authority to [act] in the afternoon. He received a reply to make the application.[9]

In the meantime, Cleveland and Kansas City made their pitches for membership. To accommodate Detroit, the Association did not convene again until the following afternoon so Watkins could receive further instructions and prepare an application. Upon resuming, delegates gave the floor to Watkins, who read a telegram from president Stearns, saying that the National League "had granted them all the concessions they had demanded and they would remain where they were." With that, delegates voted unanimously to accept Cleveland and rejected Kansas City, which had struggled financially and was too far west to suit Eastern teams.[10]

The *New York Clipper* disputed Stearns' claim of victory and the seriousness of his threat to jump leagues.

> It seems to be the general opinion that the Detroit Club's ultimatum to withdraw from the National League was a bluff made only to prevent the guarantee system from being carried out. President Stearns said that the Detroit Club had received concessions from Chicago, New York, Philadelphia, Pittsburgh and Boston Clubs which satisfied the Detroit management. He was not disposed to say what the concessions were that had induced the club to remain in the League, but finally stated that the clubs named had agreed to waive the guarantee rule in the case of the Detroits.[11]

Soden of Boston said Stearns' claim that the League had given in to Detroit was "all bosh." He said Detroit would receive $125 when playing in Boston. "The Boston Club made no concessions to Detroit, and will make none," he declared. Soden did agree, however, to play Detroit on Decoration Day in Boston and on the Fourth of July in Detroit, when gate proceeds would be split evenly. Contacted by the *Clipper,* Al Spalding confirmed that Stearns had appealed to him for help, arguing that Detroit "could not possibly go through the season of 1887 as a League club under the guarantee method." Spalding said he agreed to continue dividing gate proceeds as before with Detroit, whose games had drawn 56,000 of the 150,000 spectators attracted to all White Stockings home games.[12] Spalding insisted he didn't know what other teams had done in response to Stearns, if anything. Pittsburgh and Philadelphia said they made no concessions to Detroit. The *Clipper* reported that New York had joined Chicago in agreeing to divide gate proceeds with Detroit under the old formula.[13] The arrangements with Chicago and New York were enough to satisfy Stearns because Detroit's most lucrative games were usually in those cities. He extended the same gate-splitting scheme to Chicago and New York when they visited Recreation Park. The Wolverines would remain viable, Stearns hoped, and able to meet Detroit's high expenses. But there was real concern about the loss of revenue. Under the $125 guarantee plan, Detroit would earn $5,875 from the 47 games played in Boston, Indianapolis, Pittsburgh, Philadelphia and Washington. Had the 30 percent share remained in effect, those same games would have produced $23,500 for Detroit coffers, assuming the $500-a-game average take. Boston, in particular, would benefit at Detroit's expense.

Detroit was expecting a revenue shortfall of a bit less than $18,000 for 1887, so directors appealed to local businessmen to increase their purchase of season tickets as "a proper way of warding off the blow which the Boston schemers aimed at the club."[14] Payroll amounted to $46,650 for the 17 players, manager Watkins, secretary Leadley, ticket-sellers and grounds crew. Top earner was Fred Dunlap at $4,500, followed by Brouthers and Richardson at $4,000 each. Rowe and White earned $3,500 each, and Bennett received about $3,000. Baldwin, paid $2,500 in 1886, sought about $3,000, while Hanlon received $2,250 and Thompson got $2,000. Watkins was paid $2,000 and was expecting a raise, while Leadley received $1,000.[15] Sensing Detroit would struggle financially, New York offered $15,000 for two Wolverines who were not named publicly, and $10,000 for Hardy Richardson. Detroit didn't bite. Stopping at Rochester on his way home from New York in March, Stearns was blunt when asked about selling players: "I will not let a man go off the team, for any sum."[16]

In *The Sporting News,* Alfred Spink continued to blast "an ignorant boor named Watkins" for spreading a rumor that Spink's St. Louis Maroons were headed for extinction and for "trying to make people believe that Detroit is the biggest city in the League. How foolish." For good measure, Spinks took a swipe at the Wolverines. "The Detroits will no longer be called the 'Big Four,' but the 'Big Bluffers,' and when the team finishes next season in about fifth place the title may be changed to 'Big Duffers.'"[17] Spink said Detroit would be forced out the League, because the new guarantee system meant Detroit directors "see no way of making both ends meet." The writer seemed to enjoy that the majority of League clubs refused to yield to Stearns and his demands.[18] Early in 1887, when Spink's League-ousted Maroons were sold to a group from Kansas City and then flipped to Indianapolis businessmen headed by John T. Brush for $15,000, Spink had new enemies and lost interest in attacking Watkins.[19] The Maroons became the Indianapolis Hoosiers in the League.

Detroiters were optimistic about the 1887 campaign, a feeling that was buoyed by changes in Chicago, the League champions in 1886. Al Spalding let Boston acquire the high-living and difficult-to-discipline King Kelly for $10,000, an amount that turned heads—especially when the buyer was the parsimonious Beaneaters management. Right fielder Kelly was the batting leader for 1886 and a pillar for the White Stockings for seven years. Also released were veteran center fielder George Gore and left fielder Abner Dalrymple, both of whom had been with Chicago a year longer than Kelly. Gore signed with the New York Giants, while Dalrymple went to the Pittsburgh Alleghenys. With its entire outfield gone, Chicago would rely on younger players and was soon nicknamed "Anson's Colts." By contrast, nearly the entire Wolverines roster would return for a second run at the League title.

Manager Watkins arranged for spring training to begin in Macon, Georgia, in early March, after which the team would work its way as far north as Minneapolis and St. Paul. It was expected that the tour would cost about $4,200 and ensure the team was in peak form when it opened its season on April 28 in Indianapolis. A Southern tour included stops in Savannah, Georgia, New Orleans, Charleston, South Carolina, Mobile, Alabama, Memphis, Tennessee, and Louisville. The best and most profitable games were played in New Orleans and Memphis, but the Wolverines incurred high transportation costs and lost money in every other city. Overall, Detroit won all 31 of its spring training games.[20] New Orleans drew good crowds to its nicely appointed park, and one of the more bizarre episodes of the Southern campaign occurred there on April 5 in an 11–4 Detroit victory. Charles Mathison, the *Detroit Free Press* sporting editor, accompanied the Wolverines in the South and filed this report:

> The feature of today's game was a performance by [Abner] Powell, who played right field for the home team. A ball was knocked foul over the right field fence. Powell jumped up on the fence and saw a wicked small boy seize the sphere and run off with it. Powell skipped over the fence and chased the boy for three-quarters of a mile and brought back the ball. The game was delayed fifteen minutes.[21]

Added to the lineup were backup catcher was Charles "Fatty" Briody, from Kansas City, and rookie infielder Billy Shindle. Pitching was a problem with lefty Lady Baldwin struggling to get in shape and Larry Twitchell and Pete Conway complaining of sore arms early in April. So Detroit re-signed popular hurler Stump Weidman, giving them six pitchers on the roster, including Pretzels Getzien and a rookie named Knowlton. With the addition of Weidman, the roster stood at 18 men, most of them members of the Brotherhood of Professional Base Ball Players. Deacon White was a notable exception. The Brotherhood, formed to defend player rights, had elected Detroit slugger Dan Brouthers as its vice-president.

On the eve of the season, the annual meeting of the Detroit Base Ball Club disclosed that 600 season tickets had been purchased and that orders for more were coming in daily. The appeal to the Detroit public to rally around the team appeared to be working. President Stearns reported that although the previous season began with $20,000 in debt, it ended on the positive side of the ledger, although he didn't say by how much. He was returned as president. Meanwhile, director and past president Joseph Marsh was replaced on the board, having already sold his shares to Stearns.[22] On the last day before

The National League champion Detroit Wolverines of 1887 were the toast of the city after winning a 15-game world championship series against the St. Louis Browns. Back row, from left: Charlie Bennett, Dan Brouthers, Sam Thompson, Charlie Ganzel, Larry Twitchell, Lady Baldwin. Deacon White is in front of Ganzel. Middle row: Fatty Briody, Fred Dunlap, manager Bill Watkins, Ned Hanlon, Billy Shindle, Pretzels Getzien. Front row: Jack Rowe, Stump Weidman, Hardy Richardson (National Baseball Hall of Fame Library, Cooperstown, New York).

Detroit's opening series in Indianapolis, the papers reported that second baseman Fred Dunlap was offered $15,000 in a two-year contract with the New York Giants. The Detroit Free Press said it was yet another example that the "greedy Eastern clubs" expected Detroit to fail financially and coveted its players.[23]

The Wolverines disappointed 5,000 Indianapolis fans in the April 28 season opener when Jack Rowe drove Charlie Bennett home in the ninth inning for 4–3 Detroit victory over the Hoosiers (the former Maroons). Two more wins, by scores of 10–8 and 15–12, were notched before Detroit headed east to Pittsburgh for three games. The series began with an 8–3 loss to the Alleghenys, who received strong pitching from Pud Galvin. It was Detroit's first defeat after 31 exhibition and three League games. Bennett was idled by a sore arm, later attributed to "rheumatism." He tried to return to the lineup a month later, but fared poorly and did not return to regular duty until July 25, appearing in only 46 of 127 League games. "Rheumatism" and "malaria" were often used in newspapers of the day to describe the poor play or absences of players who were actually suffering from sexually transmitted diseases such as syphilis and gonorrhea. Many players were hard-drinking *bon vivants*, with no shortage of female admirers in various cities. Team owners often sent their ailing stars for treatment at spas and hot springs.[24] Bennett was dispatched to the popular mineral baths in Mount Clemens, just north of Detroit. While it is not known for certain whether Bennett contracted a venereal disease that 1887 season, he was a handsome and exceedingly popular Wolverine.

Detroit's home opener was May 5 against Indianapolis, amid reports that the sale of season tickets was "unprecedented" in the history of the home club.[25] In all, about 3,500 supporters braved cold, wet weather to witness sharp fielding by the Wolverines and a strong outing for Pretzels Getzien. Detroit won, 5–3. The next day, Detroit bats produced eight runs in the first inning and the Wolverines pounded the Hoosiers, 11–3, before 2,000 fans. Detroit swept the series with an 18–2 shellacking of the visitors on May 7 before 3,600 spectators. Slugger Sam Thompson had a terrific day at the plate. He swatted two bases-loaded triples and, in so doing, set a major league record for a single game. Detroit belted 18 actual, or "true" hits (once walks, which that season only were counted as hits, were excluded), including a homer by Jack Rowe. With the sweep, the Wolverines stood first in the League with an 8–1 record. Meanwhile, ace hurler Lady Baldwin remained at his home in Hastings, Michigan, nursing his lame arm, and pitcher Pete Conway was sidelined with an injury.

The Allegheny club of Pittsburgh was swept in three games at Recreation Park by scores of 10–3, 6–4, and 18–2. Crowds ranged from 2,000 to 2,500. In the first game, Allegheny pitcher Ed Morris refused to pitch, claiming he had a sore arm. He was replaced by an inexperienced Bill Bishop, who surrendered 11 true hits. Morris was troubled by the new rule that shrank the pitching box, claiming it restricted his movement, and came up with the sore-arm excuse. He was suspended by manager "Hustling" Horace Phillips for three weeks. In the final contest, on May 11, the hapless Bishop gave up nine runs in the first inning and issued 10 walks in the 18–2 blowout.

With an 11–1 record, first-place Detroit travelled to Chicago, whose 4–5 season start left it tied for fifth place. On May 12, John Clarkson was once again effective against Detroit batters in a come-from-behind, 10–8 White Stockings win. The three winning runs came off Getzien in the ninth inning, much to the delight of the 6,000 fans gathered at West Side Park. In the second game, Detroit's Weidman easily handled Anson's Colts and belted a homer in the 17–7 victory. Thompson added to the offense with three triples, and Dunlap had his second six-hit game in a week (including several walks, scored this season only as hits). The rubber match on May 14 drew 8,000 fans to see Getzien face Clarkson again. This time, the Detroit hurler came out on top, helped by a Deacon White four-bagger, and Detroit won, 7–4. In their six series during the season, Chicago would take 10 games, while the Wolverines won eight.

In Philadelphia, Detroit swept four games from the Phillies, including a 10–8 victory in the opener with Lady Baldwin back in the lineup. The following day, it was Dan Brouthers' time for heroics, pounding a bases-loaded triple and then a bases-loaded homer in a 19–10 rout. Ailing Pete Conway returned for the third game on May 18, when Brouthers and Rowe each homered in a 9–7 win. By the time the visitors downed the Phillies, 16–5, on May 19, more than 30,000 fans had witnessed the powerful Wolverines dominate the home team. Detroit's financial takeaway from the series amounted to a mere $500, however, because of the $125-a-game guarantee.

Detroit did not lose again until May 23, when Washington hit Getzien hard and eked out a 7–6 win in 10 innings. The Wolverines' record stood at 19–3, and *The Sporting News* was already predicting that the race for the world's championship in October would be between Detroit and the St. Louis Browns of the American Association.[26] The Wolverines lost two out of three games in New York that attracted 17,500 fans, before facing second-place Boston for two games on Decoration Day, May 30. More than 13,000 spectators crammed into the 10,000-capacity South End Grounds for the first clash. Detroit prevailed, 2–1, in 10 innings as its bats earned ten true hits off Hoss Radbourn. The afternoon game attracted 11,000 more fans, who saw rookie pitching phenomenon Kid Madden, 19, lead the Beaneaters to a 4–3 win. As agreed earlier, Detroit collected half the $12,000 in proceeds generated by the holiday games. The following day, with the $125 guarantee back in place, Hoss Radbourn allowed only four true Detroit hits in a 3–1 victory. Despite losing two out of three games to Boston, Detroit remained 1½ games ahead of the Beaneaters. It was reported about this time that Boston directors expected to turn a profit of from $60,000 to $70,000 in the 1887 season. The team's determination to impose the $125 guarantee for visitors was proving a boon for its bottom line.[27]

Back home at Recreation Park, Detroit prepared for Chicago, which was growing stronger and had defeated New York twice on Decoration Day. The game set for June 2 was rained out, and Chicago won the remaining two, Clarkson picking up the 4–2 win on June 3 and Kid Baldwin a 2–1 victory the following day. The slumping Wolverines had lost four games straight, reducing their lead to a half-game over second-place Boston. A total of 6,500 fans witnessed the two games. The Wolverines soon rediscovered their bats to beat the Alleghenys of Pittsburgh and then sweep a three-game series from Indianapolis. In the final game with the Hoosiers on June 11, second baseman Fred

Dunlap set a major league record by *starting* four double plays in a 7–6, come-from-behind victory. He took part in a fifth, to tie the record for the most double plays in which a single player *participated*. Injuries had beset the Wolverines. Lady Baldwin complained of a sore arm and was dispatched to the mineral baths at Mount Clemens where Bennett was being treated. Pete Conway was ailing and could not pitch, while Dan Brouthers developed a growth on his finger which kept him out of several games. But Detroit clung to first place ahead of Boston, which was enduring its own troubles.

Detroit took to the road, winning two out of three games in Pittsburgh before rolling into Chicago on June 16 where pitcher John Clarkson was effective and the home bats came alive, hammering the visitors 8–1. Detroit roared back with five home runs the following day off Kid Baldwin for a 14–10 win, but the Wolverines' nemesis, Clarkson, returned on June 18 in an 18–6 White Stockings victory. A total of 25,000 fans attended the three games, and Detroit walked away with a healthy share of the gate. On the road in Washington, manager Watkins was criticized for retaining Ned Hanlon as captain despite his poor leadership and for benching Getzien, who seemed to be pitching well. Watkins told directors: "I must have full control. In case you interfere I must ask you to appoint my successor." The directors quickly backed down.[28]

Detroit returned home and won seven of its next 10 games before playing host to Boston for a July 4 holiday doubleheader. With their struggles, primarily related to Radbourn's pitching, the Beaneaters had lost ground to Detroit. The Wolverines sat alone in first with 35 wins and 15 losses, while Boston had 32 wins and 20 defeats. On the eve of the clash, president Stearns denied another rumor floated in Philadelphia that the Phillies were negotiating to buy Brouthers, Richardson, Dunlap and Thompson. He dismissed it as a malicious bid to sow discord within the Detroit ranks, and he assured the players that management had no intention of selling any of them.[29]

Fully 8,000 Detroiters descended on Recreation Park on the morning of July 4 for the first game the much-anticipated doubleheader with Boston. Lady Baldwin was especially sharp in handling the Beaneaters lineup, which this day was missing its captain, King Kelly. Hardy Richardson homered twice and the Wolverines took the first game, 7–3. Despite threatening skies, 7,000 fans turned up for the afternoon clash, which ended in a 7–7 tie, called on account of rain after five innings. Richardson and catcher Fatty Briody both homered off Radbourn. The following day, 3,000 fans watched Detroit down the visitors, 16–8, in a slugfest in which Brouthers homered. Fred Dunlap collided with Sam Thompson while chasing a fly ball and broke bones in his foot, an injury that would keep him out of action for two months. Larry Twitchell's arm gave out, so Detroit was left with only Getzien and Baldwin and began pursuing more pitching talent. The loss by Boston dropped it to third place, while a surging Chicago claimed second.

After the home stand, the Wolverines embarked on a 12-game Eastern road trip and found victories hard to earn. Playing in New York, Boston, Philadelphia and Washington, they managed only three wins and a tie while losing eight games. The pitching of Baldwin and Getzien was largely ineffective. The hitters were in a slump, and fielding was often sloppy. Part way through the Eastern swing, president Stearns said Detroit would demand a percentage cut of the gate at League games next season or it would jump to the American Association, a comment suggesting that his club was suffering financially.[30] The AA had used a $65 guarantee since it was founded, but was widely expected to switch to a percentage system. During the trip, Boston embarrassed Detroit, 15–3 and 12–4, in consecutive games. Twitchell resumed his pitching duties and helped Detroit down the Beaneaters and Radbourn, 7–4, in the final game.

After a third straight loss to Philadelphia, in which Weidman was tagged for three home runs, manager Bill Watkins could take it no longer. He suspended Baldwin indefinitely without pay. The lefty was accused of "indifferent play" and returned to his home in Hastings, Michigan. He was earning $3,200, making him the second-highest-paid pitcher in the League after Radbourn, but Baldwin had won only six games. He was troubled by the new rule that required pitchers to keep one foot on the back line of the box and take only one step during delivery. Baldwin had also been overworked during 1886, and he seemed weaker as a result. Catcher Fatty Briody and pitcher Stump Weidman were also laid off, and Briody was fined. The reason, the newspapers surmised, was because of "dissipation" (drinking).

Watkins was developing a reputation for fining the lesser lights on the team but turning a blind eye to indiscretions and poor play on the part of the stars like Brouthers, Rowe, White, Richardson and Thompson. This tendency only fueled the dissension that was beginning to emerge. The *Detroit Free Press* supported Watkins' moves, but suggested more could be done. "There is no doubt the team needed a shaking up. There is also a very robust impression prevalent in Detroit that Watkins himself was entitled to a lion's share of the shaking up from the execrable judgment displayed by him in placing the pitchers."[31] Stearns promised that "a procession of pitchers" would be arriving to buttress the team. "We must have them, no matter how high [in price] they come." One of the first to appear, Turk Burke, pitched in only two games, recording a loss and a no-decision.

Anson's Colts appeared in Detroit for a four-game series that began July 23. It was a dispirited Wolverines club they faced, beset with injuries, ailments and a hitting slump. Chicago entered the series tied for second place, two games back of Detroit, and its youngsters were performing well. The visitors prevailed, 8–4, in the first game, hitting Getzien freely while the home club committed five errors in allowing Clarkson to take yet another Wolverines pelt. Two days later, with Bennett finally back from his "rheumatism," Detroit pounded new White Stockings pitcher George Van Haltren for 24 true hits in a 15–3 victory, including an eighth-inning homer by Sam Thompson over the distant center field fence. On July 26, Clarkson again led Chicago to victory, this time by an 8–1 score. Conway's return to the pitcher's box did not go well, and he was replaced by Twitchell. Detroit took the fourth game, 10–4, when Chicago's Kid Baldwin was pounded hard. Getzien picked up the win and a raise of $50 a month as a reward. Detroit had split the series 2–2 with Chicago, its sluggers unable to bother Clarkson, More than 12,000 fans saw the four games.

A new pitcher, Henry Gruber, a rookie from Connecticut, appeared in Detroit against New York on July 28 and did fairly well. But the Giants came from behind to win, 5–4, largely because of sloppy fielding. Gruber won four games and lost three before being released, while president Stearns' hunt for pitchers continued. With the win, New York moved to within 2½ games of Detroit, which remained in first place. The following day, Brouthers was out of the lineup with "malaria," while Rowe was out with an unspecified ailment. Getzien's pitching and sharp fielding gave Detroit the game, 8–5. The following day, Twitchell picked up one of his 11 wins in the season and Detroit edged the visitors, 8–7, to keep the Giants at bay. Despite a difficult July, Detroit still clung to first place by month's end, with 44 wins, two more than Chicago.

Yet another pitcher, Ed Beatin, from Baltimore, appeared in early August. He won one game and lost another before being released, as Stearns' "procession of pitchers" continued. Twitchell outlasted Hoss Radbourn August 4 in a 12–11 Detroit win over Boston, but his arm bothered him. Twitchell did not pitch again that season, but because of his strong bat and solid play in the outfield, Watkins kept him in the lineup. In the same game, Radbourn was punished by Detroit's sluggers, with homers by Rowe, Thompson and Brouthers, the latter just back from his illness. Despite their pitching woes, Detroit sold Stump Weidman to the New York Metropolitans of the AA for $1,000 in early August. At one point, the Wolverines carried eight pitchers among the 22 men on the payroll.

After taking two out of four games against Boston and two of three from Washington, on August 13 the Wolverines began a 17-game road trip with three games in Chicago. Success on the road was crucial if the club was to retain the League lead and avoid the late-season troubles that plagued it in the 1886 campaign. They responded by winning 11, including one of three from Chicago and one of three from tail-ender Indianapolis, before sweeping three games from Washington. They split two games with Philadelphia, took three from struggling Boston and then two of three in New York. Fully 16,000 fans watched Clarkson dominate Detroit on August 13, despite a sore arm. Clarkson struck out six Wolverines, allowed only six hits and homered twice himself in the game that was called after eight innings because of darkness. The win brought Chicago to within one game of Detroit. Large crowds on the road swelled Detroit coffers at a time when home crowds were light, often as small as 1,000 or 1,500. Two days later Clarkson repeated his mastery of Detroit in a 6–4 win.

At this point, the National League announced that a game previously awarded to Detroit, but protested, was thrown out, leaving the Wolverines and White Stockings deadlocked in first place. Detroit took the third game, 5–3, regaining first place and earning a rare victory from Clarkson, who pitched his third straight game. Total attendance came to 28,000, producing $4,000 in much-needed gate receipts for the Wolverines.

Soon afterward, when Detroit directors rescinded some of the fines he had levied, Watkins complained about a lack of support from Detroit management. Watkins said management was also interfering in his decisions about which players deserved playing time. The *Detroit Free Press* questioned Watkins' choice of pitchers on occasion and suggested that the interference from management was warranted.[32] The newspaper continued to complain about Watkins and his "asinine experiments."[33] It cited his benching and attempt to trade away Getzien, despite the pitcher's good work. Such internal strife came at a critical time with Detroit fighting for the pennant in a race considered the most exciting in League history. Boston and New York fell back and Chicago faltered, slipping to 4½ games back of Detroit by the end of August.

Detroit's 20-game final home stand got underway on September 5, when Clarkson led Chicago to a come-from-behind, 11–7 win, disappointing 7,000 fans in Recreation Park. It marked his ninth victory over Detroit in 1887. A rainout led to a doubleheader on September 7. The first game attracted only 800 fans, and Detroit's Conway earned one of his eight victories in an 8–2 win. Attendance swelled for the afternoon game when Detroit faced a tired Clarkson, who surrendered 18 true hits and lost, 8–4. The 4,000 spectators welcomed back Lady Baldwin, starting for the first time since July 16. The lefty allowed six true hits and went four-for-four at the plate. Reports out of the Chicago clubhouse hinted at player dissension, focused primarily on playing manager Cap Anson. President Al Spalding, in Detroit for the series, stepped in to quell discontent.

Despite the success of the Wolverines, fans were often scarce at home. In the morning game of a September 10 doubleheader with the Alleghenys of Pittsburgh, only 700 fans appeared at the ballpark. Detroit won both games,

14–6 and 17–3, Conway and Baldwin prevailing over Pud Galvin and Ed Morris, respectively. On September 12, after allowing only two true hits in a 6–0 shutout of Boston, Getzien was presented with a $300 gold watch, a gift from directors and prominent Detroiters, in appreciation of his solid work. The next day, Kid Madden was sharp, leading Boston to a 2–0 shutout of Detroit. Detroit roared back to pummel Boston's Dick Conway for a 15–6 win. Eight more wins with only three losses were recorded by the Wolverines as they completed their home stand against Washington, Philadelphia, New York and Indianapolis. During that time, president Stearns predicted that his club would finish the season with a profit of $5,000, despite having a payroll that was 50 percent higher than any other team. He also predicted confidently that the National League would revert to the percentage system for gate receipts in 1888.[34]

Stearns and St. Louis president Chris Von der Ahe agreed to a world championship series on the assumption that their clubs would capture their respective league pennants. After negotiations with Stearns, the Detroit players agreed to extend their services to November 1 and accept $400 each in additional pay for the series plus a $100 bonus if they won it.[35] Toward the end of the home stand, Fred Dunlap, whose broken foot bones had healed, returned to the lineup. Meanwhile, directors of the club grew concerned about local support for the Wolverines. The final three home games attracted crowds of 800, 500 and 1,000, respectively, as the last-place Indianapolis Hoosiers were dispatched with ease. Meanwhile, the American Association voted to divide gate receipts in 1888 with 30 percent allocated to visiting clubs, an arrangement similar to that which the National League had abandoned.[36] Stearns now had a bargaining chip with League magnates in his bid to push them to revert to the old system. He could threaten to bolt. But Stearns would have to be at his wily best because reports from Boston and Chicago said they were enjoying net profits of $100,000 under the new guarantee system.[37]

The final eight games for the Wolverines were on the road, beginning September 30 with a four-game series in Pittsburgh. Detroit led Chicago by six games and Philadelphia by seven. Regardless, the cushion was a comfortable one, and the Wolverines seemed to ease up. They split the four games with the Alleghenys but took only one of the four games from Indianapolis, the League's last-place club with only 37 wins. On October 8, after an 11–8 loss to the Hoosiers, Detroit captured the League pennant with a record of 79 wins and 45 losses, 3½ games ahead of the Phillies and 6½ up on the White Stockings. Detroit had taken first place on May 4 and never relinquished it, although in August it was tied for one day with Chicago.

Dan Brouthers hurt his ankle in the last game of the season and saw action in only one of the 15 games that Detroit and St. Louis had agreed to play for

Another look at the 1887 National League and world champion Detroit Wolverines. From top right, inner, clockwise: Hardy Richardson, Dan Brouthers, Lady Baldwin, Charlie Bennett, Jack Rowe, Charlie Ganzel, Peter Conway, Deacon White, Fred Dunlap, Pretzels Getzien. Inner circle, from top, clockwise, manager Bill Watkins, Sam Thompson, Ned Hanlon, Larry Twitchell (Detroit Historical Society).

the championship series. Brouthers had the League's third-best batting average at .338, second-best slugging average at .562, and top on-base percentage at .426, was fourth in runs batted in at 101 and tied for fifth with 12 home runs. He had the most runs with 153, his 169 hits placed him fifth, and he was tied for fourth-most walks with 71.

The *Detroit Free Press* was giddy at the accomplishment of the Wolverines and saluted it on the front page.

> For a town of its size Detroit has performed marvels in the base ball line. It has had the enterprise to get together a team able to mop the earth with the clubs representing threefold its population, wealth and base ball experience. It is naturally galling to these ancient landmarks of base ball to have a stripling step in and capture the honors, but at the same time they are forced into admiration at the feats of the youngster.[38]

Management was praised for bringing glory to the City of the Straits with so little financial return for directors.

Detroit's parade of sluggers dominated the League's batting categories. Sam Thompson had the best batting average at .372, the top slugging average at .571, was first in runs batted in with 166, and had the most total bases with 311. He led the League with 203 hits, his on-base percentage of .416 placed him third, and he tied for fifth with 118 runs. Hardy Richardson had third-most hits with 178, was third in runs with 131, and third in total bases with 263. Jack Rowe was second with 135 runs and fourth with 171 hits. On the pitching side, the doughty Pretzels Getzien recorded the League's highest winning percentage at .690 and the third-most wins with 29. The only other Detroit hurler to rank among the League's best was Pete Conway, whose earned run average of 2.90 was eclipsed only by Philadelphia's Dan Casey.

In the American Association, the St. Louis took the pennant as expected, finishing 14 games ahead of Cincinnati. The Browns were an aggressive and speedy team and led the major leagues with an all-time record of 581 stolen bases. By contrast, Detroit had stolen only 267. Aside from that, their left fielder Tip O'Neill, the young Canadian hurler once rejected by Detroit, had been outstanding, having quit pitching and making his mark with his bat. O'Neill led in 10 AA batting categories: batting average, .435; doubles, 52; triples, 19; slugging average, .691; on-base percentage, .490; total bases, 357; home runs, 14; hits, 225; runs, 167; and runs batted in, 123. He is the only player ever to lead in all those categories. O'Neill's batting average, adjusted to remove the walks that for 1887 were recorded as hits, is the second highest in the history of the major leagues.

The 15-game world's series was split between League and Association cities, with admission doubled to one dollar in League parks and to 50 cents in Association parks. Stearns and Von der Ahe were hoping to cash in on the success of their teams because revenue had fallen short of expectations. It was Stearns who suggested the 15-game format, expanded from the best-of-seven series of the previous year. Von der Ahe had agreed to pay his Browns $100 apiece for the series, one-third of the amount paid the Wolverines. The 15 games were to be played in 10 cities, regardless of the first team to reach eight wins, and proceeds would be shared. The first two contests were scheduled for St. Louis, beginning October 10, followed by one in Detroit before both teams hit the road in a special train of parlor cars for games in Pittsburgh, Brooklyn, New York, Philadelphia, Boston, Washington, Baltimore and Chicago. Stearns was banking on the drawing power of his Wolverines on the road to fill team coffers. He didn't mind playing only one game at home, where crowds had been thin. Stearns also came up with the novel idea of employing two umpires for the series, Honest John Gaffney and Honest John Kelly.

The reigning world champion St. Louis took the first game, 6–1, when Detroit's sluggers had trouble solving Browns pitcher Bob Caruthers, getting only five hits. The League champions came within a whisker of being shut out, scoring their only run in the ninth inning when Getzien was brought home on a single by Twitchell. Caruthers helped himself with three of the 12 true hits off Getzien. The crowd at Sportsman's Park was estimated at from 7,000 to 10,000. Pete Conway was sharp the following day when Detroit capitalized on seven errors by the Browns to win, 5–3, before 7,000 spectators.

With that split of the first two games, the teams moved to Detroit. On October 12, about 7,000 fans packed Recreation Park for a pitching duel and saw Detroit come from behind to tie the game, then win it, 2–1, in 13 innings. Getzien allowed 13 true hits, singled and scored the game's winning run when Charlie Comiskey at first base muffed a throw from second baseman Yank Robinson, who had fielded a Jack Rowe grounder. Caruthers had been sharp in the exciting game and limited Detroit to six true hits.

In Pittsburgh the following day, Lady Baldwin was outstanding. He held the Browns to two true hits in an 8–0 shutout before 5,000 fans. Charlie Bennett was able to stymie the much-vaunted stealing game of the AA champions, while Detroit stole five bases on Browns pitcher Silver King. St. Louis continued to commit uncharacteristic errors, and Tip O'Neill struggled at the plate. Game five was October 14 in Brooklyn, and Detroit's Pete Conway had poor control while Caruthers largely curbed Detroit's heavy artillery. About 10,000 fans saw St. Louis take the game, 5–2. The next day, in New York, Detroit roared back with a 9–0 shutout of the Browns before a crowd of 6,000. Getzien took a no-hitter into the ninth inning before giving up three hits. Charlie Ganzel, who had replaced the injured Dan Brouthers at first base, led the Wolverines with four of the 14 hits off Dave Foutz. Detroit led the series, four games to two, at this point.

The next venue was Philadelphia, and Stearns was in a fine mood, having already sent $15,000 in proceeds back to Detroit.[39] Detroit took its fifth win, 3–1, before 9,000 fans as Baldwin had fine control. Charlie Bennett picked off two Browns runners at third base and dissuaded others from stealing. The St. Louis club again demonstrated uncharacteristically sloppy fielding behind Caruthers. Tip O'Neill finally made his presence known with a ninth inning home run, the best of his 13 hits during the series. Detroit hammered the Browns 9–2 on October 18 before 6,000 fans in Boston. Caruthers allowed 13 true hits, including two home runs by Sam Thompson. The next day, in Philadelphia, 3,000 spectators, the smallest crowd in the series to date, watched Detroit prevail, 4–2, O'Neill again failing to lead his team's offense and Bennett easily picking off Browns base runners.

A game slated for October 20 in Washington was rained out. It was agreed to play the game the following morning, after which the teams would travel to Baltimore for a second game that afternoon. In the morning, St. Louis picked up its third win, 11–4, before 2,000 fans, pulling off a rare triple play in the third inning. Thompson came to the plate with the bases loaded and hit a line drive caught by shortstop Bill Gleason, who flipped the ball to third baseman Arlie Latham, who doubled off Richardson, who had started for home plate. Latham then fired the ball to Yank Robinson at second, who caught Charlie Ganzel before he could return to the bag. The 6–5–4 triple play was the first in a world series championship. Meanwhile, center fielder Curt Welch drilled a bases-loaded homer for the Browns while Latham, Gleason, Comiskey and Foutz each contributed three hits. The vaunted bat of Tip O'Neill remained silent. In Baltimore that afternoon, Detroit clinched the series with its eighth win, before a crowd of 3,000. Detroit sluggers made mincemeat of Browns pitcher Dave Foutz, scoring 11 runs in the middle three innings on their way to a 13–3 blowout.

In winning the championship, Detroit was awarded the new Dauvray Cup. By previous arrangement, and to milk the series for every nickel, the championship continued on October 22 in Brooklyn. However, with suspense gone, only 800 diehard fans bothered to turn out in blizzard-like conditions. Silver King outpitched Pete Conway in the contest, called after seven innings on account of coldness, with the score 5–1 for St. Louis. Dan Brouthers was back in the lineup for his only appearance in the series and made two of the five Wolverines hits. His ankle still bothered him and he could not run. Several Wolverines were also injured or ill, and Getzien's arm was tired. Stearns picked up Sy Sutcliffe from Des Moines to play first base for Brouthers. Meanwhile, player dissension beset the St. Louis clubhouse, and catcher Doc Bushong sought his release so he could join a National League team.[40]

The 13th game in the series was to have been played in Cincinnati, but a disagreement about finances led Stearns and Von der Ahe to agree to play on October 24 back in Detroit. A lively and happy crowd of 4,000 greeted the teams at Recreation Park after they had been welcomed with a parade and luncheon. During the reception for both teams at the Russell House Hotel, Detroit Mayor Marvin Chamberlain saluted the new world champions. "Detroit is famed for beauty, culture, intelligence, energy and enterprise," he said. "But Detroit's base ball club has carried far and wide, even beyond the bounds of our nation, the renown of our fair city, and in honoring the club we simply honor the city."[41]

At the ballpark, the fans were especially happy to see veteran catcher Charlie Bennett, a popular Wolverine since 1881, for whom special recognition had been planned. In the fourth inning, moments after Jack Rowe reached first base on a hit, the shrill sounds of a fife and drum band erupted. The musicians marched onto the field, followed by two Detroit directors pushing a wheelbarrow full to the brim with 520 silver dollars. They stopped at home plate and called Bennett to join them. He was not in the lineup that day, enjoying a rest. At the plate, three big policemen informed Bennett that if he didn't take custody of the wheelbarrow and wheel it around the bases they would be "compelled to take him in." With a police escort and the band playing "Yankee Doodle Dandy," Bennett complied, to the delight of the cheering throng who "shouted themselves into hysterics."[42] Two other players received recognition that day. Brouthers was given a bat made of "zylonite" (or xylonite, an early form of plastic) in recognition of his hitting, but Sam Thompson, the team's actual batting leader, was overlooked. Ganzel was presented a gold watch for his solid work in spelling Brouthers at first base and Bennett behind the plate. After the interruption, Detroit went on to win the game, 6–3.

The 14th game of the series was played before 600 shivering fans in Chicago on October 25, and it reflected more of the same play that had characterized the series: sloppy defensive work by the Browns, little contribution from Tip O'Neill, and Bennett sharp at picking off base runners. Neither Dunlap nor Brouthers played and Detroit won, 4–3, Getzien picking up yet another victory. The final game of the longest-ever world series was played October 26, when only 659 fans turned out on another cold day in St. Louis. Getzien and Caruthers each gave up nine hits, but Detroit committed seven errors and the Browns won, 9–2.

Detroit had dominated the Browns, taking 10 of the 15 games and scoring 73 runs to 54 for St. Louis. The team batting average was .243 to .232 in favor of Detroit. Sam Thompson wielded the hottest bat in the series with a .362 batting average and .621 slugging average. Meanwhile, Tip O'Neill, whose AA season batting average had been .435, managed to bat just .200. The best Browns hitter had been Yank Robinson with a .325 average. Detroit pitchers' earned run average was 2.30, while St. Louis' was 2.39. Charlie Bennett's arm stymied the St. Louis base-stealing game, and the Browns managed only 28 in the 15 games while Detroit stole 42. Chris Von der Ahe told the *New York Clipper* that Detroit had been the better team, and his banged-up nine couldn't match the determination of its opposition. "I don't think they tried quite as hard as they might to win," he said of the Browns.[43] Von der Ahe was angry at the loss and threatened to withhold the $12,500 earned from the series, rather than share it with his players as he had with the $13,920 from the previous year's victory over Chicago.[44]

More than 40,000 spectators attended the series, despite the doubled admission prices. It was costly to arrange, however, and the *Clipper* reported the "alleged" profit was $25,000. Historian Harold Seymour calculated that each team netted about $12,000 after expenses.[45] For his part, Stearns insisted that Detroit earned a net profit of only $3,000, "and he ought to know," said the *Clipper*. But, as was their custom, Detroit directors were reluctant to disclose solid, reliable financial information. Stearns, a large shareholder, revealed only what he felt was necessary.

Regardless of the financial picture, Detroit and its directors could crow about the success the Wolverines had achieved. It had taken seven seasons, but Detroit had finally risen to the top of the baseball world, no small feat for a comparatively small city that harbored big-league aspirations.

11

Collapse

Fred Dunlap couldn't wait to get out of Detroit. The best second baseman of his day refused to play another inning for manager Bill Watkins. He had returned to the lineup on September 20 after a 10-week absence because of his foot injury and appeared in 11 of the 15 games of the world's championship, during which Watkins was sharply critical of his play. Watkins complained that his star player and top earner was moving too slowly when he failed to corral ground balls. Dunlap angrily retorted that some of those drives couldn't have been collared if he had used "a scoop net."[1] With the season over, Dunlap believed he could easily find a new team interested in services, based on New York's expressed willingness earlier to pay him $15,000 in a two-year pact. For his part, Watkins was more than anxious to unload a large salary and bad attitude, and by early November Dunlap was sold to the Pittsburgh Alleghenys. Detroit received $5,500, with Dunlap receiving half, at his insistence.

Eight other Wolverines took a different tack. They wanted Watkins out of Detroit and by early December formed a "combine," telling management they would not sign new contracts if Watkins remained. Captain Ned Hanlon urged president Frederick Stearns to replace Watkins with secretary Bob Leadley, but Stearns refused.[2] Watkins knew the players wanted him out, but he insisted it was merely part of a Brotherhood of Professional Base Ball Players scheme to force all non-playing managers from the game. "I am not lying awake thinking about it at night," the embattled manager said. "I treated my men so loyally this year that I cannot understand why there should be any objection to me."[3] The standoff lingered for a few months and produced some uncertainty about Detroit's chances of repeating as pennant winners and world champions.

In the meantime, Detroit won an important battle off the field when, in November, the National League resurrected the percentage system to split gate

11. Collapse   171

receipts. Stearns wanted 30 percent, but the figure was set at 25 percent. Regardless, he touted the decision as an important victory for Detroit. In other business, the Brotherhood was formally recognized by League magnates, who agreed to a uniform, "model" contract for players in which the reserve provisions were spelled out. League bosses deferred consideration of salary limits for the time being. In rules changes, three strikes were restored for an out (reduced from four), and bases on balls were no longer to be counted as hits. Five balls still constituted a walk.

Fresh from his world's series and gate-receipts triumphs, Stearns dropped a bombshell. He resigned his post as club president, saying he needed to tend to business. His father, Frederick S. Stearns, had retired, so he was now in charge of Stearns Pharmaceuticals. Baseball, he said, was interfering with his greatly expanded responsibilities. In a December 17 note to his fellow directors, Stearns reminded them that they had agreed he could step down when he saw fit. He now saw fit. Stearns noted that the team's financial troubles were cured, harmony existed among directors, and the League pennant and world championship had been secured, so "it seems to me that no time could be more appropriate than the present to insist upon your relieving me of my official duties as Executive." He said he planned to retain his 60 shares in the club because he believed the team had a bright future.[4] His fellow directors urged him to remain as president, but he was steadfast, agreeing only to continue as a director. Stearns made his resignation effective January 1, and until then he said he would continue signing players for 1888. Sam Thompson was persuaded to agree to a contract at a salary of $2,500, but the others remained unsigned. Director Charles H. Smith, a retired shoe manufacturer, was named club president, and he readily acknowledged that his knowledge of the game was not nearly as broad as that of Stearns. He therefore planned to delegate many tasks to other directors.[5] Smith promised, however, that player salaries would remain the same as the previous year, when Detroit was the highest-paid team in the League.

In the weeks that followed, fearing they might become unemployed and faced with continued management support for Watkins, several members of the "combine" weakened and agreed to contracts. Among them was reliable backstop Charlie Bennett, a Wolverine since Detroit's first campaign in 1881. Third baseman Deacon White, however, said he was planning to retire, a gambit he had used since his early days in Buffalo to fatten his contract. His "annual retirement announcement" was definitely more forceful this year than in the past. "He asserts that he has been so badly treated by Watkins that he could not think of playing for him. He affirms that Watkins made an attempt last summer to run him out of the club, took unfair advantage of him, and misrepresented him in a shameful manner."[6] White was steadfast and didn't join the team for spring training in the South, so directors announced they were seeking to replace him. Late in March, however, after extracting a promise of better treatment from Watkins, White joined the team in Mobile. Hanlon, meanwhile, remained a holdout, threatening to remain at the hat shop he owned in Detroit.[7] In early April Hanlon relented, signing on and joining Bennett as the only other Wolverine on the roster since day one. The lineup was complete and, minus Dunlap, looked very much like that fielded the previous year.

Spring training in 1888 proved to be far different from 1887, when the Wolverines won 31 straight games. Rust was evident in sloppy play and poor pitching, with Detroit losing five straight games to St. Louis in their first meeting since the world's series. Sam Thompson hurt his throwing arm in one of the exhibition games, and it bothered him all season. The situation didn't improve when League play began on April 20. Detroit dropped three games in Pittsburgh to the Alleghenys, 5–2, 10–3, and 10–9, before picking up its first win of the season, 6–4, on April 24. The home team's new second baseman, Fred Dunlap, shunned his old Wolverines teammates during the series, refusing to their shake hands. "His demeanor was cold and proud," it was reported.[8] The Wolverines travelled to Indianapolis, the League's last-place team in 1887, and lost two games, 8–3 and 16–7. After five losses in six games, Watkins was disgusted and said so. "I cannot imagine how a club composed of the same players who did so well last season can play such poor ball this season. And this is all the more surprising when it is considered that there is not a man of all of them out of condition." He laid off Baldwin, without pay, for allowing 12 runs in the 16–7 debacle, and he fined Hanlon $10 for failing to slide during a stolen base attempt.[9] On April 28, the Wolverines eked out their second win, a 1–0 shutout of the Hoosiers, on a strong pitching performance by Pretzels Getzien. Two days later, to finish the series, the Detroit bats pounded Indianapolis into submission in a 13–1 romp.

During the May 1 home opener in Detroit, three giant flags were run up the newly erected, 151-foot flagpole at Recreation Park. Below the Stars and Stripes, a dark-blue banner proclaimed "Champions of the World," while beneath it a white pennant declared in red letters that the Wolverines were reigning National League champs. All fluttered in the wind of a bitterly cold day, warming up the 2,200 fans. Getzien allowed only five hits to the Pittsburgh Alleghenys, who were downed, 10–1, in a game called after seven innings because of the "pneumonia atmosphere."[10] Detroit relied on its bats again to beat the visitors, 16–1, the following day, then again, 18–13, on May 3 and 8–2 on May 4, to sweep the series. The latter two games drew only 1,100 and 600 fans respectively, a bad omen for the champions.

Detroit opened the 1888 season by unfurling three flags on a new pole that soared high above Recreation Park. The Stars and Stripes was joined by pennants marking the Wolverines as National League champions and winners of the world's series in 1887 (Burton Historical Collection, Detroit Public Library).

William G. Thompson, the founding president of the Wolverines, was back in action on May 5 when he became involved in another public dust-up. This one took place at the Michigan Central Railroad depot, where the former mayor, now a deputy court clerk and deputy sheriff, helped a visiting judge board a train for his home in Washington. Thompson was spotted by Daniel J. Campau, the collector of customs for Detroit and brother of Thompson's wife, Adele. Campau confronted Thompson about vile things he had heard his brother-in-law was saying about Adele in the saloons of the city. The Campau family was one of the founding French families in Detroit, wealthy and well-respected. The customs collector was visibly upset. Words were exchanged, and Thompson threw a punch, prompting Campau to reply in kind. Thompson got the worst of it before bystanders quickly pulled apart the antagonists, both prominent leaders in the local Democratic Party. Blood poured from Thompson's face, and he scurried away for medical attention. Campau, largely unscathed, boarded his train for Toledo, as planned. That same afternoon, as previously scheduled, Adele Campau filed a petition for divorce from Thompson, alleging infidelity, cruelty and habitual drunkenness.[11] A year later, she was granted the decree and settled for a lump sum of $30,000 in alimony. Charges were never filed in the train depot incident, which, unlike Thompson's barroom clash of two years earlier, could not be kept out of the papers. In fact, the story about the altercation between Detroit's Democratic heavyweights even found its way into the pages of the *New York Times*.[12] In Detroit, the affair became the talk of the town, and public sympathy lay with Campau.

The same afternoon that Thompson was bloodied by Campau, the Wolverines welcomed the Boston Beaneaters to Recreation Park. Chicago hurler John Clarkson had been traded to Boston, but the change of venue hadn't impaired his ability to tame Wolverines bats. A fine crowd of 4,000 was disappointed when Boston edged the home club, 5–4. In the next game, witnessed by 1,300 spectators two days later, Detroit batters managed to solve Clarkson in an 8–3 win. Boston took the third game, 13–6, before a crowd of 1,500. After winning two of three games against Philadelphia, the Wolverines found themselves in fourth place. They rose to third when they shut out Washington, 2–0, on May 16, before only 500 fans in Recreation Park. Detroit remained in third place for the remainder of their home stand in May, playing before crowds ranging from 1,500 to 2,000. By month's end, the Wolverines slipped to fourth. Inconsistent play made the team lose two out of three in Chicago, but take two of three in Philadelphia before sweeping four games at Washington in early June. The Wolverines were in second place, three games behind Chicago.

During the series in Washington, the team was invited to the White House to meet President Grover Cleveland, who congratulated the players on winning the world's series the previous fall. A former mayor of Buffalo and governor of New York state, Cleveland immediately recognized former Bisons Dan Brouthers and other members of the Big Four. He asked Brouthers about the welfare of former Buffalo pitcher Pud Galvin, now hurling for the Alleghenys in Pittsburgh. "Galvin was a great favorite of mine in Buffalo," Cleveland said, upon being assured the pitcher was doing well. The president congratulated the Wolverines on being "world beaters" and asked Brouthers if he was still hitting the ball as hard as in Buffalo. Brouthers replied that he was doing his best to do so. Cleveland apologized that he would be unable to attend the game

Its 1888 campaign was the eighth and final one for the Wolverines, when they briefly contended for the League pennant but finished fifth. For their final campaign they wore smart, pin-striped white shirts with dark blue pants and white stockings. Directors, it was said, lost money because of poor fan support so they sold the team. Players went to the highest bidders and the franchise to Cleveland. In this photograph, taken in June at Boston's South End Grounds, it appears that images of Brouthers and Baldwin (below Brouthers) may have been added later, the latter laid off at the time. Back row, from left: Pete Conway, Charlie Bennett, Larry Twitchell, Dan Brouthers, Charlie Ganzel, Sy Sutcliffe, Sam Thompson, Deacon White. Front row: Henry Gruber, Pretzels Getzien, Ned Hanlon, Hardy Richardson, Jack Rowe (Library of Congress).

that day because he was preoccupied with his Democratic Party nomination meeting underway in St. Louis.[13] The players wished him luck, and Cleveland replied by encouraging his visitors to retain the League pennant. The president, it turned out, would be more successful than the players.

On June 8 in Boston, Detroit exploded in the 15th inning for six runs to defeat Boston—and their nemesis Clarkson—by a score of 11–5 in the longest game of the National League season. The next day, they edged the Beaneaters, 10–9, for a seventh consecutive win, putting Detroit two games behind first-place Chicago. Along the way, however, injuries began to mount. Brouthers, Bennett and Conway missed several games, and Hanlon's throwing arm bothered him. By mid–June the team was described as being in "a badly crippled state."[14] Friction and dissension were also plaguing the club. On June 18, manager Watkins fined Pretzels Getzien $100 for "back talk."[15] This followed their clash after a June 11 game in Boston when Getzien allowed 21 hits in a 14–9 loss. Watkins drew criticism for riding Getzien and Conway too hard and not giving enough work to young hurlers Henry Gruber and Ed Beatin. Despite the problems, the Wolverines continued to play well enough to remain strong contenders for the League pennant.

Returning home after a road trip of nearly a month, only 1,200 fans greeted the Wolverines for a June 20 game against Cleveland with Bennett and Brouthers back in the lineup. Sam Thompson was sidelined with a sore throwing arm, and Hardy Richardson broke his ankle sliding into a base. Richardson tried to return to the lineup in August, but the broken bone wasn't healing properly and he was out for the season after playing only 58 games. Detroit native Charles "Count" Campau was signed to play right field in Thompson's absence and proved to be a good addition to the lineup, both in the field and at the plate. A speedster on the base paths, Campau, 24, had played for the Cass Club, Erie, Guelph, London, Savannah, New Orleans and Kansas City. He was also a member of the same prominent Detroit family into which Wolverines founder William G. Thompson had married.

On July 4 in New York, Detroit lost both ends of a doubleheader but continued to cling to second place. In early July, Sam Thompson was sent home to rest for a month, but upon his return did so poorly at the plate and in the field that he was laid off without pay. It was feared his playing days were over. Thompson played in fewer than half the Wolverines games just a year after being the hitting leader for his club and the League. The slugger's bat was sorely missed. Lady Baldwin returned to the lineup mid-month, winning games on July 11 and 24, while losing two. On July 18, before 3,000 Detroit fans, Conway was outstanding when the Wolverines blanked first-place Chicago, 5–0, a victory that landed Detroit in first place. The White Stockings bounced back the following day with a 4–3 win to reclaim the League lead. Detroit wins, combined with Chicago losses, put Detroit back in the League lead for a few days late in July, but its highest rank after that point in the season was second. Baldwin's last appearance came July 28 in a 21–17 slugfest loss in Chicago. His arm had given out, and his career was about to end. For the White Stockings, center fielder Jimmy Ryan belted two triples, a single, a double, and a home run and also pitched 7⅓ innings in relief. In so doing, Ryan became the first player ever to hit for the cycle and pitch in the same game, although his single and one of his triples were belted before he took the ball.[16]

The loss to Chicago that day was the start of a 16-game losing streak that dropped the Wolverines to a distant third place. Detroit lost four times to seventh-place Indianapolis, twice to Pittsburgh, twice to Boston, twice to last-place Washington, and three times to Philadelphia. By the first of August, New York assumed the League lead and held it for the remainder of the season to capture the League pennant. Detroit's fielding was poor during its slump, and the players were described as "devoid of spirit."[17] The impact of poor play on Detroit fans was noticeable. Attendance was light, and those fans who appeared at Recreation Park were quick to voice their displeasure, even at Charlie Bennett, the long-time local favorite upon whom they had lavished a wheelbarrow full of silver dollars. As early as June, it had been reported: "Catcher Bennett complains that the people in the grandstand behind him insult and abuse him while playing here, and he wants to be released in consequence of it."[18] The losing streak that began the next month made matters significantly worse.

Criticism of the manager also grew as the losses mounted. Watkins' decision-making was questioned in the *Detroit Free Press*, which said he gave too much playing time to pitcher Larry Twitchell and too little to outfielder Count Campau. It accused Watkins of deliberately doing "something he knows to be wrong," adding, "for some time past he has shown a remarkable lack of judgment and unless there is a speedy improvement in this respect, the team will do worse."[19] In a bit of awkward timing, on August 11, the same day the Wolverines lost their 11th straight game, the *New York Clipper* carried a profile of "genial" manager Watkins. It traced his career from his playing days in Canada and Indianapolis to his record as a manager with the Hoosiers and Detroit and his key role in acquiring the "Big Four." The *Clipper* added: "Watkins is very popular wherever he goes ... and with the team of sluggers he now has under his direction will make a big fight for the championship of the National League again this season."[20] The rosy picture painted of the Wolverines skipper was at odds with the grim reality he faced in Detroit.

As the losing streak continued, Lady Baldwin was released, Rowe came down with "malaria," Bennett's hands were injured and Conway's arm went lame after being struck by a line drive. Richardson was gone from the lineup. The injuries, the tension, and the losses were taking their toll on the players. In an interview with the *Boston Globe* when the Wolverines lost three games to the Beaneaters, Bennett conceded: "The boys don't go into a game now like winners, they feel their own weakness."[21] Also taking note of the situation was *Sporting Life*, which opined that Detroit's pennant chances were slipping away. "The team is practically disorganized for the present, and both manager Watkins and the players are greatly depressed over their ill fortune."[22]

The 16th loss was particularly difficult to take. On August 21 in Indianapolis, Detroit held a 2–0 lead over the Hoosiers after seven innings. Things quickly deteriorated. With two men out in the eighth, the home team scored two earned runs off Getzien to tie it and added another to take the lead. The Hoosiers went on to win 8–3 when Detroit committed six errors in the final two innings. "All hopes of the pennant have died in the breasts of Detroiters, and the only thing they pray for now is that the team may keep out of fourth place," said *Sporting Life*.[23] The string of injuries continued. Hanlon was spiked in Indianapolis and laid off, while Rowe, just back from his illness, sprained his knee in New York and was disabled.

The losing streak finally ended the next day in Indianapolis when the Wolverines won, 4–2. It was the end of a nightmare. With the final Hoosiers out, "Getzein [sic] ran out of the box and threw himself flat on the ground and every one of the seven Detroit fielders followed his example. Even Deacon White picked out a nice dry place and hid his face in the grass."[24] The relief was palpable, but short-lived. The following day, back in Detroit, the White Stockings came from behind to win, 3–2, before a crowd of only 1,500. Detroit lost again, 14–4, on August 24 when Getzien was clobbered for 16 Chicago base hits. The following day, Detroit salvaged a 4–1 win.

Bill Watkins could take it no longer. He resigned as manager, a decision announced after the Chicago series. Asked to comment, director Stearns, his long-time supporter, replied: "Well, he said there was too much friction in the conduct of the club and his position was so unpleasant, he concluded it would be best for himself and best for the club for him to retire." The *Detroit Free Press* noted that in his two years with the club, Watkins had endured a stormy relationship with directors and players.

> It cannot be denied that his course for some time past has not been pleasing to a majority of the directors, and his resignation was accepted without hesitation.... Mr. Watkins' retirement removes all friction that existed and opens the way for the club to go ahead and make a determined effort to retain third place and fight Chicago for second. It is to be hoped the team will take a new tack and pull all together.[25]

Club secretary Robert Leadley was appointed to fill Watkins' managerial shoes. Leadley conceded, however, that the team's outlook "is not very brilliant." He said he planned no changes other than perhaps appointing Brouthers as team captain in the continued absence of Hanlon.

Sporting Life was sympathetic to Watkins, saying he was doomed by a year's worth of friction with his players. With the talented team Watkins had assembled, winning was expected. So when the Wolverines won, he received little credit. But when they lost, he was blamed. "His enterprise in getting the team together cannot be gainsaid [contradicted]."[26] Indeed, Watkins had accomplished much in three years in Detroit. Under his watch, the Wolverines won 249 games and lost 161, for a healthy .607 winning percentage. The 1888 team stood at 49–44 upon his departure and occupied third place. During his tenure, the Wolverines had captured the League pennant and the world's championship. Watkins' abilities were widely recognized in the baseball community and, in two weeks Kansas City hired him to manage the Cowboys, then occupying the cellar in the American Association. Watkins continued managing or owning teams until 1914, in such cities as St. Paul, Rochester, St. Louis, Sioux City, Indianapolis (again), Pittsburgh, Memphis, and his adopted hometown of Port Huron, Michigan. There, he became president of Port Huron's entry in the Michigan-Ontario league in the early 1920s. Overall, his teams won the championships of 12 professional leagues, a record for a Canadian-born manager.[27] The game that nearly killed him as a player had been very, very good to Bill Watkins. He died in Port Huron in 1937, at the age of 79.

With Bob Leadley at the helm, the Wolverines went 19–19 for the remainder of the season and continued to draw poorly at Recreation Park. The last home game was played on September 22, the third in a series with the New York Giants, who had locked up the pennant. In the first contest September 20, Detroit lost 5–4, and on September 21 tied 3–3. In the final game, a crowd of 1,500 saw the Giants commit seven errors while Henry Gruber held them to six hits for a 6–5 Detroit victory. The final road trip of the season took the team to Pittsburgh, New York, Boston, Philadelphia and Washington. Detroit lost 10 of the 16 games, won five and tied one. The final game of the Wolverines' season was October 13, a 7–4 win in Washington. The club finished in fifth place with a 68–63 record. By then, rumors were rampant that Detroit directors wanted to wash their hands of the team.

The Detroit's hitters failed to deliver in 1888 after dominating most of the batting categories the previous year. They were often handicapped by injuries or completely sidelined by them. Sam Thompson, who led five hitting categories in 1887, appeared in none. His batting average plunged from .372 to .282. Dan Brouthers was the only Wolverine to hit better than .300, with a .307

average, good for fourth in the League. Brouthers had the loop's most runs with 118 and fourth-most hits with 160. His on-base percentage was second, at .399, and he tallied the fourth-most total bases at 242. But that was about it for offense. The team that so often relied on hitting to mask its occasional pitching woes came up short.

"Farewell, Sluggers," blared the headline in the October 14 edition of the *Detroit Free Press*. The club had been sold. Detroit directors Stearns and Gray, it said, had been in Cleveland and Chicago to discuss the potential sale of players to those clubs. Cleveland was unhappy with the American Association and was anxious to switch to the League by buying the entire Detroit franchise. In Chicago, president Al Spalding said that Stearns told him that Detroit planned to eliminate high salaries and continue play with "rising youngsters who can be secured comparatively cheap." Chicago and New York were not interested in the Detroit stars, however, while Indianapolis and Washington were too poor to make good offers. That left Boston, Philadelphia and Pittsburgh as potential buyers. Boston acquired Dan Brouthers, Hardy Richardson, Charlie Bennett, Charlie Ganzel and Deacon White for an estimated $30,000. Sam Thompson was sold to Philadelphia for $5,000. The Pittsburgh Alleghenys picked up Pete Conway and Jack Rowe for an undisclosed amount, and Ned Hanlon for $2,500. Cleveland bought pitchers Ed Beatin, Larry Twitchell and Henry Gruber, along with infielder Sy Sutcliffe, and the Detroit franchise, for $10,000. Pretzels Getzien later went to Indianapolis, and White, returned by Boston, was sold to Pittsburgh.

The *Free Press* was blunt in its assessment of the situation. And rather bitter:

> And what becomes of Detroit, gentle reader? Detroit will retire from the base ball business and engage enthusiastically in croquet and other violently exciting sports. It was the natural consequence of non-support of a grand base ball organization, and it serves the people of the city exactly right. Business interests have lost quite a card, and will doubtless regret it. The men who had their money risked on the venture have got out even, and no one can blame them. In fact, they are to be congratulated. Ta, ta, base ball.[28]

In November, the National League approved Cleveland's application for membership but deferred Detroit's formal resignation until the spring, when the sale of players and the franchise would be complete. Stearns took to the road to consider various deals and was authorized by his fellow directors to wrap up the baseball operation. It was said that shareholders lost $15,000 during the season and $58,000 during the eight years of the Wolverines. "The men who have their money risked on the venture have come to the conclusion that Detroit as a base ball town is in that condition of reposeful indifference characteristic of a deceased game cock," said the *Free Press*, "and that they have determined to get out as nearly whole as possible."²⁹ There was some talk that Detroit would remain in the League with a young roster, or switch to the American Association, it being noted that the latter's 25-cent admission might work, because "Detroit as a league ball town is as dead as a door nail."³⁰ But nothing came of either notion. Instead, Detroit continued in baseball with a new team that joined the International League, which included Buffalo, Toronto, Hamilton, Syracuse, London, Rochester and Toledo.

The National League reduced the number of balls required for a walk to four in 1889, the final tinkering with balls and strikes. The League's decision with the most impact on the game, however, was the adoption of a salary classification system to limit the pay of players to a maximum of $2,500. The move brought to a boil the simmering discontent within the Brotherhood of Professional Base Ball Players. John Ward and his lieutenants (with capitalist backers) began formulating plans for what became the Players' League of 1890. Detroit left the major league scene on the eve of major turmoil that created financial challenges for many teams and contributed to the demise of the shaky American Association.

Frederick Stearns was a busy man as he sought to maximize the financial return for club directors. Things became complicated in December when Jack Rowe and Deacon White purchased a controlling interest of the Buffalo Bisons of the International League, their old team when it was a member of the National League. The pair announced that they intended to manage and play for the Bisons. Rowe lived in Buffalo, where he had married a wealthy widow, while White farmed not far away in Corning, New York. The Buffalo team was a good fit for them. Both men had carefully saved their money during their careers and joined an investor group determined to return the Bisons to the National League, with White named as club president. But their playing rights were owned by Detroit, which sold both men to the Pittsburgh Alleghenys. The reserve clause barred them from playing anywhere but in Pittsburgh. Upon learning about the intentions of his former players, Stearns was indignant. "White may have been elected president of the Buffalo club or president of the United States, but that won't enable him to play ball in Buffalo," he railed. "He'll play in Pittsburgh or he'll get off the earth." Allegheny president William Nimick concurred: "If they do not want to play in Pittsburgh, they'll play nowhere."

Rowe and White were still holding out in June when they were persuaded by Brotherhood president John Ward to back down and sign with Nimick. Ward reasoned that it was better for the pair to play and stay in shape than be idled for a year. They would be among the key players in the new league that Ward and the Brotherhood were busy organizing. In July, the duo reported to

Pittsburgh. The obstinate White received $1,250 of his $7,000 sale price. He was upset at being treated like cattle and demanded a piece of the action, famously declaring: "No man can sell my carcass unless I get half." It was strong language for a normally mild-mannered and sober church-goer, but it reflected the growing militancy among players determined to challenge the National League, the American Association and the reserve clause the men hated and likened to slavery.[31] On July 14, John Ward announced plans for the Players' League and said sponsors were being lined up for the 1890 season.

Despite his irritation at White and Rowe, Frederick K. Stearns was rather pleased with his financial handiwork. A reporter for the *Detroit Free Press* found him strolling along Woodward Avenue downtown on May 21, 1889, and was struck by his sunny disposition and broad smile, despite the foul weather. Stearns was asked to explain his buoyant mood and readily did so. "I have just made my final report to a meeting of the directors of the old Detroit Base Ball Club, it was very favorably received, and the affairs of the old club, with the exception of the Rowe-White matter, are wound up," Stearns said. He was buttonholed about how much additional money directors were assessed because of the club's reported losses. "Assessment! Not so much," Stearns retorted. "We declared a dividend of $54,000, and there is still more money in bank [*sic*] to be divided." The reporter was startled at the revelation of profit. Stearns explained that holders of the club shares, valued at $50 apiece, would receive $135 for each, as of June 1. And 80 percent of the shares were held by directors like himself (Stearns owned 60 of the 400 total). No wonder his smile. Stearns predicted a further $3,000 for shareholders once the sale of Rowe and White was finalized and the pair received their share of sale proceeds.[32]

Detroit won the International League pennant in 1889 and continued in the same loop for 1890, but attendance was poor and the league collapsed in July.[33] The following year, a Detroit team joined the Northwestern League and moved its games from Recreation Park to Riverside Park, close to the Detroit River near Belle Isle. But that 1891 club folded after only 28 games.[34] By 1893, local agitation arose for Detroit to return to the National League to replace a struggling Washington franchise expected to be replaced. Buffalo was looking to fill the same spot. Frederick Stearns and other businessmen suggested that if $45,000 could be raised in Detroit, a new team could be established to pursue League membership. Stearns said he would provide advice to any interested party, but he was far too busy with his pharmaceutical firm to take an active role in such a campaign.[35] Reaction to the rumblings in both Detroit and Buffalo was negative among League magnates, however. *Sporting Life* dismissed Buffalo as a city that demonstrated poor support for baseball and "not good for anything better than 25 cent base ball."[36] As for Detroit, *The Sporting News* reported

11. Collapse

that Pittsburgh director W. W. Kerr opposed any bid from the City of the Straits. "Detroit has not the remotest chance of getting into the big league [the American Association disappeared after 1892]," Kerr declared. "It was no stayer while it was a member of the league and sold out to considerable profit."[37] In the end, Washington remained in the National League and Detroit and Buffalo were left on the sidelines.

By 1894, Cincinnati sportswriter Ban Johnson reorganized the Western League he led, with a grand plan to make it a rival for the National League, now enjoying a monopoly on top-flight professional ball. Johnson persuaded Detroit to sign on, becoming the largest city in the revamped loop that included Kansas City, Minneapolis, Indianapolis, Grand Rapids, Toledo, Sioux City and Milwaukee. The Detroit entry was known as the Creams, because owner George Vanderbeck insisted his team would be the "cream of the league." They played their games at League Park (also known as Boulevard Park), just east of the city limits near the bridge to Belle Isle. By 1895, the Creams became the "Tigers." The first time that name appeared in print was in an April 16, 1895, *Detroit Free Press* headline, "Their First Breather. Strouthers' Tigers Showed Up Very Nicely," atop a story about the team captained by Con Strouthers beating a local club known as the Athletics by a lopsided score of 13–1. Beside that story was a companion article, headlined: "Notes of the Detroit Tigers for 1895."[38] The sporting press and Detroiters soon adopted the name, which for many years had been used by the city's highly regarded Detroit Light Guard, a military unit which distinguished itself during Civil War battles at Gettysburg, Bull Run, Chancellorsville and Antietam. The Guards included several prominent citizens, some of whom had been involved in baseball locally. In 1882, the Light Guard organization formalized its nickname by adding a tiger's head to its official crest.[39] Detroit's diamond warriors had a new identity.

In 1896, the baseball Tigers leased a new site for a field at the northwest corner of Michigan and Trumbull Avenues, long occupied by a municipal haymarket and dog pound. The property was known as Woodbridge Grove because of its large stand of shade trees. Massive elms and oaks were removed to create a playing surface, although several were spared in deep left-center field. The new baseball ground was named Bennett Park, after revered Wolverines catcher Charlie Bennett. In January 1894, he had fallen under the wheels of a moving train while trying to board it during a hunting trip in Kansas, severing his left foot and mangling his right leg, which was amputated at the knee. Bennett had been playing for Boston, to whom he had been sold in 1888, and helped the Beaneaters win three pennants. His long playing career ended abruptly, but not his connection to Detroit. Wearing artificial legs, Bennett caught the ceremonial first pitch at the new park on Opening Day, April 28,

1896, and every opening day until 1926. The crowd favorite and reminder of the Wolverines died shortly before Opening Day, 1927.[40]

A new era in baseball had begun in Detroit with the Tigers. Ban Johnson's organization became the American League and by 1901 was recognized as a major league, with Detroit as one of its charter members.

This time, Detroit would be a "stayer."

Epilogue

The Detroit Wolverines were members of the National League at a pivotal time for baseball. The business model for the professional game was still being refined, and the sport itself was being altered with rule changes intended to find the proper balance between pitching and hitting and to ensure it was appealing to spectators.

Co-operative community ventures fielded teams in the earlier National Association and elsewhere, largely out of civic pride. But they lost favor as capitalists took control of the game and sought to profit from it. The businessmen tried to limit player salaries, increase attendance, set sustainable admission fees and divide them appropriately. The sale of franchises was unheard of until Detroit bought the Buffalo and Indianapolis teams in 1885. The reserve system was introduced in 1880 to prevent players from selling their services to the highest bidder, to keep team owners from battling each other over players, and to allow them to focus on profit. The players realized that the reserve clause was intended to control them and grew to hate it, likening the system to slavery. Two Wolverines were among those who rebelled, despite relatively enlightened ownership of their club. The normally mild-mannered Deacon White was particularly hostile to having his "carcass" sold and demanded a piece of the action. He was accommodated. Dan Brouthers became a leading member of the Brotherhood of Professional Base Ball Players, which declared war on the established leagues. Battle lines were being drawn between men with capital and control—the owners—and those with baseball talent, the workers. The divide grew while the Wolverines were in the League and flared into open warfare a year after Detroit left, with the advent of the Players' League.

Detroit directors treated their players fairly by paying well beyond the salary limits set by other teams and giving some players a share of the proceeds when they were sold. Such liberal treatment irritated other members of the

League, and they sought to penalize the high-flying Wolverines by imposing the $125 guarantee for visiting teams. By respecting and empowering its players, Detroit may have inadvertently contributed to their decision to create the Brotherhood, by demonstrating how they *could* be treated. When League directors adopted the salary classification scheme in 1889, players could take it no more and established their rival league.

During its time in the National League, Detroit witnessed the arrival of the American Association in 1882, with its lower admission fees, beer in the park and Sunday play. Two years later, Henry Lucas' vanity league, the Union Association, appeared and then just as quickly disappeared. Capitalists pursued different formulas to keep teams and leagues afloat and produce profits for their shareholders. Post-season play that pitted the champions of the National League against those of the American Association began in 1884, in a bid to pad club coffers. In 1887, Detroit milked it for all it was worth.

As the business model was being refined, so was the game. Rules were changed every year to provide more offense without unduly penalizing pitchers. A 50-foot pitching distance was established in 1881 (up from 45 feet), Detroit's first season. By 1887, that was incresed by another five feet, six inches. Pitchers were limited to throwing underhand until 1883, but by 1884 all restrictions were lifted and the overhand delivery was permitted. Pitchers who previously could throw both games of a doubleheader without unduly taxing their arms found the new delivery difficult to master and harder on their bodies. It forced some to retire. The strike zone was re-defined to be between the top of the batter's shoulder and the bottom of his knee, but not until 1887. And during Detroit's eight-season run, batters lost the right to call for low or high deliveries. The balls-to-strikes ratio was constantly adjusted, from seven balls for a walk in 1881 to five for the last two seasons of the Wolverines. Strikes grew from three to four for an out, then back to three for Detroit's forgettable 1888 campaign. Walks were counted as hits only during Detroit's championship season, and the unpopular move was quickly killed off. The game played by the Wolverines was noticeably different from that played by today's Tigers.

Detroit's success was largely attributable to Frederick K. Stearns. Once in charge, he spent freely to attract and retain some of the best talent available. Stearns orchestrated the acquisition of Buffalo and its Big Four, slugger Sam Thompson and Fred Dunlap, the best second baseman of his day. The Detroit president relied on gate proceeds from cities far larger than Detroit to keep the Wolverines in business. In so doing he incurred the wrath of his fellow directors, who retaliated with the guarantee scheme. Stearns stirred things up in the gentleman's club the National League had become, and he micro-managed the affairs of his team when he felt it was necessary. He was an early-day George

Steinbrenner of New York Yankees fame, doing whatever he could and by paying whatever he felt was needed to achieve success. Stearns, with his competitive drive, his desire to have Detroit become a player among America's big cities, and his willingness to forgo profit for baseball fame, was the power behind the Wolverines. Stearns won battles both on the ball field and in the smoke-filled meeting rooms of the League. Without him, Detroit would likely have been relegated to history after its woeful 1884 season.

Many Wolverines went on to baseball glory. Despite his injury-plagued 1888, Detroit's big slugger, Sam Thompson, did not retire as had been predicted. He played 11 more seasons, all but the last with Philadelphia, and recorded a lifetime batting average of .331, reaching .415 in 1894. He belted 126 home runs, good for second highest before Babe Ruth came on the baseball scene. In all, the lanky right fielder played in 1,410 games, the first 368 with Detroit. He was elected to the National Baseball Hall of Fame in 1974, one of four Wolverines so honored. First baseman Dan Brouthers played 19 years in the big leagues, winning five batting titles and two home run titles, among other accomplishments. The big lefty never batted worse than .300 after 1880, and his career average stood at .342. Brouthers was elected to the Hall in 1945. Catcher-turned-third-baseman Deacon White ended his 20-year career in 1890 and went back to farm in Corning. He recorded 2,067 hits in his 1,560 games, with a .312 batting average, making him one of the game's most prolific hitters. A member of six championship clubs in three leagues, the sure-handed White was elected to the Hall of Fame in 2013. Outfielder Ned Hanlon became a formidable manager and in that category he was elected to the Hall of Fame in 1996. His teams won five pennants between 1894 and 1900. He cut his teeth as captain of the Wolverines, overseeing his fellow players from his position in center field. After Detroit folded, he managed the League and Players' League teams in Pittsburgh, then in Baltimore, Brooklyn, and Cincinnati. Charlie Bennett, considered the best catcher of his day, has not been honored by the Hall of Fame, in what seems a strange omission. But Deacon White's relatively recent induction demonstrates that Bennett's day may yet come.

Detroit doubled in size to about 200,000 inhabitants while the Wolverines were competing against far larger cities. The Paris of the West was an attractive and bustling city that drew compliments from the tourists who arrived by boat and train. Its economy was booming and diversified. Henry Ford spent most of the decade tinkering at his family farm in Dearborn, and it was several years before his automobile transformed America, his $5-a-day pay for workers created the Motor City, and economic diversity perished. Detroit became the automotive capital of the world.

After its key role in the Arsenal of Democracy during the Second World

War, decline set in for Detroit. Its peak population of 1.8 million was reached in 1950. The flight to the suburbs, ironically made possible by the same automobiles it built, left the City of the Straits in "straits" that could never have been imagined by former Wolverines presidents William G. Thompson and Frederick K. Stearns. In 2013, with a population of about 700,000 in the city proper, and unable to replace streetlights, repair roads, fund capital projects or provide needed city services, Detroit declared bankruptcy, the largest city ever to do so.

Today, out of bankruptcy, the city is pulling itself together. It is a slow process and there is a long way to go. Streetlights are being replaced, potholes filled, and funding is improving for the police and fire departments and for schools. The latter is especially important in a city whose residents need better education to build their futures—and that of the city. With 40 percent of the landscape vacant and more than 70,000 abandoned buildings, opportunity beckons in the low prices for real estate of all kinds. Investors and builders have moved in with plans for new residential, office and commercial developments and to repurpose old properties. The vandalized, vacant and desolate-looking Packard plant, once a symbol of Detroit's automotive dominance, but which hasn't produced a vehicle since 1956, became a symbol of the city's decline, urban blight and decay. It has found a buyer. So, too, has the abandoned American Motors headquarters and factory. Both former car plants were sold at tax foreclosure auctions at rock-bottom prices to entrepreneurs who sense opportunity and plan to profit by transforming them in coming years. The new QLine streetcar, running three miles along Woodward Avenue, has been touted as a catalyst for change downtown with predictions that it will generate $3 billion in economic development and much-needed jobs. The $142 million project was funded partly by the optimistic Quicken Loans, which is investing heavily in Detroit. Little Caesars Arena, a new, more than $800 million home for the Detroit Red Wings hockey club, with associated residential, retail and office uses, is a huge new attraction along Woodward, not far from Comerica Park and Ford Field, both of which are relative newcomers to the core. Detroit has been a great sports town, and it can be no surprise that investment in sport is helping to bring Detroit back from its darkest days.

Recreation Park was dismantled in 1894 and the land subdivided for housing. Today, all that remains is an historical plaque in a parkette amid the massive Detroit Medical Center complex. The marker is located in what was once left field of one of the most beautiful baseball grounds in America. Meanwhile, on the green patch at the northwest corner of Michigan and Trumbull Avenues that for a century was home to the Tigers, a $12 million, mixed-use project sprouted. A baseball diamond continues on the site, operated by the Police

Epilogue

Detroit, "The Paris of the West," became the Motor City and automotive capital of the world. But hard times hit the industry and the city. The massive, abandoned plant that once produced luxury Packard automobiles served for decades as a ghostly symbol of Detroit's fall. But the city may have hit bottom with its bankruptcy. Signs of better things to come abound, with investors seeing opportunity in rock-bottom prices for property. A Spanish firm acquired the Packard plant in a 2013 tax sale, with plans to give it new life. Another firm bought the vacant American Motors headquarters and factory for $500 in another tax sale, with plans to redevelop it. Throughout Detroit's industrial boom, depression, race riots, recession, bankruptcy and today's glimmer of hope, the city has enjoyed its baseball (Chip Martin photograph).

Athletic League for its youth sports programs. The legacy of the historic corner has been preserved and may some day produce future stars of the game.

Detroit was late to embrace professional baseball compared to places like Chicago, St. Louis, Cincinnati, Boston, and Philadelphia. And during the eight seasons of the Wolverines, the city's support for its team was far from automatic. There were lean times and good times, and club directors were oftentimes frustrated that baseball fever raged and then ebbed so quickly.

Since the arrival of the Tigers, Detroit has not been without a team to cheer for and to be cheered by. The Tigers won 11 American League pennants, beginning in 1907, and the World Series four times, in 1935, 1945, 1968 and

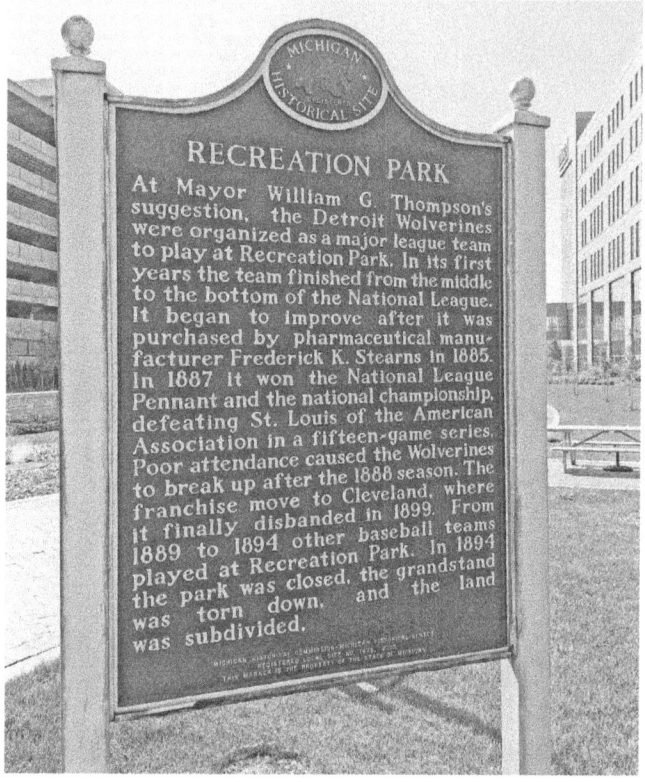

Today, the only reminder of Recreation Park, once considered one of the most attractive baseball parks in America, is this plaque in a parkette at the massive Detroit Medical Center. The marker is located in what was once left field. For 15 years, Recreation Park served as the place where Detroiters enjoyed baseball and other sports and diversions (Chip Martin photograph).

1984. Their early games were played in a park named after popular Wolverine Charlie Bennett, for whom Detroiters retained lasting affection. So there is a link between Detroit's National League history and its American League team. The city has had its ups and downs over the decades, with booms, depression, race riots, and recession, but baseball has been constant in a city that strongly identifies itself with the American League. There was a time, however, when baseball's future was far from assured in the vibrant City of the Straits.

Once widely used in Michigan and Detroit, the Wolverines name today is associated primarily with the University of Michigan and its athletic programs. The Detroit Wolverines, however, were the first team to make it famous. Their story is little known, but deserved to be told.

Appendix: Detroit Baseball Rosters, 1879, 1881 to 1888

Hollinger Nine 1879
Affiliation: Independent
Record: 20–9
Manager: William Hollinger
Pitchers: Harry Salisbury, Isaac Van Burkalow (change, or relief)
Catcher: Emil Gross
First Base: Steve Libby
Second Base: Sam Barkley
Third Base: J. B. "Trick" McSorley
Shortstop: Tom Shaughnessy
Left Field: Charlie Morton
Center Field: Isaac Van Burkalow
Right Field: Ed Swartwood

Detroit Wolverines 1881
Affiliation: National League
Record: 41–43, Fourth Place
Manager: Frank Bancroft
Pitcher (appearances): George Derby (56), Stump Weidman (13), Frank Mountain (7), Tony Mullane (5), Will White, Jack Leary (2)
Catcher: Charlie Bennett
First Base: Martin Powell
Second Base: Joe Gerhardt
Third Base: Art Whitney
Shortstop: Sadie Houck
Left Field: George Wood

Center Field: Ned Hanlon
Right Field: Lon Knight
Substitutes (games played): Lew Brown (27), Charlie Reilley (19), Dasher Troy (11), Mike Dorgan (8), Sam Trott (6), Will Foley (5), Jack Leary (3), Dan Stearns (3), Dan O'Leary (2), Billy Taylor, Sam Wise, Mike Moynahan and George Bradley (1)

Detroit Wolverines 1882
Affiliation: National League
Record: 42–41, Sixth Place
Manager: Frank Bancroft
Pitcher (appearances): Stump Weidman (46), George Derby (40), Art Whitney (3), Yank Robinson (1)
Catcher: Charlie Bennett
First Base: Martin Powell
Second Base: Dasher Troy (40), Tom Forster (21) Joe Farrell (18)
Third Base: Joe Farrell
Shortstop: Mike McGeary (33), Walt Kinzie (13), Dasher Troy (11), Yank Robinson (10)
Left Field: George Wood
Center Field: Ned Hanlon
Right Field: Lon Knight
Substitutes (games played): Sam Trott (32), Art Whitney (31), Yank Robinson (11), Bob Casey (9), Tom Kearns (4), Henry Luff (3), Tom Morrissey (2), Julius Willigrod (1)

Detroit Wolverines 1883
Affiliation: National League
Record: 40–58, Seventh Place
Manager: Jack Chapman
Pitcher (appearances): Stump Weidman (52), Dupee Shaw (26), Dick Burns (17), Jack Jones (12), George Radbourn (3), Frank McIntyre, Tom Mansell, George Wood (1)
Catchers: Charlie Bennett (72), Sam Trott (34)
First Base: Martin Powell
Second Base: Sam Trott (42), Joe Quest (37)
Third Base: Joe Farrell
Shortstop: Sadie Houck
Left Field: George Wood
Center Field: Ned Hanlon
Right Field: Tom Mansell
Utility: Sam Trott (75)
Substitutes (games played): Ben Guiney (1)

Detroit Wolverines 1884
Affiliation: National League
Record: 28–84 Eighth Place (last)
Manager: Jack Chapman
Pitcher (appearances): Frank Meinke (35), Dupee Shaw (28), Stump Weidman (26), Charlie Getzien (17), Frank Brill (12), Bill Geiss (1)
Catcher: Charlie Bennett
First Base: Milt Scott
Second Base: Bill Geiss (73), Tom Kearns (21)
Third Base: Joe Farrell
Shortstop: Frank Meinke (51), Frank Cox (27)
Left Field: George Wood
Center Field: Ned Hanlon
Right Field: Stump Weidman
Substitutes (games played): Henry Jones (34), Harry Buker (30), Ed Gastfield (23), Fred Wood (12), Chief Zimmer (8), Walter Prince (7), Ed Santry (6), Frank Jones, Joe Weber, Ben Guiney (2), Walt Walker, Dickie Lowe, Dave Beadle (1)

Detroit Wolverines 1885
Affiliation: National League
Record: 41–67, Sixth Place
Manager: Charlie Morton (7–31), Bill Watkins (34–36)
Pitcher (appearances): Stump Weidman (38), Charlie Getzien (37), Lady Baldwin (21), Dan Casey (12), Frank Meinke, George Wood, Gene Moriarty (1)
Catchers: Charlie Bennett (62), Deacon McGuire (31)
First Base: Mox McQuery (70), Milt Scott (38)
Second Base: Sam Crane (68), Joe Quest (39)
Third Base: Jim Donnelly (56), Charlie Morton (18), George Wood (12)
Shortstop: Marr Phillips (33), Jim Manning (20), Jim Halpin (15), Joe Quest (15), Chub Collins (14)
Left Field: George Wood
Center Field: Ned Hanlon
Right Field: Sam Thompson
Substitutes (games played): Joe Quest (55), Jerry Dorgan (39), Charlie Morton (22), Frank Ringo (17), Gene Moriarty (11), Jerrie Moore (6), Nate Kellogg (5), Frank Olin, George Bryant, Ed Gastfield (1)

Detroit Wolverines 1886
Affiliation: National League
Record: 87–36, Second Place
Manager: Bill Watkins
Pitcher (appearances): Lady Baldwin (56), Charlie Getzien, (43), Pete Conway (11), Bill Smith (9), Larry Twitchell, Hardy Richardson (4), Phenomenal Smith (3)

Catchers: Charlie Bennett (69), Charlie Ganzel (45)
First Base: Dan Brouthers
Second Base: Fred Dunlap (51), Hardy Richardson (42), Sam Crane (38)
Third Base: Deacon White
Shortstop: Jack Rowe
Left Field: Hardy Richardson
Center Field: Ned Hanlon
Right Field: Sam Thompson
Substitutes (games played): Sam Crane (47), Jim Manning (26), Harry Decker (14), Bill Shindle (7), Jack McGeachy (6), Tom Gillen (2)

Detroit Wolverines 1887
Affiliation: National League
Record: 79–45, First Place. Defeated St. Louis in world's series
Manager: Bill Watkins
Pitcher (appearances): Charlie Getzien (43), Lady Baldwin (24), Stump Weidman (21), Pete Conway (17), Larry Twitchell (15), Henry Gruber (7), Ed Beatin, Turk Burke (2), Fred Dunlap (1)
Catchers: Charlie Ganzel (51), Charlie Bennett (45), Fatty Briody (33)
First Base: Dan Brouthers
Second Base: Fred Dunlap (65), Hardy Richardson (64)
Third Base: Deacon White
Shortstop: Jack Rowe
Left Field: Larry Twitchell, Hardy Richardson (58)
Center Field: Ned Hanlon
Right Field: Sam Thompson
Utility: Hardy Richardson (120)
Substitutes (games played): Billy Shindle (22), Jim Manning (13)

Detroit Wolverines 1888
Affiliation: National League
Record: 68–63, Fifth Place
Manager: Bill Watkins (49–44), Bob Leadley (19–19)
Pitcher (appearances): Charlie Getzien (46), Pete Conway (45), Henry Gruber (27), Ed Beatin (12), Lady Baldwin (6), Larry Twitchell (2)
Catchers: Charlie Bennett (73), Charlie Ganzel (28)
First Base: Dan Brouthers
Second Base: Hardy Richardson (58), Charlie Ganzel (49), Parson Nicholson (24)
Third Base: Deacon White
Shortstop: Jack Rowe
Left Field: Larry Twitchell
Center Field: Ned Hanlon
Right Field: Count Campau (70), Sam Thompson (56)

Appendix 195

Substitutes (games played): Sy Sutcliffe (49), Ted Scheffler (27), Jake Wells (16), Deacon McGuire (3), Sam LaRoque (2), Barney Gilligan, Frank Scheibeck, Cal Broughton (1)

Sources: David Nemec. *The Great Encyclopedia of 19th Century Major League Baseball* (New York: Donald I. Fine Books, 1997); *Detroit Free Press*

Chapter Notes

Chapter 1

1. Peter Morris, *Baseball Fever: Early Baseball in Michigan* (Ann Arbor: University of Michigan Press, 2003), 27.
2. Peter Morris, "Detroit Base Ball Club," quoting *Detroit Post*, April 17, 1868, in *Base Ball Pioneers: 1850–1870*, eds. Peter Morris, William J. Ryczek, Jan Finkel, Leonard Levin and Richard Malatzky (Jefferson, NC: McFarland, 2012), 178.
3. Morris, *Baseball Fever*, 348.
4. Peter Morris, "Forest City Base Ball Club of Cleveland," *Base Ball Pioneers: 1850–1870*, eds. Peter Morris, William J. Ryczek, Jan Finkel, Leonard Levin and Richard Malatzky (Jefferson, NC: McFarland, 2012), 125.
5. *Ibid.*, 129.
6. David Nemec, *The Rank and File of 19th Century Major League Baseball: Biographies of 1,084 Players, Owners, Managers and Umpires* (Jefferson, NC: McFarland, 2012), 268.
7. Richard Bak, *A Place for Summer: A Narrative History of Tiger Stadium* (Detroit: Wayne State University Press, 1998), 23. The specific newspaper and date are not cited.
8. David Nemec, *The Great Encyclopedia of 19th Century Major League Baseball* (New York: Donald I. Fine Books, 1997), 83–84.
9. James M. Egan, Jr., *Base Ball on the Western Reserve: The Early Game in Cleveland and Northeastern Ohio* (Jefferson, NC: McFarland, 2008), 81–84.
10. "International Bulletin," *New York Clipper*, November 2, 1878, 250.
11. Egan, *Base Ball on the Western Reserve*, 85.
12. "The League Convention of 1878," *New York Clipper*, December 14, 1878, 298.
13. "Base Ball," *Detroit Free Press*, January 28, 1879, 1.
14. "Base Ball News," *Detroit Free Press*, February 16, 1879, 6.
15. "Recreation Park," *Detroit Free Press*, February 28, 1879, 1.
16. "Sayings and Doings," *Detroit Free Press*, February 27, 1879, 1.
17. "Recreation Park," *Detroit Free Press*, March 19, 1879, 1.
18. Geoffrey G. Drutchas, "Gray Eminence in a Gilded Age: The Forgotten Career of Senator James McMillan of Michigan," *Michigan Historical Review* 28, no. 2 (Fall 2002), 78–113.
19. Robert Conot, *American Odyssey: A Unique History of America Told Through the Life of a Great City* (New York: William Morrow, 1974), 66–67.
20. Thomas Arbaugh, "James McMillan: The Nation's Capital Owes Much to This Early Grosse Pointe Resident," *Heritage: A Journal of Grosse Pointe Life* 3, no. 5 (September 1986), 13–16.
21. Morris, "Detroit Base Ball Club," in *Base Ball Pioneers*, 182, and "Early Risers of Detroit," in *Base Ball Pioneers*, 186.
22. Bak, *A Place for Summer*, 25.
23. Scott Martelle, *Detroit: A Biography* (Chicago: Chicago Review Press, 2012), 59–61.

24. *Dictionary of Canadian Biography,* Volume 13, 1901 to 1910 (Toronto: University of Toronto Press, 1994), 466–469.
25. "The Runners," *Detroit Free Press,* June 10, 1879, 6.
26. Martelle, *Detroit,* 55.
27. "Local Matters," *Detroit Free Press,* April 8, 1879, 6.
28. "Local Matters," *Detroit Free Press,* March 11, 1879, 1.
29. "The Base Ball Club," *Detroit Free Press,* April 4, 1879, 6.
30. "Recreation Park and the Peninsulars," *Detroit Free Press,* April 4, 1879, 6.
31. *Ibid.*
32. "Recreation Park. Something About This Admirable Enterprise," *Detroit Post and Tribune,* April 13, 1879, 1.
33. *Ibid.*
34. "The Great Base Ball Match," *New York Clipper,* July 24, 1858, 110.
35. John Thorn, "History Buried: America's All-Star Game of 1858," *Voices: The Journal of New York Folklore* 39 (Spring-Summer 2013), accessed September 13, 2015, http://www.nyfolklore.org/pubs/voic39-1-2/play.html.
36. "Recreation Park," *Detroit Free Press,* April 27, 1879, 7.
37. "Base Ball Brevities," *Detroit Free Press,* April 22, 1879, 8.
38. "Sayings and Doings," *Detroit Free Press,* May 2, 1879, 1.

Chapter 2

1. David Pietrusza, *Major Leagues: The Formation, Sometimes Absorption and Mostly Inevitable Demise of 18 Professional Baseball Organizations, 1871 to Present* (Jefferson, NC: McFarland, 1991), 43.
2. "Local Matters," *Detroit Free Press,* March 11, 1879, 1.
3. "Later Baseball Notes," *New York Clipper,* April 26, 1879, 35.
4. Baseball-reference.com credits him with only five wins in 1878, but *New York Clipper* box scores show him pitching every game for Rochester beginning July 28, and from that point on the team went 14–16–3.
5. Richard Bak, *A Place for Summer: A Narrative History of Tiger Stadium* (Detroit: Wayne State University Press, 1998), 26.
6. "The Base Ball Match," *Detroit Free Press,* May 10, 1879, 1.
7. "Recreation Park," *Detroit Post and Tribune,* May 13, 1879, 4.
8. "Recreation Park," *Detroit Free Press,* May 13, 1879, 1.
9. "Recreation Park," *Detroit Post and Tribune,* May 13, 1879, 4.
10. *Ibid.*
11. "Where the First Paid Professional Baseball Team Scored for Detroit in 1879," *Detroit Sunday News,* August 31, 1919, 12.
12. "Base Ball Brevities," *Detroit Free Press,* May 18, 1879, 6.
13. "Base Ball," *Detroit Free Press,* May 23, 1879, 1, and "Local Matters," *Detroit Free Press,* May 25, 1879, 6.
14. Base Ball, *Detroit Free Press,* May 28, 1879, 1.
15. "Base Ball," *Detroit Free Press,* June 8, 1879.
16. "Assistance Needed," *Detroit Free Press,* June 11, 1879, 6.
17. Baseball-reference.com, accessed October 7, 2015, http://www.baseball-reference.com/register/league.cgi?id=9db35b65.
18. "Base Ball," *Detroit Free Press,* June 22, 1879, 1.
19. "Base Ball," *Detroit Free Press,* June 27, 1879, 1.
20. "Base Ball," *Detroit Free Press,* July 1, 1879, 6.
21. "Base Ball," *Detroit Free Press,* July 4, 1879, 2.
22. "Sayings and Doings," *Detroit Free Press,* July 12, 1879, 1.
23. "Recreation Park Points," newspaper article in the Recreation Park file at the Burton Historical Collection, Detroit Public Library. It is indicated as being clipped from the *Detroit Free Press* of July 8, 1878, but a search of *Free Press* microfilm for several days around that time failed to find it.

24. "Baseball Notes," *New York Clipper*, July 26, 1879, 139.
25. "Amusements" classified advertisement, *Detroit Free Press*, July 2, 1879, 6.
26. "Patriotic Pastimes," *Detroit Free Press*, July 6, 1879, 6.
27. "Recreation," *Detroit Free Press*, July 29, 1879, 1.
28. "Batters and Bases," *Detroit Free Press*, July 19, 1879, 1.
29. "Where the First Paid Professional Team Scored for Detroit in 1879," *Detroit Sunday News*, August 31, 1919, 12.
30. "Ten to Nothing," *Detroit Free Press*, July 16, 1879, 1.
31. "One to Nothing," *Detroit Free Press*, July 18, 1879, 6.
32. "Out-Door Sports," *Detroit Free Press*, July 20, 1879, 1.
33. "Recreation Park," *Detroit Free Press*, August 6, 1879, 6.
34. "Base Ball Brevities," *Detroit Free Press*, August 7, 1879, 1.
35. "Exit Detroits," *Detroit Free Press*, August 13, 1879, 6.
36. "The Detroit Club's Record," *New York Clipper*, August 30, 1879, 181.
37. "Base Ball Brevities," *Detroit Free Press*, September 12, 1879, 1.
38. "Base Ball Brevities," *Detroit Free Press*, October 18, 1879, 1.
39. "Later Baseball Notes," *New York Clipper*, November 1, 1879, 251.
40. "Looking Ahead," *Detroit Free Press*, November 15, 1879, 1.
41. "Recreation Park," *Detroit Free Press*, January 23, 1881, 7.
42. "Bill Hollinger One of the Real Veterans of Billiards," *Detroit Free Press*, January 25, 1912, 11.

Chapter 3

1. "Cincinnati, Ohio," Ohio History Central, accessed October 22, 2015, http://www.ohiohistorycentral.org/w/Cincinnati,_Ohio?rec=681.
2. David Pietrusza, *Major Leagues: The Formation, Sometimes Absorption and Mostly Inevitable Demise of 18 Professional Baseball Organizations, 1871 to Present* (Jefferson, NC: McFarland, 1991), 2–4.
3. "Cincinnati Reds II," Society for Cincinnati Sports Research, accessed October 21, 2015, http://www.scsr.org/19CCBB/Teams/CR2.htm.
4. David Nemec, *The Great Encyclopedia of 19th Century Major League Baseball* (New York: Donald I. Fine Books, 1997), 125.
5. "Welcome to 19th Century Cincinnati Base Ball," Society for Cincinnati Sports Research, accessed October 21, 2015, http://www.scsr.org/19CCBB/Teams/CR2.htm.
6. "The Rochester Meeting," *New York Clipper*, October 16, 1880, 238.
7. "The Cincinnati Club," *New York Clipper*, November 6, 1880, 261.
8. "Base Ball," *Detroit Free Press*, October 8, 1880, 2.
9. "Base Ball," *Detroit Free Press*, October 27, 1880, 2.
10. "A New League," *New York Clipper*, November 6, 1880, 238.
11. David Nemec, *The Beer and Whisky League: The Illustrated History of the American Association—Baseball's Renegade Major League* (New York: Lyons & Burford, 1994), 15–16.
12. "Later Baseball Notes," *New York Clipper*, January 17, 1880, 338.
13. "Sayings and Doings. Recreation Park," *Detroit Free Press*, April 27, 1880, 1.
14. "The Runners," *Detroit Free Press*, April 15, 1880, 6.
15. William G. Thompson," *The History of Detroit and Michigan or The Metropolis Illustrated: A Chronological Cyclopedia of the Past and Present* (Detroit: Silas Farmer and Company, 1889), 1048.
16. Richard Bak, *A Place for Summer: A Narrative History of Tiger Stadium* (Detroit: Wayne State University Press, 1998), 30.
17. "Thompson From a Republican Standpoint," *Detroit Free Press*, October 26, 1879, 4.
18. "In a Business Light," *Detroit Free Press*, October 31, 1879, 4.
19. "Sayings and Doings," *Detroit Free Press*, June 29, 1880, 1.
20. "Base Ball," *Detroit Free Press*, August 22, 1880, 2.
21. "Worcester vs. Cass," *New York Clipper*, September 4, 1880, 187.
22. "Base Ball," *Detroit Free Press*, August 28, 1880, 1.
23. "Baseball Notes," *New York Clipper*, September 4, 1880, 187.

24. "Local Brevities," *Detroit Free Press*, September 11, 1880, 6.
25. "The National Game," *Detroit Free Press*, September 15, 1880, 2.
26. "Local Matters. Base Ball," *Detroit Free Press*, September 19, 1880, 3.
27. "City Personals," *Detroit Free Press*, September 21, 1880, 8.
28. Michael Haupert, "William Hulbert," SABR BioProject, accessed October 27, 2015, http://sabr.org/bioproj/person/d1d420b3
29. "Baseball Notes," *New York Clipper*, October 2, 1880, 218.
30. "Baseball Notes," *New York Clipper*, October 9, 1880, 229.
31. "The Base Ball Boom," *Detroit Free Press*, October 26, 1880, 6.
32. "The Five Men Rule," *New York Clipper*, October 23, 1880, 245.
33. "F. C. Bancroft," *New York Clipper*, October 30, 1880, 250.
34. "1880 Detroit National League Membership Application Signed by William Hulbert," Robert Edward Auctions 2005, accessed July 21, 2015, http://www.robertedwardauctions.com/auction/2005/15.html#photos
35. "The Detroit Club," *New York Clipper*, November 13, 1880, 266.
36. *Nineteenth Century Stars, 2012 Edition*, eds. Robert L. Tiemann and Mark Rucker (Phoenix: Society for American Baseball Research, 2012), 100.
37. "Manager Bancroft," *New York Clipper*, November 27, 1880, 282.
38. "First Inning," *Detroit Free Press*, November 30, 1880, 1.
39. "The Base Ball Club," *Detroit Free Press*, December 7, 1880, 4.
40. "The League Convention," *New York Clipper*, December 18, 1880, 309.

Chapter 4

1. David Nemec, *The Great Encyclopedia of 19th Century Major League Baseball* (New York: Donald I. Fine Books, 1997), 148.
2. "The Wolverine," from University of Michigan campus information, accessed December 21, 2015, https://campusinfo.umich.edu/article/wolverine.
3. Henry Chadwick, SABR BioProject, accessed November 16, 2015, http://sabr.org/bioproj/person/436e570c.
4. "Frank Bancroft: A Life in Baseball," accessed November 15, 2015, http://seamheads.com/2008/11/21/frank-bancroft-a-life-in-baseball/.
5. "Sayings and Doings," *Detroit Free Press*, March 12, 1881, 1.
6. "Base Ball Match," *Detroit Free Press*, April 3, 1881, 6.
7. "Sporting Matters," *Detroit Free Press*, April 6, 1881, 1.
8. "Sporting Matters," *Detroit Free Press*, May 22, 1881, 6.
9. "Sporting Matters," *Detroit Free Press*, April 21, 1881, 1.
10. *Nineteenth Century Stars 2012 Edition*, eds. Robert L. Tiemann and Mark Rucker (Phoenix: The Society for American Baseball Research, 2012), 205, and "James 'Tip' O'Neill," Canadian Baseball Hall of Fame, accessed November 6, 2105, http://baseballhalloffame.ca/inductees/james-tip-oneill.
11. "Sporting Matters," *Detroit Free Press*, May 10, 1881, 6.
12. "Sporting Matters," *Detroit Free Press*, May 11, 1881, 1.
13. "Sporting Matters," *Detroit Free Press*, May 13, 1881, 1.
14. "Sporting Matters," *Detroit Free Press*, May 14, 1881, 1.
15. "Sporting Matters," *Detroit Free Press*, May 28, 1881, 1.
16. "Sporting Matters," *Detroit Free Press*, May 29, 1881, 6.
17. *Ibid*.
18. "Sporting Matters," *Detroit Free Press*, June 18, 1881, 1.
19. As quoted in "Sporting Matters," *Detroit Free Press*, July 19, 1881, 1.
20. "Sporting Matters," *Detroit Free Press*, July 29, 1881, 1.
21. "Sporting Matters," *Detroit Free Press*, August 2, 1881, 1.
22. "The Detroit Club," *New York Clipper*, August 6, 1881, 314.
23. "Sayings and Doings," *Detroit Free Press*, July 30, 1881, 1.
24. "The Detroit Club Management," *New York Clipper*, August 13, 1881, 330.
25. "Sporting Matters," *Detroit Free Press*, October 1, 1881, 1.

Chapter 5

1. David Nemec, *The Beer and Whisky League* (New York: Lyons and Burford, 1994), 19–23.
2. David Pietrusza, *Major Leagues: The Formation, Sometimes Absorption and Mostly Inevitable Demise of 18 Professional Baseball Organizations, 1871 to Present* (Jefferson, NC: McFarland, 1991), 72.
3. "Baseball," *New York Clipper*, April 8, 1882, 44.
4. "Sporting Matters," *Detroit Free Press*, October 5, 1882, 6, and "Sporting Matters," *Detroit Free Press*, November 18, 1882, 4.
5. As quoted in "Base Ball," *Detroit Free Press*, March 7, 1882, 8.
6. "Sporting Matters," *Detroit Free Press*, March 15, 1882, 1.
7. "Base Ball," *Detroit Free Press*, February 8, 1882, 1.
8. As quoted in "Sporting Matters," *Detroit Free Press*, April 1, 1882, 8.
9. "Sporting Matters," *Detroit Free Press*, April 6, 1882, 1.
10. "Sporting Matters," *Detroit Free Press*, April 13, 1882, 1.
11. No title, *New York Clipper*, May 20, 1882, 139.
12. "Sporting Matters," *Detroit Free Press*, May 13, 1883, 7.
13. "Sporting Matters," *Detroit Free Press*, January 31, 1882, 1.
14. Charlton's Baseball Chronology—1882, accessed November 12, 2015, http://www.baseballlibrary.com/chronology/byyear.php?year=1882.
15. Pietrusza, 73.
16. David Nemec, *The Great Encyclopedia of 19th Century Major League Baseball* (New York: Donald I. Fine Books, 1997), 167.
17. "Dick Higham," Baseball-reference.com, accessed December 9, 2015, http://www.baseball-reference.com/bullpen/Dick_Higham.
18. "The 'Dick' Letter," *Detroit Free Press*, June 27, 1882, 8.
19. "Sporting Matters," *Detroit Free Press*, June 25, 1882, 7.
20. "The 'Dick' Letter."
21. Nemec, *The Great Encyclopedia*, 168–69.
22. Edward Achorn, "Radbourn the Slugger," *Inventing Baseball: The 100 Greatest Games of the Nineteenth Century*, edited by Bill Felber (Phoenix: Society for American Baseball Research, 2013), 141–143.
23. "Sporting Matters," *Detroit Free Press*, August 18, 1882, 6.
24. "Sporting Matters," *Detroit Free Press*, September 26, 1882, 6.
25. "Sporting Matters," *Detroit Free Press*, September 29, 1882, 6.
26. "Sporting Matters," *Detroit Free Press*, October 8, 7.
27. "Sporting Matters," *Detroit Free Press*, October 15, 1882, 4.
28. "Baseball," *New York Clipper*, October 21, 1882, 499.
29. "Sporting Matters," *Detroit Free Press*, November 22, 1882, 1.
30. Harold Seymour and Dorothy Seymour Mills, *Baseball: The Early Years* (New York: Oxford University Press, 1989), 343.
31. "Baseball," *New York Clipper*, November 25, 1882, 583.
32. Joe Overfield, "John Curtis Chapman," *Nineteenth Century Stars: 2012 Edition*, eds. Robert L. Tiemann and Mark Rucker (Phoenix: Society for American Baseball Research, 2012), 57.
33. "Sporting Matters," *Detroit Free Press*, March 4, 1883, 1.
34. "Sporting Matters," *Detroit Free Press*, November 21, 1882, 6.
35. Pietrusza, *Major Leagues*, 77–79.

Chapter 6

1. "Sporting Matters," *Detroit Free Press*, March 28, 1883, 6.
2. "Sporting Matters," *Detroit Free Press*, April 3, 1883, 6.
3. "Sporting Matters," *Detroit Free Press*, April 8, 1883, 7.
4. "Sporting Matters," *Detroit Free Press*, May 10, 1883, 1.
5. "Sporting Matters," *Detroit Free Press*, May 19, 1883, 1.
6. "Sporting Matters," *Detroit Free Press*, June 23, 1883, 1.
7. "Sporting Matters," *Detroit Free Press*, June 27, 1883, 1.

8. "Sporting Matters," *Detroit Free Press*, June 28, 1883, 1.
9. "Sporting Matters," *Detroit Free Press*, July 2, 1883, 7.
10. "Sayings and Doings," *Detroit Free Press*, July 29, 1883, 9.
11. "Sporting Matters," *Detroit Free Press*, August 11, 1883, 6.
12. "Sporting Matters," *Detroit Free Press*, September 4, 1883, 1.
13. "Sporting Matters," *Detroit Free Press*, September 7, 1883, 1.
14. "Diamond Dust," *Detroit Free Press*, October 21, 1883, 15.
15. "Base Ball," *Detroit Free Press*, November 23, 1883, 6.
16. David Pietrusza, *Major Leagues: The Formation, Sometimes Absorption and Mostly Inevitable Demise of 18 Professional Baseball Organizations, 1871 to Present* (Jefferson, NC: McFarland, 1991), 93.
17. David Nemec, *The Great Encyclopedia of 19th Century Major League Baseball* (New York: Donald I. Fine Books, 18897), 214–215.
18. "Sporting Matters," *Detroit Free Press*, December 23, 1883, 12.
19. "Sporting Matters," *Detroit Free Press*, March 30, 1884, 11.
20. "Manager Chapman," *New York Clipper*, May 3, 1884, 99.
21. "Charlton's Baseball Chronology—1884," accessed December 10, 2015, http://www.baseballlibrary.com/chronology/byyear.php?year=1884.
22. "Sporting Matters," *Detroit Free Press*, June 1, 1884, 11.
23. "Sporting Matters," *Detroit Free Press*, July 8, 1884, 8.
24. "Sporting Matters," *Detroit Free Press*, September 23, 1884, 8.
25. "Sporting Matters," *Detroit Free Press*, September 29, 1884, 1.
26. Frederick Kimball Stearns, "The Growth of Manufacturing Pharmacy in Detroit During the Nineteenth Century," a brief paper about the major players and accomplishments in Detroit's pharmaceutical industry, in the holdings of the Detroit Historical Society.
27. "Sporting Matters," *Detroit Free Press*, October 8, 1884, 8.
28. "Sporting Matters," *Detroit Free Press*, October 15, 1884, 5.
29. James Egan, Jr., *Baseball on the Western Reserve: The Early Game in Cleveland and Northeast Ohio, Year by Year and Town by Town, 1865–1900* (Jefferson, NC: McFarland, 2008), 138–140.
30. Harold Seymour and Dorothy Seymour Mills, *Baseball: The Early Years* (New York: Oxford University Press, 1989), 164.
31. "This Rattles Us," *Detroit Free Press*, January 6, 1885, 2.
32. "Sporting Matters," *Detroit Free Press*, January 11, 1885, 6.

Chapter 7

1. J.W. Leonard, *The Industries of Detroit: Her Relations as a Centre of Trade. Manufacturing Establishments and Business Houses* (Detroit: J. M. Elstner & Co., 1887), 197.
2. Peter Morris, *Baseball Fever: Early Baseball in Michigan* (Ann Arbor: University of Michigan Press, 2003), 97.
3. *Ibid.*, 240.
4. "Baseball in Early Days: Frederick K. Stearns and the '75 Team," *The Michigan Alumnus*, November 2, 1922, 103.
5. *Successful Men of Michigan: A Compilation of Useful Biographical Sketches of Prominent Men* (Detroit: SI. U. Collins, 1914), 6, quoted in Roy Kerr, *Big Sam Thompson* (Jefferson, NC: McFarland, 2015), 45.
6. James J. Mitchell, *Detroit in History and Commerce* (Detroit: Rogers and Thorpe Publishers, 1891), 34.
7. "Sporting Matters," *Detroit Free Press*, June 6, 1885, 3.
8. "Sporting Matters," *Detroit Free Press*, June 14, 1885, 7.
9. "Sporting Matters," *Detroit Free Press*, June 15, 1885, 4.
10. "Sporting Matters," *Detroit Free Press*, June 16, 1885, 8.
11. "Sporting Matters," *Detroit Free Press*, June 17, 1885, 8.
12. Guy M. Smith, "He Could Catch Anything," article in Jim McGuire file at National Baseball Hall of Fame Library, quoted in Peter Morris, *A Game of Inches* (Chicago: Ivan R. Dee, 2010), 358.
13. "Baseball in Early Days: Frederick K. Stearns and the '75 Team," *The Michigan Alumnus*, November 2, 1922, 103.

14. George W. Stark, "Detroit's Veteran Magnate Tells How He Kidnapped Ball Players," unsourced newspaper article, no date, in Don Thompson's Sam Thompson clipping file, as quoted in Roy Kerr, *Big Sam Thompson: Baseball's Greatest Clutch Hitter* (Jefferson, NC: McFarland, 2015), 46. (George W. Stark became a reporter for the *Detroit Free Press* in 1905. Four years later he moved to the *Detroit News*, where he worked as a reporter, drama critic, city editor and columnist. His column "Town Talk" dealt mainly with Detroit history and led to his participation in the city's historical activities. He authored two books, *In Old Detroit* and *City of Destiny*, both histories of the city. Stark died in Detroit on Jan. 29, 1966. A search of the *Free Press* failed to turn up the article, suggesting it was published in the *News* in 1909 or later.)

15. Don Thompson, "Sam Thompson," SABR BioProject, accessed January 22, 2016, http://sabr.org/bioproj/person/b3e0fab8.

16. Maclean Kennedy, "Sam Thompson Ranks as One of the Great Sluggers of Baseball History," *Detroit Free Press*, February 16, 1913, 22.

17. *Washington Post*, January 28, 1906, quoted in David L. Fleitz, *More Ghosts in the Gallery: Another Sixteen Little-Known Greats at Cooperstown* (Jefferson, NC: McFarland, 2007), 155.

18. "Sporting Matters," *Detroit Free Press*, June 23, 1885, 8.

19. Robert W. Bigelow, "Deacon McGuire," SABR BioProject, accessed January 19, 2016, http://sabr.org/bioproj/person/62d7cf30.

20. "Fair Balls," *Detroit Free Press*, July 3, 1885, 2.

21. George W. Stark, "Detroit's Veteran Magnate," quoted in Roy Kerr, *Big Sam Thompson*.

22. Bill Lamb, "Bill Watkins," SABR BioProject, accessed November 4, 2015, http://sabr.org/bioproj/person/c568f927.

23. "From Detroit," *Sporting Life*, July 22, 1885, 1.

24. Frank Vaccaro, "Origins of the Pitching Rotation," Society for American Baseball Research, accessed January 25, 2016, http://sabr.org/research/origins-pitching-rotation.

25. "Base Hits," *New York Clipper*, August 8, 1885, 323.

26. "The Buffalo Club," *New York Clipper*, July 25, 1885, 291.

27. "A Stunner: Bisons Sell Out," *Sporting Life*, September 23, 1885, 1.

28. "Detroit to Get Radbourn," *Ibid*.

29. Brian McKenna, "Old Hoss Radbourn," SABR BioProject, accessed January 28, http://sabr.org/bioproj/person/83bf739e.

30. "Mean But Legal," *Detroit Free Press*, September 13, 1885, 5.

31. "Outside Spectators," *Detroit Free Press*, April 25, 1886, 4.

32. Jared S. Hopkins, "Cubs Owner Ricketts Buys Wrigley Rooftop Buildings," *Chicago Tribune*, May 21, 2015, accessed January 26, 2016, http://www.chicagotribune.com/sports/baseball/cubs/ct-ricketts-family-buys-more-wrigley-rooftops-20150521-story.html.

Chapter 8

1. "Bought Another Club," *Detroit Free Press*, September 16, 1885, 8.
2. "Big Four Coming," *Detroit Free Press*, September 18, 1885, 8.
3. "Sporting Sensations," *Detroit Free Press*, September 17, 1885, 8.
4. "A Stunner. Bisons Sell Out," *Sporting Life*, September 23, 1885, 1.
5. "Nick Young Opposed," *Ibid*.
6. "Buffalo's View," *Ibid*.
7. "A Strong Kick from New York," *Ibid*.
8. "A Big Four Fuss," *Detroit Free Press*, September 19, 1885, 4.
9. "Detroit vs. New York," *New York Clipper*, September 26, 1885, 441.
10. "The Base Ball Situation," *Detroit Free Press*, September 21, 1885, 4.
11. "Au Revoir, Big Four," *Detroit Free Press*, September 22, 1885, 8.
12. "Sporting Events," *Detroit Free Press*, September 23, 1885, 8.
13. "Blocked. The Big Four Free," *Sporting Life*, September 30, 1885, 1.
14. Joe Overfield, *The 100 Seasons of Buffalo Baseball* (Kenmore, NY: Partners' Press, 1985), 25.
15. "From Chicago," *Sporting Life*, September 30, 1885, 5.
16. "Base Ball," *Sporting Life*, October 7, 1885, 1.

17. "The 'Big Four,'" *Sporting Life*, October 7, 1885, 1.
18. *Ibid.*
19. "Base Ball Prospects," *Detroit Free Press*, October 21, 1885, 3.
20. "The Famous Four," *Detroit Free Press*, October 22, 1885, 3.
21. *Detroit Free Press*, October 21, 1885, 3.
22. David Pietrusza, *Major Leagues: The Formation, Sometimes Absorption and Mostly Inevitable Demise of 18 Professional Baseball Organizations, 1871 to Present* (Jefferson, NC: McFarland, 1991), 99.
23. "Base Ball," *Detroit Free Press*, November 18, 1885, 8.
24. "The League Convention," *New York Clipper*, November 28, 1885, 584–585.
25. "The Big Four Are Ours," *Detroit Free Press*, November 20, 1885, 8.
26. "Secrets. Now Leaking Out," *Sporting Life*, December 2, 1885, 1.
27. "Base Ball. Detroit Happy," *Sporting Life*, November 24, 1885, 1.
28. Untitled, *New York Clipper*, November 28, 1885, 587.
29. Untitled, *New York Clipper*, February 6, 1886, 745.
30. "From the City of the Straits," *Sporting Life*, December 9, 1885, 1.
31. "Base Ball," *Detroit Free Press*, November 21, 1885, 8.
32. "Polishing Up The Park," *Detroit Free Press*, February 26, 1886, 8.
33. "From the City of the Straits," *Sporting Life*, December 9, 1885, 1.
34. "Liners," *Detroit Free Press*, May 1, 1886, 3.
35. "A Statement Concerning Salaries," *Detroit Free Press*, September 19, 1885, 4.
36. "Liners," *Detroit Free Press*, December 14, 1885, 7.
37. "Watkins' Latest," *Detroit Free Press*, December 14, 1885, 7.
38. "The Cowboy City Wins," *Detroit Free Press*, February 10, 1886, 8.
39. David Nemec, *The Great Encyclopedia of 19th Century Major League Baseball* (New York: Donald I. Fine Books, 1997), 287.
40. Untitled, *New York Clipper*, February 20, 1886, 779.

Chapter 9

1. "A $300,000 Block," *Detroit Free Press*, February 26, 1886, 8.
2. "Struck With a Cane," *Chicago Daily Tribune*, February 4, 1886, 2, and untitled, *New York Clipper*, February 13, 1886, 762.
3. "A Funny Fracas," *Chicago Daily Tribune*, February 5, 1886, 3.
4. "The Sluggers Home," *Detroit Free Press*, April 27, 1886, 8.
5. "Bradstreet's Review," *Detroit Free Press*, May 1, 1886, 7.
6. "Haymarket and May Day," Encyclopedia of Chicago, accessed February 12, 2016, www.encyclopedia.chicagohistory.org/pages/571.html.
7. "Liners," *Detroit Free Press*, May 13, 1886, 8.
8. "Unanimous Hitting," *Detroit Free Press*, May 24, 1886, 5.
9. "Liners," *Detroit Free Press*, May 12, 1886, 8.
10. Peter Morris, *A Game of Inches: The Stories Behind the Innovations That Shaped Baseball* (Chicago: Ivan R. Dee, 2006), 490.
11. "Liners," *Detroit Free Press*, June 5, 1886, 5.
12. "The Michigan Giants," *Detroit Free Press*, June 1, 1886, 8.
13. "Sporting News," *Detroit Free Press*, June 14, 1886, 5.
14. "Liners," *Detroit Free Press*, June 4, 1886, 8.
15. "A Drawn Battle," *Detroit Free Press*, June 5, 1886, 5.
16. Charlton's Baseball Chronology 1886, Baseballlibrary.com, accessed August 24, 2014, http://www.baseballlibrary.com/chronology/byyear.php?year=1886.
17. "Malicious Invention," *Detroit Free Press*, August 2, 1886, 1.
18. "More Sensations," *Sporting Life*, August 11, 1886, 1.
19. "Notes and Comments," *Sporting Life*, August 11, 1886, 5.
20. *Ibid.*
21. "Lucas Quits," *Sporting Life*, August 25, 1886, 1.
22. "Shaking up the Detroits," *Detroit Free Press*, August 27, 1886, 8.

23. "Liners," *Detroit Free Press*, August 24, 1886, 8.
24. "A Board of Five," *Detroit Free Press*, September 27, 1886, 4, and "A Change of Base," *Detroit Free Press*, September 28, 1886, 6.
25. "Detroit's Great Team," *Sporting News*, September 13, 1886, 1.
26. "Beaten by the Babes," *Detroit Free Press*, September 21, 1886, 8.
27. "Bold Diamond Robbery," *Detroit Free Press*, September 23, 1886, 3.
28. "St. Louis vs. Chicago," *New York Clipper*, November 6, 1886, 537.
29. Untitled, *Sporting News*, October 25, 1886, 4.

Chapter 10

1. "The Detroit Club," *Sporting News*, October 25, 1886, 1.
2. "Caught on the Fly," *Sporting News*, October 25, 1886, 5.
3. "The League Meeting," *Sporting News*, October 25, 1886, 1.
4. Untitled, *New York Clipper*, March 5, 1887, 810.
5. "Detroit May Drop Out," *Detroit Free Press*, November 20, 1886, 2.
6. "Detroit Will Fight," *Detroit Free Press*, November 21, 1886, 2.
7. "Detroit's Ultimatum," *Detroit Free Press*, November 22, 1886, 1.
8. "A Sensation: Detroit Threatens to Jump the League," *Sporting Life*, November 24, 1886, 1.
9. "Cleveland Got There," *Sporting News*, November 27, 1886, 1.
10. "The Cleveland Club Joins the American Association," *New York Clipper*, December 4, 1886, 601.
11. Ibid.
12. Attendance figures from Untitled, *Sporting News*, December 11, 1886, 3.
13. "Detroit's Game of Bluff," *New York Clipper*, December 4, 1886, 601.
14. "From Detroit," *Sporting Life*, March 9, 1887, 6.
15. "Pretty Hefty. What the Detroit Club Disburses Annually in the Way of Salaries," *Sporting Life*, December 1, 1886, 1.
16. "How President Stearns Thinks the Clubs Will Come Out," *Detroit Free Press*, March 21, 1887, 5.
17. Untitled, *Sporting News*, December 11, 1886, 4.
18. "Detroit May Be Dropped," *Sporting News*, December 11, 1886, 5.
19. "Bill Watkins," SABR BioProject, accessed November 4, 2015, http://sabr.org/bioproj/person/c568f927.
20. "The Pennant Struggle," *Detroit Free Press*, April 28, 1887, 8.
21. "Change of Base," *Detroit Free Press*, April 6, 1887, 8.
22. "Sporting Matters," *Detroit Free Press*, April 19, 1887, 8.
23. "Base Ball," *Detroit Free Press*, April 27, 1887, 8.
24. Harold Seymour, *Baseball: The Golden Age* (New York: Oxford University Press, 1971), 106.
25. "To-day's Sport," *Detroit Free Press*, May 5, 1887, 1.
26. Untitled, *Sporting News*, May 21, 1887, 4.
27. "Liners," quoting the *Boston Herald*, *Detroit Free Press*, June 5, 1887, 6.
28. "First-Class Ball," *Detroit Free Press*, June 23, 1887, 2.
29. "Here it is Again," *Detroit Free Press*, July 2, 1887, 2.
30. "Must Have Percentage," *Detroit Free Press*, July 11, 1887, 4.
31. "A Lively Shaking Up," *Detroit Free Press*, July 19, 1887, 2.
32. "Managerial Gall," *Detroit Free Press*, August 18, 1887, 2.
33. "Liners," *Detroit Free Press*, August 20, 1887, 2.
34. "Rushing Pennantward," *Detroit Free Press*, September 18, 1887, 6.
35. "Everything Lovely," *Detroit Free Press*, September 23, 1887, 2.
36. "The Association Meeting," *New York Clipper*, September 17, 1887, 427.
37. Untitled, *New York Clipper*, October 1, 1887, 460, for Boston, and "Sport-Pastime Talk," *Brooklyn Eagle*, October 27, 1887, 6, for Chicago figures.
38. "We Can't Lose the Flag," *Detroit Free Press*, October 5, 1887, 1.

39. "In the Quaker City," *Detroit Free Press*, October 17, 1887, 4.
40. "It Was a Cold Day," *Detroit Free Press*, October 23, 1887, 5.
41. "Our Champions," *Detroit Free Press*, October 25, 1887, 4.
42. "A Grand Finale," *Detroit Free Press*, October 25, 1887, 2.
43. Untitled, *New York Clipper*, November 12, 1887, 559.
44. David Nemec, *The Beer and Whisky League* (New York: Lyons and Burford, 1994), 140.
45. Harold Seymour and Dorothy Seymour Mills, *Baseball: The Early Years* (New York: Oxford University Press, 1989), 187.

Chapter 11

1. Frederick C. Dunlap, *Major League Baseball Profiles: 1871–1900, Volume 1*, comp. and ed. David Nemec (Lincoln: University of Nebraska Press, 2011), 352.
2. "Sporting Matters," *Detroit Free Press*, December 5, 1887, 11.
3. "Watkins Feels Easy," *Detroit Free Press*, December 9, 1887, 2.
4. "President Stearns Resigns," *Detroit Free Press*, December 19, 1887, 11.
5. "Sporting Matters," *Detroit Free Press*, January 16, 1888, 5
6. "Deacon Won't Sign," *Detroit Free Press*, March 13, 1888, 7.
7. "The Base Ball Crank," *Detroit Free Press*, March 25, 1888, 4.
8. "The League Season," *Detroit Free Press*, April 21, 1888, 8.
9. "Watkins Can't Account For It—Baldwin Laid Off," *Detroit Free Press*, April 28, 1888, 8.
10. "Rallied Round the Flags," *Detroit Free Press*, May 2, 1888, 8.
11. "They Come to Blows," *Detroit Free Press*, May 6, 1888, 5, and "The Fiats of Justice," *Detroit Free Press*, May 6, 1888, 12.
12. "Both Men Laid Up," *New York Times*, May 6, 1888.
13. "The President Knew Them," *New York Times*, June 9, 1888, 2.
14. "We Lose the Last Game," *Detroit Free Press*, June 17, 1888, 4.
15. "Notes and Comment," *Sporting Life*, June 20, 1888, 7.
16. Arthur Ahrens, "An Assist for Jimmy Ryan," Society for American Baseball Research, Research Journals Archive, accessed May 28, 2016, http://research.sabr.org/journals/assist-for-jimmy-ryan.
17. "Second Place Again," *Detroit Free Press*, August 1, 1888, 8.
18. "All Broken Hearted," *Sporting Life*, June 2, 1888, 4.
19. "Bad Judgment or What?," *Detroit Free Press*, August 5, 1888, 4.
20. "Manager W. H. Watkins of the Detroits," *New York Clipper*, August 11, 1888, 349.
21. "Gossip. The Trouble With the Detroits," *Detroit Free Press*, August 16, 1888, 8, which referenced the *Boston Globe* story.
22. Untitled, *Sporting Life*, August 15, 1888, 6.
23. "Disgusted Detroit," *Sporting Life*, August 22, 1888, 3.
24. "Wasn't it Glorious," *Detroit Free Press*, August 23, 1888, 8.
25. "Watkins Steps Down," *Detroit Free Press*, August 28, 1888, 8.
26. No title, *Sporting Life*, September 5, 1888, 2.
27. Bill Lamb, "Bill Watkins," SABR BioProject, accessed November 4, 2015, http://sabr.org/bioproj/person/c568f927.
28. "Farewell, Sluggers," *Detroit Free Press*, October 14, 1888, 18.
29. "Yes, They All Will Go," *Detroit Free Press*, October 16, 1888, 8.
30. "Do We Want Base Ball?," *Detroit Free Press*, October 18, 1888, 8.
31. Lee Lowenfish, *The Imperfect Diamond: A History of Baseball's Labor Wars* (Lincoln: University of Nebraska Press, 2010), 33–34.
32. "Gossip. Just Look at This," *Detroit Free Press*, May 22, 1889, 8.
33. "Base Ball. The Death of the International," *Detroit Free Press*, July 9, 1890, 8.
34. Richard Bak, *A Place for Summer: A Narrative History of Tiger Stadium* (Detroit: Wayne State University Press, 1998), 38.
35. "Can Have a League Club," *Detroit Free Press*, October 31, 1893, 3.
36. "No Chance at All," *Sporting Life*, November 4, 1893, 5.

37. "Detroit Not Wanted," *Sporting News*, October 14, 1893, 3.
38. "Their First Breather. Strouthers's Tigers Showed up Very Nicely," *Detroit Free Press*, April 16, 1895, 2.
39. Bak, *A Place for Summer*, 46–48.
40. Ibid., 59n.

Bibliography

Books

Bak, Richard. *A Place for Summer: A Narrative History of Tiger Stadium*. Detroit: Wayne State University Press, 1998.
Batesel, Paul. *Players and Teams of the National Association, 1871–1875*. Jefferson, NC: McFarland, 2012.
Block, David. *Baseball Before We Knew It*. Lincoln: University of Nebraska Press, 2005.
Conot, Robert. *An American Odyssey: A Unique History of America Told Through the Life of a Great City*. New York: William Morrow, 1974.
Dewey, Donald, and Nicholas Acocella. *The Biographical History of Baseball*. Chicago: Triumph, 2012.
Dictionary of Canadian Biography, 1901 to 1910. Volume 13. Toronto: University of Toronto Press, 1994.
Egan, James M., Jr. *Base Ball on the Western Reserve: The Early Game in Cleveland and Northeast Ohio, Year by Year and Town by Town, 1865–1900*. Jefferson, NC: McFarland, 2008.
Felber, Bill, ed. *Inventing Baseball: The 100 Greatest Games of the Nineteenth Century*. Phoenix: Society for American Baseball Research, 2013.
Ginsburg, Daniel E. *The Fix Is In: A History of Baseball Gambling and Game Fixing Scandals*. Jefferson, NC: McFarland, 1995.
The History of Detroit and Michigan, or The Metropolis Illustrated: A Chronological Cyclopedia of the Past and Present. Detroit: Silas Farmer, 1889.
The Industries of Detroit: Her Relations as a Centre of Trade. Manufacturing Establishments and Business Houses. Detroit: J. M. Elstner, 1887.
Ivor-Campbell, Frederick, and Mark Rucker, eds. *Baseball's First Stars*. Cleveland: Society for American Baseball Research, 1996.
Kerr, Roy. *Big Dan Brouthers: Baseball's First Great Slugger*. Jefferson, NC: McFarland, 2013.
_____. *Big Sam Thompson: Baseball's Greatest Clutch Hitter*. Jefferson, NC: McFarland, 2015.
Kossik, John. *63 Alfred Street, Where Capitalism Failed: The Life and Times of a Venetian Gothic Mansion in Downtown Detroit*. Detroit: self-published, 2012.
LeDuff, Charlie. *Detroit: An American Autopsy*. New York: Penguin, 2013.
Lieb, Frederick G. *The Detroit Tigers*. Kent, OH: Kent State University Press, 2008. First published 1946 by G.P. Putnam's Sons.
Lowenfish, Lee. *The Imperfect Diamond: A History of Baseball's Labor Wars*. Lincoln: University of Nebraska Press, 2010.
Martelle, Scott. *Detroit (A Biography)*. Chicago: Chicago Review Press, 2012.

Martin, Brian. *The Tecumsehs of the International Association: Canada's First Major League Baseball Champions.* Jefferson, NC: McFarland, 2015.
Mitchell, James J. *Detroit in History and Commerce.* Detroit: Rogers & Thorpe, 1891.
Morris, Peter. *Baseball Fever: Early Baseball in Michigan.* Ann Arbor: University of Michigan Press, 2003.
_____. *A Game of Inches: The Story Behind the Innovations That Shaped Baseball.* Revised and Expanded One-Volume Edition. Chicago: Ivan R. Dee, 2006.
Morris, Peter, et al., eds. *Base Ball Pioneers: 1850–1870.* Jefferson, NC: McFarland, 2012.
National Baseball Hall of Fame and Museum 2015 Yearbook. Lynn, MA: H.O. Zimman, 2014.
Nemec, David. *The Beer and Whisky League: The Illustrated History of the American Association— Baseball's Renegade Major League.* New York: Lyons and Burford, 1994.
_____. *The Great Encyclopedia of 19th Century Major League Baseball.* New York: Donald I. Fine Books, 1997.
_____, ed. *Major League Baseball Profiles. 1871–1900.* Volume 1, *The Players Who Built the Game.* Lincoln: University of Nebraska Press, 2011.
Overfield, Joseph M. *The 100 Seasons of Buffalo Baseball.* Kenmore, NY: Partners' Press, 1985.
Pietrusza, David. *Major Leagues: The Formation, Sometimes Absorption and Mostly Inevitable Demise of 18 Professional Baseball Organizations, 1871 to Present.* Jefferson, NC: McFarland, 1991.
Ryczek, William J. *Blackguards and Red Stocking: A History of Baseball's National Association, 1871–1875.* Wallingford, CT: Colebrook Press, 1999. First published 1992 by McFarland.
Seymour, Harold, and Dorothy Seymour Mills. *Baseball: The Early Years.* New York: Oxford University Press, 1989.
Thorn, John. *Baseball in the Garden of Eden: The Secret History of the Early Game.* New York: Simon & Schuster, 2011.
Tiemann, Robert L., and Mark Rucker, eds. *Nineteenth Century Stars.* Phoenix: Society for American Baseball Research, 2012.
Vincent, Ted. *The Rise & Fall of American Sport: Mudville's Revenge.* Lincoln: University of Nebraska Press, 1994. First published 1981 by HarperCollins.
Voigt, David Q. *American Baseball.* Norman: University of Oklahoma Press, 1966.

Articles

Ahrens, Arthur. "An Assist for Jimmy Ryan." *Baseball Research Journal* 12 (1983): 66–70. http://research.sabr.org/journals/assist-for-jimmy-ryan.
Arbaugh, Thomas. "James McMillan: The Nation's Capital Owes Much to This Early Grosse Pointe Resident." *Heritage: A Journal of Grosse Pointe Life* 3, no. 5 (September 1986): 13–16. http://http://digitize.gp.lib.mi.us/digitize/magazines/heritage/1985-89/86/1986-09.pdf.
"Baseball in Early Days: Frederick K. Stearns and the '75 Team." *Michigan Alumnus* 29, no. 304 (November 2, 1922): 101–103.
"Cincinnati, Ohio." Ohio History Central (website). Accessed October 22, 2015. http://www.ohiohistorycentral.org/w/Cincinnati,_Ohio?rec=681.
"Cincinnati Reds II." Society for Cincinnati Sports Research. http://www.scsr.org/19CCBB/Teams/CR2.htm.
Drutchas, Geoffrey G. "Gray Eminence in a Gilded Age: The Forgotten Career of Senator James McMillan of Michigan." *Michigan Historical Review* 28, no. 2 (Fall 2002): 78–113.
Fleitz, David. "Fred Goldsmith." SABR Baseball Biography Project. http://sabr.org/bioproj/person/99c4a5f5.
"The Great Railroad Strike." *Digital History.* Accessed February 4, 2015. http://www.digitalhistory.uh.edu/disp_textbook.cfm?smtID=2&psid=3189.
Haupert, Michael. "William Hulbert." SABR Baseball Biography Project. http://sabr.org/bioproj/person/38c553ff.
Hausberg, Charles. "Pud Galvin." SABR BioProject, http://sabr.org/bioproj/person/38c553ff.

Macgranachan, Brendan. "Frank Bancroft: A Life in Baseball." Seamheads (website). Accessed November 15, 2015. http://seamheads.com/2008/11/21/frank-bancroft-a-life-in-baseball/.
McKenna, Brian. "Mark Baldwin." SABR Baseball Biography Project. http://sabr.org/bioproj/person/41f65388.
Schiff, Andrew. "Henry Chadwick." SABR Baseball Biography Project. http://sabr.org/bioproj/person/436e570c.
Stearns, Frederick Kimball. "Growth of Manufacturing Pharmacy in Detroit During the Nineteenth Century." Working Paper, Detroit Historical Society.
Thorn, John. "History Buried: America's All-Star Game of 1858." *Voices: The Journal of New York Folklore* 39 (Spring-Summer 2013): 31. Accessed September 13, 2015. http://www.nyfolklore.org/pubs/voic39-1-2/play.html.
Vaccaro, Frank. "Hugh Daily." SABR Baseball Biography Project. http://sabr.org/bioproj/person/8d8c99e4.
"William G. Thompson." *The History of Detroit and Michigan, or The Metropolis Illustrated: A Chronological Cyclopedia of the Past and Present.* Detroit: Silas Farmer, 1889.

Baseball Periodicals

New York Clipper
Sporting Life
The Sporting News

Newspapers

Brooklyn Eagle
Buffalo Courier
Buffalo Courier Express
Buffalo Evening News
Buffalo Express
Chicago Tribune
Detroit Free Press
Detroit Post and Tribune
Detroit Sunday News
London (Ontario) Advertiser
London (Ontario) Free Press
New York Daily News
New York Times
Pittsburgh Dispatch

Other Publications

The [University of] Michigan Alumnus Magazine

Online Resources

ancestry.com
baseballalmanac.com
baseball-reference.com
bioproj.sabr.com
Charlton's Baseball Chronology
ProQuest Historical Newspapers: Detroit Free Press
retrosheet.org

Index

Numbers in **bold italics** indicate pages with photographs

Actives Base Ball Club, Detroit 101
Aetnas Base Ball Club, Detroit 5, 6, 8, 26, 53, 95, 101–102
Alerts Base Ball Club, Detroit 5
Alleghenys of Pittsburgh 9, 67–68, 71–72, 90, 98, 103, 109, 112–113, 131, 143, 151, 155–158, 162–163, 170, 172, 175, 180–181
American Association (AA) 9, 67–68, 71–72, 90, 98, 103, 109, 112–113, 131, 143, 151, 155–158, 162–163, 170, 172, 175, 180–181
American League 2, 184, 189–190
Anson, Cap 60, 63–64, 91, 95, 128, 136, 140–142, 146, 148, 162
Anson's Colts 155, 157, 160
Athletics Base Ball Club, Detroit 183
Athletics of Philadelphia 53, 67, 78
Atkins, George 5

Bagard, Edward 132–133
Baldwin, Lady 109, ***110***, 112–113, 115, 122, 128, 135–136, ***137***, 138–142, 144–148, 154–155, ***156***, 157–160, 162–163, ***164***, 167, 172, ***175***, 176–177
Baldwin, Mark "Kid" 161
Baltimore Canaries 73
Bancroft, Frank 43–48, 51–57, 60–66, 69–74, 76–80
Barkley, Sam 21–23, 25–28, 30, 33
Barnes, Ross 37
Barnum, Eugene T. 47
Barr, Bob 139
Beatin, Eb "Ed" 161, 176, 180
"Beer and Whisky League" 39, 68
Bennett, Charlie 46, 52, 54, 56, ***57***, 59–63, 66, 68–70, 73, 77–79, 83–84, 87–88, 90, ***92***, 97, 103, 106, 115, 128, 135, 140, 142, 144, 154, ***156***, 157, 159, 161, ***164***, 167–169, 171–172, ***175***, 176–178, 180, 183, 187, 190

Bennett Park 35, 183, 190
Bierbauer, Louis 121
Big Four 2, 103, 107, 113, 116–119, 121–130, 134, 136, 139, 142, 151, 154, 175, 177, 185–186
Bishop, Bill 157
Bond, Tommy 30, 59
Bonfield, Police Inspector John 135
Boston Beaneaters 84–85, 87, 91, 97, 123, 136, 154, 158–160, 174, 176, 178, 183
Boston Red Caps 29–30, 42, 59, 61, 65
Boyle, Henry 115, 144
Boyton, Captain Paul 115, 144
Bradley, George H. "Foghorn" 42, 77–78
Bradley, George Washington "Grin" 47, 53–54, 57, 62, 64, 72, 77–78
Brill, Frank 92
Briody, Fatty 97, 155–156, ***156***, 159–160
Brooklyn Atlantics 37, 79–80
Brotherhood of Professional Base Ball Players 127, 155, 170–171, 181, 185–186
Brouthers, Dan 2, 92–93, 103, 113, 116, ***117***, 118–119, 122–123, 125–126, 128, ***137***, 138, 140–141, 145–146, 148, 154, ***156***, 158–161, 163, ***164***, 165–168, ***175***, 176, 179–180, 185, 187
Brown, Lew 53, 59–60
Brush, Adelaide 41
Brush, Alfred 15, 24, 34, 40, 46
Brush, Alfred E. 14, 47
Brush, Edmund 14–15, 132
Brush, John T. 154
Buffalo Base Ball Club 46, 113, 119, 181
Buffalo Bisons 21, 25, 47, 56, 62, 64, 72, 78, 85, 92–93, 103–104, 109, 112–113, 115–116, 121, 124–125, 175, 181
Buker, Henry 93
Burke, Turk 160

211

Burns, Dick 79, 82—88
Bushong, Doc 168
Byrne, Charlie 120

Campau, Adele 41, 133, 174
Campau, Charles "Count" 176–177
Campau, Daniel J. 132, 174
Campau, Mary 132
Canadian Baseball Hall of Fame 56
Caruthers, Bob 166–168
Casey, Dan 109, 112–113, 115, 127–129, 139, 165
Cass Base Ball Club 5–6, 8, 14, 18, 21, 26–27, 29, 32, 39, 42, 55, 95, 99, 102, 110, 111, 176
Caylor, O.P. 67
Chadwick, Henry 44–46, 51
Chamberlain, Mayor Marvin 168
Champion, Aaron 36
Chapman, Jack 80, 82, 86, 89, **90**, 92, 98, 124
Chicago Cubs 115
Chicago White Stockings 7–8, 44, 48, 52–53, 62–64, 71–73, 75, 79, 83–84, 87, 91–92, 102, 104, 125, 135–136, 140–141, 144–146, 148, 153–154, 157, 159, 161–163, 176–178
Chipman, Judge J. Logan 114
Chittenden, William 95, 97
Cincinnati Outlaw Reds 89, 109
Cincinnati Red Stockings 6–7, 36–38, 44, 67, 72, 78, 80
Cincinnati Star Base Ball Association 37
Clarkson, John 135, 140–141, 144, 146–147, 157–159, 161–162, 174, 176
Cleveland, President Grover 133, 174–176
Cleveland Blues, or Blue Stockings 9, 21, 62, 94, 97
Cleveland Forest Citys 7–9, 11, 21
Cobb, Ty 2
Collins, Chub 109
Comerica Park 5, 14, 188
Comiskey, Charlie 166–167
Connor, Roger 79, 137
Conway, Pete 115, 145–145, 155, 157–159, **164**, 165–167, **175**, 180
Corcoran, Larry 75, 83–84, 91–92
Corcoran, Mike 92
Corey, Fred 42, 60
Crane, Sam 109, 112, 121–123, **137**, 138, 140, 143
Crawford, Sam 2
Creightons Base Ball Club, Detroit 5
Croft, Art 21

Daily, Hugh "One Arm" 136
Dalrymple, Abner 155
Dauvray Cup 167
Davenport, Francis O. 23, 31–32, 40
Davenport (Iowa) Brown Stockings 28–29

Davis, Lily M. 129
Dempsey, Michael 5
Denny, Jerry 76
Deppert, John Jr. 114–115, 129, 136
Derby, George 49, 53–66, 72, 75–78, 85
Detroit Base Ball Club 1–2, 5–7, 9, 13–14, 19, 30–33, 45–47, 59, 82, 94–97, 99–102, 114, 142, 155, 171, 182
Detroit Creams 183
Detroit Hiawathas ball club 55
Detroit Jockey Club 15, 40
Detroit Light Guard 183
Detroit Medical Center 14–15, 188, 190
Detroit Medical College 35
Detroit Red Wings 188
Detroit Tigers 2, 35, 52, 183–184, 186, 188–189
Detroit Velocipedes 101
Donnelly, Jim 110, 112, 121–123, 130
Dorgan, Jerry 103, 109, 112
Dorgan, Mike 66, 127
Doscher, Herm 79–81
Dubuque (Iowa) Red Stockings 28
Dunlap, Fred 142, **143**, 147, 150, 152, 154, 157, 159, 163, **164**, 170, 172, 186
Durfee, Judge E.O. 145

Early Risers Base Ball Club, Detroit 5, 13–14
Eastern League 106
Edson, James L. 145–152
Ely, Bones 21
Eureka Base Ball Club, Detroit 5
Evans, Ford 7–10, 21, 32, 43, 46

Farrell, Joe 71, 79, 88, **90**, 91, 103
Fashion Race Course, Queens 18
Ferguson, Bob 80, 122
Flint, Frank "Silver" 63–64
Flynn, Jocko 140, 146
Foley, Will 63
Ford, Henry 1, 187
Ford Field, Detroit 188
Forest City Base Ball Club, Cleveland 7–9, 11, 21
Foutz, Dave 167
Fox, John 61
Franklin Base Ball Club, Detroit 5, 7
Fulmer, Chick 47

Gaffney, Honest John 166
Gaffney, Jim 140
Galvin, James Francis "Pud" 35, 56, 64, 76, 85, 92–94, 98, 104, 112–113, 115, 156, 163
Ganzel, Charlie 140, **156**, **164**, 166–168, **175**, 180
Gastfield, Ed 103
Gault, Ed 21

Gehringer, Charlie 2
Geiss, Bill 89, *90*
Gerhardt, Joe 47, 59, 64, 66, 69–71, 127
Getzien, Charles "Pretzels" *90*, 93–94, 103–104, 109, 112–113, 115, 128, 136, *137*, 138–142, 144, 146, 148, 155, *156*, 157–163, *164*, 165–172, *175*, 176, 178, 180
Gillean, Thomas 23, 25
Glasscock, Jack 8, 97, 144
Gleason, Bill 167
Goldsmith, Fred 63, 73, 84, 87, 92
Gore, George 126, 154
Greenberg, Hank 2
Gross, Emil 21
Gruber, Henry 161, *175*, 176, 179–180
Guelph (Ontario) Maple Leafs 102, 111

Hamilton, Ontario 12, 15, 89, 110
Hanlon, Edward "Ned" 47, 53, 56, *57*, 63, 66, 76, 78–79, 84, 88, *90*, 91, 103, 106, 113, 117, 128, *137*, 142, 144–145, 154, *156*, 159, *164*, 170, 172, *175*, 176, 178–180, 187
Harper Hospital 11, 17, 19, 59
Harris, Colonel Len A. 39
Harrison, Chicago Mayor Carter H. 135
Hartford Dark Blues Base Ball Club 9, 73, 134
Hayden, Professor J. W. 30
Haymarket Riot, Chicago 135
Hendrie, George 15, 35, 40, 46, 82, 95
Higham, Dick 59, 66, 73–74
Hines, Paul 76, 114, 118
Hollinger Nine 10, 16–17, 19–21, 35, 98
Hollinger, William "Bill" 8–10, 15–16, 19, 21, 23–25, 27–29, 35
Houck, Sadie 47, 58–59, 66, 68, 79, 81, 83–84, 88
Hughson, George 119
Hulbert, William 7–10, 37, 43–44, 46–49, 53–54, 71–72, 81, 86
Hunkidori Base Ball Club, Detroit 101

Indianapolis Hoosiers 104–107, 109, 111–113, 154, 156–157, 163, 172, 177–178
International Association of Professional Base-Ball Players 8–10, 32, 73, 89
International League 181–184
Irwin, Art 52

Johnson, Ban 183–184
Jones, Jack 86–87

Kalamazoo (Baseball) Club 6, 8, 31–33, 55, 102
Kaline, Al 2
Kansas City Cowboys 130, 135, 141, 144, 179
Keefe, Tim 61, 110, 136, 147
Keenan, Jim 109, 113

Kell, George 2
Kelly, Honest John 166
Kelly, Mike "King" 38, 146–148, 154, 159
Kennard Street Park, Cleveland 97
Kennedy, Doc 21
Kennedy, Maclean 107
Kennett, John 138
Kerr, W. W. 183
kidnapping of Indianapolis players 106–109
King, Silver 166–167
Knight, Lon 46–47, 52–53, 56, 66, 75
Kurtz, Mel 26

Lake Front Park, Chicago 83, 91
Langdon, Mayor George 35
Latham, Arlie 167
Leadley, Bob 109, 117, 129, 145, 184, 170, 179
League Alliance 48, 49
League (Boulevard) Park, Detroit 183
Leary, Jack 60–61
Libby, Steve 21–23, 25–28, 32–33
Little Caesars Arena 188
London (Ontario) Tecumsehs 9, 26–27, 42, 79, 102
Lucas, Henry V. 89, 97, 130, 142, 144, 186
Lynch, Jack 56

Madden, Kid 158, 163
Mahoney, William 132
Manning, Jim 121–123, 128, 136–138
Mansell, Tom 79, 83–85
Marsh, Joseph A. 95, 97, 99, 104–105, 116, 124–125, 127, 129–130, 141–143, 145, 155
Mathison, Charles 87, 108–109, 119, 128, 145, 155
Maxwell, Charles 89
McCormick, Jim 97, 135, 145
McGeary, Mike 69, 71, 73
McGuire, Deacon 106, 109–110, 112, 128–129
McIntyre, Frank 84
McKee, James 21
McKeon, Larry 109, 113
McKnight, Denny 67–68, 81
McMillan, James 12–15, 40, 43, 47, 82, 95
McQuery, Mox 109, 112, 121–123, 130
McSorley, John "Trick" 21–22, 25–26, 29–30, 32–33
McVey, Cal 37–38
Meinke, Frank 89, *90*, 92, 94, 103
Menderson, Nathan 38
Miller, Joe 21
Mills, Abraham 44, 81, 88, 96
Miner, Captain John 49
Molony, John B. 106, 117, 124–125, 127–128, 145
Moore, Jerrie 103
Moriarty, Gene 110

Morris, Ed 157
Morris, Peter 6
Morton, Charlie 21–22, 33, 98, 103–104, 106
Mountain, Frank 61–63
Mountjoy, Billy 85
Muir, W.K. 35
Mullane, Tony 63–65
Murnane, Tim 39
Mutrie, Jim 68, 120–122

National Agreement 81, 88, 106, 113, 119, 128
National Association of Professional Base Ball Players 6–8, 37
National Base-Ball Association 9, 11, 32, 52
National Baseball Hall of Fame 7, 52, 187
National League 1, 7–10, 19–20, 22, 29, 31–40, 42–48, 50–53, 56, 66–73, 79–82, 88–91, 96–99, 101, 105–107, 110, 113, 117–120, 122, 124–128, 130, 137, 143, 145, 147–148, 150–151, 153, 156, 162–164, 168, 170, 172–173, 176–177, 180–183, 185–187, 190
Nava, Sandy 76
Neagle, Jack 84
Neff, J. Wayne 37
New York Giants 111, 120, 122, 127–128, 136–138, 147, 155–156, 161, 179
New York Gothams 111, 120, 122, 127–128, 136–138, 147, 155–156, 161, 179
New York Metropolitans 54, 60, 68, 73, 161
New York Mutuals 73
Newberry, John S. 13–15, 35, 43, 95
Nimick, William 181
Nobby Base Ball Club, Detroit 101
Normandie Pool and Billiards Room 35
Northwestern League 21, 27–28, 81–82, 89, 94, 111, 182

O'Leary, Daniel 34, 42, 47
Olympic Park, Buffalo 112, 124, 129
Omaha Green Stockings 28
O'Neill, James "Tip" 55–56, 86, 165–169

Peninsular Cricket Club 16, 25, 39
Philadelphia Athletics 53, 67, 78
Philadelphia Quakers 84–86, 88–90
Phillips, Horace 67, 157
Phillips, Marr 103, 109
Players' League 127, 181–182, 185, 187
Powell, Abner 155
Powell, Martin 60–61, 76, 79, 89
Powers, Phil 146–147
Preston, Frank B. 145
Providence Grays 32, 58, 73, 75–78, 91, 94, 114
Purcell, William "Blondie" 38
Purroy, Charles 21

QLine streetcar line, Detroit 188
Quest, Joe 79, 83–87, 103, 109, 121

Radbourn, Charles "Hoss" 58, 76–77, 84–85, 94, 114, 118, 126, 142, 158–159, 160–161
Radbourn, George 84–85
Railway Union Base Ball Club, Cleveland 7
Recreation Park, Detroit 1, 11–12, 14–19, 21–26, **27**, 28–35, 39–40, 42, 49, 55–64, **70**, 72–73, 75, 82, 84, 87, 90–92, 94, 98, 110, 114, 122, 128, 136, **139**, 140, 143–144, 147, 153, 157–159, 162–166, 168, 172, **173**, 174, 177, 179, 182, 188, **190**
Reid, William 72–73
Reilley, Charles 53–54, 61, 64
reserve clause 20, 35, 37, 45–46, 51, 89, 126, 181–182, 185
Richardson, Arthur "Addie" 89
Richardson, Hardy 103, 113, 116–119, 121–123, 125–126, 128–129, 136, **137**, 138, 141–142, 144–145, 148, 154, **156**, 159–160, **164**, 165, 167, **175**, 176, 178, 180
Richmond, Lee 42, 52, 60, 78
Ringo, Frank 103, 131
Riverside Park, Detroit 182
Robinson, Yank 166–167, 169
Rochester Hop Bitters 32, 39
Rockford White Stockings 28
Rowe, Jack 2, 92, 103, 113, 116–117, **118**, 119, 122–123, 125–126, 128–129, **137**, 138, 140, 144, 148, 154, **156**, 157–158, 160–161, **164**, 165–166, 168, **175**, 177–178, 180–182
Rudolph Speil's Opera House Orchestra 30, 59
Rulison, Professor Walliky 30
Russell, Ned 24
Russell House Hotel **13**, 14–15, 43, 47, 121, 151, 168
Ruth, Babe 56, 91, 187
Ryan, Jimmy 177

Sage, J.B. 125
St. Louis Brown Stockings, or Browns 21, 124, 148, 156, 158, 165–169
St. Louis Maroons 104, 124, 154
St. Thomas (Ontario) Atlantics 111
Salisbury, Harry 21, 24–26, 28–30, 33
Saratoga Agreement 119–120, 122, 124, 126, 128
Schachtel, Ernst 129
Schachtel, Louisa 129
Scott, Milt 89, **90**, 103, 109
Scripps, James Edward 99
Serad, Bill 115
Seymour, Harold 169
Shallix, Gene 112
Shaughnessy, Tommy 21–22, 24–27, 29, 33

Shaw, Fred "Dupee" 85–88, **90**, 91–92, 94, 96–97, 112, 136
Sheeran, William 47
Shindle, Billy 155, **156**
Shoupe, John 23–24
Simmons, Joe 35
Simmons, Lew 120
Smith, Billy 142, 144
Smith, Charles H. 145, 171
Smith, John "Phenomenal" 147
Smith, Tommy 23
Soden, Arthur 43, 46, 72, 81, 120, 123, 143, 151–153
South Bend Green Stockings 25–26
Spalding, Albert Goodwill 7–8, 10, 71, 109, 120, 124–125, 130, 142, 150, 152–154, 162, 180
Spink, Alfred 147, 150, 154
Sportsman's Park, St. Louis 166
Starkey, Henry 5
Stearns, Dan 57
Stearns, Frederick K. 2, 95, 103, 112–113, 116–117, 141, 143, 145, 155, 159, 163, 166–168, 180, 182, 187
Steinbrenner, George 100, 103, 187
Sutcliffe, Sy 167, 180
Swampdoodle Grounds, Washington 138
Swartwood, Ed 21–22, 24, 26–27, 33
Sweeney, Charlie 134, 140
Syracuse Stars 73

Taylor, Joseph 23–24
Thompson, Sam 2, 107–108, 110–112, 122, 136, **137**, 140, 142, 148, 154, **156**, 157, 159, 161, **164**, 165, 167–169, 171–172, **175**, 176, 179–180, 186–187
Thompson, William G. 1, 34–35, **40**, 43–45, 47–48, 68, 70–71, 82, 86, 97, 129, 132, 174, 176, 188
Thorner, Justus 37–38, 67, 97
Titus, Jonas H. 5
Toledo Modocs 25
Tripartite Agreement 81–82, 88
Trott, Sam 64, 75–77, 79, 88
Troy, Dasher 64, 68, 70, 72–73, 75
Troy Trojans 22–24, 33, 58, 61, 65, 75, 77–79
Twitchell, Larry 126, 128, 134, **137**, 141–142, 144, 146, 155, **156**, 159–161, **164**, 166, **175**, 177, 180

Unas of Kalamazoo 102
Union Association 89, 92, 94, 96–97, 143, 186

Vail, George M. 145
Van Burkalow, Isaac 21–25, 29, 33
Van Depoele, Charles 30–31
Vanderbeck, George 183

Van Haltren, George 161
Van Norman, Jonathan 6
Voltz, William 127
Von der Ahe, Chris 120, 124, 148, 163, 166, 168–169

Walker, Walt 89
Ward, John Montgomery 58, 76, 127, 137–138, 181–182
Washington Nationals 53, 60, 136, 138
Watkins, William "Bill" 104, **105**, 106–113, 115–118, 121–122, 124, 126–131, 133–134, **137**, 138–145, 147, 150, 152–155, **156**, 159–162, **164**, 170–172, 176–179
Weidman, Stump 64–66, 72–73, 75–78, 83–88, **90**, 92–93, 103–104, 106, 109, 113, 128, 131, 155, **156**, 157, 160–161
Weiss, Joe 145
Welch, Curt 167
Welch, Mickey 58, 136, 138
West Side Park, Chicago 135, 141
Western League 2, 104–106, 109, 112, 151, 183
White, Jim "Deacon" 2, 7, 37–38, 93, 103, 113, 116, 118, 123, 126, 136, **137**, 139, 144, 155, **156**, 158, **164**, 171, **175**, 178, 180–181, 185, 187
White, Will 55–58
White, William (writer) 109, 116
Whitney, Art 59
Whitney, Jim 59
Williamson, Ned 91
Wise, Sam 68
Wolverines: acquire Big Four 116; acquire Indianapolis Hoosiers 106; finish in 1881 65; finish in 1882 78; finish in 1883 88; finish in 1884 94; finish in 1885 124; finish in 1886 148; finish in 1887 163; finish in 1888 179; okayed by League 128; team established 42–45; team sold 180; win National League pennant in 1887 163; win World Series of 1887 168
Wood, Fred 89, 91
Wood, George 47, 63, 106
Wood, Pete 115
Woodbridge Grove 183
Woodstock (Ontario) Actives 31
Worcester Ruby Legs 34, 42, 44, 47, 52–53, 57, 60–61, 65, 75, 78
"World's Series" of 1887 2, 101, 156, 158, 163, 165–169, 171–173, 175, 179
Wright, George 36, 77
Wright, Harry 36
Wrigley Field, Chicago 115
Wykoff, Wheeler 120

Young, Nick 46, 74, 80, 96, 118, 120, 122, 128, 147, 151

www.ingramcontent.com/pod-product-compliance
Ingram Content Group UK Ltd.
Pitfield, Milton Keynes, MK11 3LW, UK
UKHW031827070125
453106UK00011B/152